Myth, Cosmos, and Society

Myth, Cosmos, and Society

Indo-European Themes of Creation and Destruction

Bruce Lincoln

Harvard University Press
Cambridge, Massachusetts, and London, England

Publication of this book was assisted by a grant from the
Publications Program of the National Endowment for the
Humanities, an independent federal agency.

This book is printed on acid-free paper, and its binding
materials have been chosen for strength and durability.

Library of Congress Cataloging-in-Publication Data

Lincoln, Bruce.
    Myth, cosmos, and society.

    Bibliography: p.
    Includes indexes.
    1. Mythology, Indo-European—Addresses, essays,
lectures.   I. Title.
BL660.L45   1986   291.1'3   85-24733
ISBN 0-674-59775-3 (alk. paper)

For Cristiano Grottanelli

Acknowledgments

While preparing this book, I received aid, support, guidance, and counsel from a large number of talented and generous persons. It is my great pleasure to thank them now for their invaluable contributions, without—I hope—implicating them in any of the inevitable errors and shortcomings that remain in the work.

Above all, I am grateful to my wife, Louise Lincoln, who offered countless suggestions and criticisms on matters of content, style, and argumentation at every stage of my research and writing. Without her input the book would be immeasurably poorer, and I can hardly do justice to her many contributions. Moreover, I could never have seen the project through without her confidence, encouragement, patience, and affection, as well as that of our children, Rebecca and Martha.

Several close colleagues were kind enough to read earlier versions of the manuscript and to offer detailed and probing critiques. Such generosity is all too rare, and I have been privileged to benefit from the expertise, perspicacity, and scholarly acumen of these individuals: Françoise Bader, Cristiano Grottanelli, Gregory Nagy, and Edgar Polomé.

Many others have read portions of the work, heard pieces presented in lecture form, or helped shape my thinking on various points via correspondence or conversation. I have thanked some of these in the notes, but I am sure I have failed to give ample credit to all those who contributed substantially. Among those to whom I am indebted are Paul Bauschatz, Mary Boyce, Walter Burkert, Pietro Clemente, Carsten Colpe, Richard Dieterle, Ulf Drobin, Daniel Dubuisson, Mircea Eliade, Marija Gimbutas, Don Handelman, Alf Hiltebeitel, Vittorio Lanternari, William Malandra, Wendy O'Flaherty, Jaan Puhvel, William Sayers, John Scheid, Hanns-Peter Schmidt, Brian Smith, Pier-Giorgio Solinas, Jesper Svenbro, and H. S. Versnel.

Typists are rarely given their due, and it is difficult to tender sufficient praise or thanks to Marlos Rudie. In its first incarnation— before the expense of printing and composition became an issue— this work included notes quoting all primary sources in their original language, and without complaint Mrs. Rudie produced virtually letter-perfect copy in a host of unfamiliar tongues and scripts. The many hours of care and attention she gave to my work are richly appreciated, as is her kind friendship. I am also grateful to Nancy Leeper, who on short notice did an excellent job in preparing the illustrations.

Preliminary versions of Chapters 3 and 6 appeared in the *Journal of Indo-European Studies* and an earlier version of Chapter 4 in *History of Religions*. I thank the editors of these journals for permission to make use of these materials in their expanded and modified forms. I am also grateful to Harper and Row for permission to use Carolyn Forché's poem "Return" from her collection *The Country between Us*.

Lastly, I would like to express my sincere gratitude to the John Simon Guggenheim Memorial Foundation, which gave me fellowship support during the 1982–83 academic year when I was preparing the first full draft of this work, and to the University of Minnesota, which granted me a sabbatical leave during the same period.

Contents

Tables

Figures

Abbreviations

AB: *Aitareya Brāhmaṇa*
AitUp: Aitareya Upaniṣad
Alb: Albanian
Arm: Armenian
ASS: Āpastamba Śrauta Sūtra
Av: Avestan
AV: Atharva Veda
Beow: Beowulf
BG: Caesar, De Bello Gallico
Bibl: Apollodoros, Bibliotheka
BL: Book of Leinster
Bret: Breton
BṛhadUp: Bṛhadāraṇyaka Upaniṣad
Byel: Byelorussian
BYt: Bahman Yašt
CMT: Cath Maige Turedh
Codex Vat: Codex Vaticanus
Corn: Cornish
Dan: Danish
DeAbst: Porphyry, *De Abstinentia*
Dind: Rennes Dindsenchas
Dion Hal: Dionysius of
  Halicarnassus
Dk: Dēnkart
Eng: English
etym Wb: etymologisches
  Wörterbuch
Gall: Gallic
GBd: Greater Bundahišn

GGS: Gobhila Gṛhya Sūtra
Gk: Greek
Gmc: Germanic
Goth: Gothic
Grm: Grímnismál
Gylf: Snorri Sturlason, *Gylfaginning*
Hdt: Herodotos
HGS: Hiranyakeśin Gṛhya Sūtra
Hitt: Hittite
IE: Indo-European
II: Indo-Iranian
Il: Iliad
KGS: Khādira Gṛhya Sūtra
KS: Kauśika Sūtra
LG: Lebor Gabála Érenn
Lith: Lithuanian
Lok: Lokasenna
Lt: Latin
Manu: Manāva Dharmaśāstra
MEng: Middle English
Met: Ovid, *Metamorphoses*
MHG: Middle High German
MIr: Middle Irish
MSS: Manāva Śrauta Sūtra
MUp: Maitri Upaniṣad
MX: Mēnōg i Xrad
NH: Pliny, *Natural History*
NHG: New High German
Norw: Norwegian

OBulg: Old Bulgarian
OCS: Old Church Slavonic
Od: Odyssey
OE: Old English
OFris: Old Frisian
OHG: Old High German
OIr: Old Irish
ON: Old Norse
OPers: Old Persian
OPruss: Old Prussian
ORuss: Old Russian
Osc: Oscan
Pahl: Pahlavi
PeriHeb: Peri Hebdomadōn
PIE: Proto-Indo-European
PRDD: Pahlavi Rivāyat
  accompanying the Dādestān i Dēnīg
Proto-Gmc: Proto-Germanic
Rep: Plato, Republic
Rum: Rumanian
Russ: Russian
RV: Ṛg Veda
SB: Śatapatha Brāhmaṇa
SCr: Serbo-Croatian
SGS: Śankhāyana Gṛhya Sūtra
SGW: Škend Gumānīg Wizār

Skaldskp: Snorri Sturlason,
  Skaldskaparmál
Skt: Sanskrit
Slovo: Slovo o P"lku Igorevě
SNS: Šāyast nē Šāyast
Sogd: Sogdian
TaitUp: Taittirīya Upaniṣad
TB: Taittirīya Brāhmaṇa
TD MS: TD Manuscript no. 2 of
  the *Greater Bundahišn*, ed. T. D.
  Anklesaria
Theog: Hesiod, Theogony
Tim: Plato, Timaios
Tokh: Tokharian
TS: Taittirīya Saṃhitā
Up: Upaniṣad
Vaf: Vafþrúðnismál
Vd: Vīdēvdāt
VS: Vajasaneyi Saṃhitā
Vsp: Vǫluspá
W: Welsh
WD: Hesiod, Works and Days
Y: Yasna
YBL: Yellow Book of Lecan
Yt: Yašt
ZS: Zad Spram

Alternating continuously, these processes never stop:
Sometimes things come together into one whole through the power
    of Love,
And sometimes they are all borne apart again through the
    hatefulness of Strife.
Thus, insofar as the One has learned to issue from the Many
And the Many result from separating out of the One again,
By this process they come into being, and their allotted time is not
    lasting.
Insofar as they never stop alternating continuously,
Thus they are ever motionless in the cycle.

Empedokles, fragment B17, ll. 6–13

a labor leader was cut to pieces and buried,
Tell them how his friends found
the soldiers and made them dig up
and ask forgiveness of the corpse, once
it was assembled on the ground
like a man.

Carolyn Forché, "Return"

1

Cosmogony, Anthropogony, Homology

> From Ymir's flesh   the earth was made
>   and from his sweat (or: blood), the sea;
> Mountains from his bones,   trees from his hair,
>   and heaven from his skull.
> From his brows   built the gentle gods
>   Miðgarð (the human realm) for the sons of men;
> And from his brain   shaped they all the clouds,
>   Which were hard in mood.

So an ancient Germanic poem—verses 40–41 of the *Grímnismál*—recounts the origin of the cosmos. Elsewhere, in Snorri Sturlason's *Gylfaginning* 6–8, a fuller narrative is presented, in which we are told that Ymir ("Twin"), a frost-giant, was the first living being within the universe. Actually it is difficult to speak of "the universe" as such for the time when he was alive; rather, Ymir inhabited a primordial realm, rich in potential but as yet unformed.

The event that changed this realm into the world as we know it was Ymir's death, a death that—according to Snorri—came at the hands of the first gods, Oðinn and his shadowy brothers, Vili and Vé. Then, using pieces of Ymir's body as (quite literally) raw material, those deities constructed our physical universe, along the lines described in the verses I have quoted.

Narratives resembling this one are well attested throughout the world, as has long been recognized by students of mythology and folklore.[1] I take as the data for this book the large set of such stories

---

*All translations are my own. For sources where the original-language texts may be located, see the list of primary sources, pp. 231–234.

preserved in the ancient literatures of the various peoples speaking Indo-European languages.[2] The general narrative is that a primordial being is killed and dismembered, and that from that being's body the cosmos or some important aspects of it are created. On this basic theme, a great number of variants occur, as outlined in table 1.

Table 1. Generalized account of creation in Indo-European myths.

Creation results from:

I. The death
  A. usually violent
      1. by sacrifice
      2. by murder
      3. in battle
  B. but sometimes by natural causes

II. and dismemberment
  A. usually literal and corporeal
  B. but sometimes figurative (e.g., the "dismemberment" of a primordial king's realm among his heirs)

III. of a primordial being
  A. usually human
      1. usually the first man
      2. the first king (often the first man is also the first king)
      3. sometimes other primordial specialists: e.g., the first healer
  B. sometimes super- or sub-human beings
      1. a god
      2. a demon
      3. a giant
  C. a domestic animal
      1. most often, a bovine, as representative of all domestic animals (and often in combination with a primordial human)
      2. sometimes the first exemplar of other species: horse, goat, etc.

IV. and the formation of the universe—or some significant portion thereof—from the pieces of the victim's body
  A. the physical universe
      1. as a totality

Table 1 (*continued*)

---

       2. or with local reference only: e.g., the features of a specific region

  B. the social universe

       1. as a set of vertically stratified classes

       2. or as a set of horizontally separated kingdoms (which regularly have also strong associations to stratified classes)

  C. other specialized items

       1. animal species

       2. vegetable species

       3. foodstuffs

       4. elemental matter

       5. etc.

Beside the features listed in table 1, there are others that tend to recur in the specifically Indo-European myths of the "creative death" type—central characters are often named "Man" and "Twin," for instance[3]—but these details are less important than the general shape of the narrative. As examples, two other stories can be added to that of Ymir. First, *Ṛg Veda* 10.90, the celebrated "Song of Puruṣa" (*Puruṣasūkta*), composed around 900 B.C.:

(A) When they divided Puruṣa ("Man"), how many pieces did they prepare?
What was his mouth? What are his arms, thighs, and feet called?
The priest was his mouth, the warrior was made from his arms;
His thighs were the commoner, and the servant was made from his feet.

(B) The moon was born of his mind; of his eye, the sun was born;
From his mouth, Indra and fire; from his breath, wind was born.
From his navel there was the atmosphere; from his head, heaven was rolled together;
From his feet, the earth; from his ear, the cardinal directions.

This text contains a dimension lacking from the *Grímnismál* passage. For whereas the latter offered a straightforwardly cosmogonic account—that is, a story of the creation of the universe—the *Puruṣasūkta* contains both a cosmogonic section (*RV* 10.90.13–14, which I have labeled B) and a sociogony: a story of the creation of society (*RV* 10.90.11–12, labeled A). More complex still is a Slavic variant, the

Old Russian "Poem on the Dove King" (*Stič o golubinoj knig"*), a popular work collected from oral tradition early in the nineteenth century, although literary references to this poem exist in texts dating six hundred years earlier:[4]

(B) Our bright light comes from the Lord,
The red sun from the face of God,
The young shining moon from his breast,
The bright dawn from the eyes of God,
The sparkling stars from his vestments,
The wild winds from the Holy Spirit.

(A) From this our little Czars are on earth:
From the holy head of Adam.
From this princes and heroes come into being:
From the holy bones of Adam.
From this are the orthodox peasants:
From the holy knee of Adam.

(C) Strong bones come from stones,
Our bodies from the damp earth.

This source presents not only sociogonic and cosmogonic accounts (labeled A and B respectively) but also an anthropogony—that is, a story of the creation of man (labeled C).

Although the *Puruşasūkta* lacks an anthropogonic account of the sort encountered here, and the *Grímnismál* lacks both an anthropogony and a sociogony, such discussions are to be found in other important Indic and Germanic sources, as we will see in later chapters. In general, within the Indo-European tradition, issues of creation and destruction were considered at all three of these levels: that of the individual human body or microcosm; that of the macrocosm, or universe writ large; and that of the entity intermediate to individual and cosmos—the mesocosm, if you will—human society. For the sake of analytic clarity, I will tend to keep these levels separate from one another, concentrating initially upon the individual and cosmic levels and moving explicitly to the social level only in the final chapter.

Such a separation, to be sure, is rather artificial, for the individual, social, and cosmic levels of discourse are, as we will see, intimately interwoven: mutually implicative and mutually reinforcing. Theories about the nature of the universe, for instance, have other referents in addition, being also—at least implicitly—theories about (and programs for) the "proper" nature of society.[5] Ultimately, I will consider these myths of creation as one of the world's most successful systems

of ideology, given that they provided the mystifications and legiti-
mations that sustained an extremely widespread, stable, and durable
but also extremely rigid, hierarchic, and exploitative social system.
This analysis will have to wait, however, until the final chapter. A great
many other questions, many of them rather detailed and some quite
arcane, must be pondered first.

The cosmogonic and anthropogonic sections of the three texts presented above provide a convenient starting point. Before I discuss the
details of these passages, however, it is helpful to observe that the
general thrust in each instance is to establish a set of homologies
between bodily parts and corresponding parts of the cosmos: eyes
and sun, flesh and earth, and so forth. Note also that these texts do
not just call attention, in the manner of poetic imagery, to some perceived similarity between two disparate entities. They state not that
"X is like Y," but rather that "X was made from Y." Between the two
items linked in such a homology, there is thus posited a fundamental
consubstantiality, whereby the one entity may be created out of the
material substance of the other. The two are understood as *alloforms*,
alternative shapes, of one another. Viewed thus, flesh and earth, to
take one example, are seen as consisting of the same material stuff:
matter that may be temporarily incarnated in either one of two superficially—and only superficially—different forms. To put it somewhat differently, flesh and earth are viewed as alternate moments in
a continuous process, whereby one continually is transmuted into the
other.

Turning to the details of the homologies that are presented in these
three texts, we can note numerous similarities among them, but also
some significant divergences, as becomes clear when their contents
are plotted in tabular form (see table 2). Some of these divergences
may be straightened out readily, as for instance in the case of the
alloforms posited for heaven. For whether the comparison is to the
skull (ON *hauss*) or to the head more broadly (Skt *śirṣṇa-*), the homology rests upon a positional similarity: heaven is the highest part
of the cosmos, just as the head or skull is the highest part of the body.
When the skull is taken as heaven's alloform, a morphological dimension is added to the homology, for the shape of the cranial cap
suggests the perceived "rim of heaven."

Similarly, a positional comparison underlies the homology of earth
and feet in the Indic text, for in Indic cosmology the universe is
regularly considered to possess three vertical levels: heaven, atmosphere, and earth.[6] Heaven being associated to the top of the human
body, the head, earth is associated to its bottom, the feet. This line of

Table 2. Comparison of the homologic sets in *Grímnismál* 40–41, the *Puruṣasūkta*, and the "Poem on the Dove King."

	Heaven	Sun or Dawn	Moon	Stars	Clouds	Wind	Fire
Grímnismál	Skull	—	—	—	Brain	—	—
Puruṣasūkta	Head	Eye	Mind	—	—	Breath	Mouth
"Dove King"	—	Eyes and Face	Breast	Vestments	—	Holy Spirit	—

	Atmosphere	Trees	Mountains or Stones	Sea	Miðgarð	Cardinal Points	Earth
Grímnismál	—	Hair	Bones	Sweat or Blood	Brows	—	Flesh
Puruṣasūkta	Navel	—	—	—	—	Ear	Feet
"Dove King"	—	—	Bones	—	—	—	Body

analysis also applies to the homology of atmosphere and navel posited in the *Puruṣasūkta,* for each of these marks the midpoint of an encompassing vertical structure. We thus have here an extended homology or a homologic set, in which not two but six items are brought into relation with one another: three from the body (or microcosm) and three from the universe (or macrocosm).

Head : Heaven
Navel : Atmosphere
Feet : Earth

This elegant set is not, however, attested anywhere outside of Indic sources. It would thus appear to be an extension constructed upon the traditional Indo-European homology of head (or skull) and heaven—which, as we will see, is well attested elsewhere—making creative use of the general principles of homologic thought.

Elsewhere, the usual alloform for earth is flesh, as shown in the *Grímnismál* and—less obviously—in the "Dove King," where the term used for "body," ORuss *tĕlo,* denotes primarily the external, visible, fleshy surface of the body, being derived from the PIE root *tel-,* which marks surfaces of all kinds, including the surface of the body and also that of the earth (as for instance, in Lt *tellus* and OIr *talam* "earth," as well as ORuss *t'lo* "soil".[7] Together with this homology of flesh and earth, another is often grouped to form a four-item homologic set posited upon substantive (that is, material) and positional resemblances. For just as bones are the dense matter located within the softer flesh, so stones are related to the soil. This set could be graphed as follows:

Flesh : Earth
Stones : Bones

It is articulated concisely and forcefully in the anthropogonic section (section C) of the "Poem on the Dove King":

Strong bones come from stones,
Our bodies (*tĕlesa*) from the damp earth.

An ambiguity to consider in the data laid out in table 2 is the subtle alternance in the alloforms posited for the sun (or dawn). For whereas the Indic text gives "eye" (*cakṣoḥ,* singular ablative), its Slavic counterpart gives "eyes" (*očej,* in the dual). The question is, do both eyes correspond to the sun, or does only one, and if the latter, what becomes of the other eye? One might expect the occurrence of another four-member homologic set, correlating the eyes to the chief heavenly bodies:

> Right Eye : Sun
> Left Eye : Moon

This set, however, does not occur in any of the texts I have considered so far, nor is it frequent elsewhere.[8] Rather, the alloform given for the moon in the *Puruṣasūkta* is the mind, and in the "Dove King" the breast. The logic of these comparisons is rather difficult to fathom. The issues are whether there is any correspondence between mind and breast, and further, what led to their homologization to the moon. The latter problem proves easier to resolve, and its resolution leads to resolution of the former.

It would appear that the basis for the Indic comparison of mind and moon is folk etymology, specifically the resemblance between the words *manas-* "mind" and *mās-* "moon" (or, as it is given in the *Puruṣasūkta, candra-mās-* "radiant moon"), a resemblance that is also apparent in the PIE forms from which they are derived: *menos-* ("mind," from a verb "to think") and **mē̄(n)s-* ("moon," from a verb "to measure," with probable reference to the measurement of time).[9] The philological value of this comparison is nil: it is more word play than scientific linguistic analysis. But once posited, the homology exerted powerful influence on the history of ideas, and the various theories of "lunacy" that flourished until quite recently—whereby mental and emotional states are correlated to the phases of the moon—in all likelihood derive from the ancient homology of mind and moon. If this is so, it might also help to explain why another bodily part commonly understood as the seat of the emotions—the breast—appears as the alloform of the moon in the "Poem on the Dove King."

What all these materials reveal is a common pattern of creation mythology, traditional among the Indo-European peoples, in which the world is formed from the dismembered body of the first man and—in some versions—the body of the first bovine.[10] An important aspect of this tradition was the use of detailed homologies, relating the parts of the human body to parts of the cosmos, and also to parts of society (I will postpone study of the latter system until Chapter 7). As should already be evident (and will become more so), certain specific homologies recur consistently in a fairly fixed form. Others are subject to considerable variation. But even in the most stable homologies—flesh and earth, for instance—a certain amount of innovation or play was always possible, for the tradition rests more upon the logic of homology than on the details of any given comparisons. The methodological implication of this is that we ought not attempt to reconstruct pristine PIE homologies, from which all deviations may be dismissed as degenerate forms or subsequent transformations. Rather, my goal is the identification of more or less well-defined semantic ranges in which homologies regularly recur, but always with some degree of variation.

With this in mind, let us turn to an Iranian creation account that makes use of the same pattern of homologic analysis: the Manichaean cosmogony described in a Pahlavi (Middle Persian) text, from the ninth century A.D., *Škend Gumānīg Wizār* 16.8–20.[11]

> This also is said [by the Manichaeans]: the bodily, material creation is of Ahriman ("the Evil Spirit"). More precisely, the sky is from the skin, the earth is from the flesh, the mountains are from the bone, and the plants are from the hair of the demon Kūnī . . . Kūnī was the general of Ahriman's army, who at the beginning of the first battle swallowed the light in order to steal it from the god Ohrmazd ("the Wise Lord"). And in the second battle, [Ohrmazd] seized the demon Kūnī and many demons, and he bound them on the sphere, and killed the demon Kūnī. This macrocosm (*ēn dām ī wuzurg*) was created and made from her.

Within this doctrine—which is also alluded to in *Dēnkart* 3.200.7—the negative Manichaean valuation of the material world is forcefully expressed, for the cosmos derives from the body of a demon (Pahl *dēw*) bearing the name Kūnī, which would seem to mean nothing other than "Anus."[12] Consistent with other Manichaean views, the only redeeming feature of the material world is the fact that particles of light exist trapped within matter, by virtue of Kūnī's having swallowed up the light in her initial assault. This light, after the death and dismemberment of Kūnī, presumably became the spiritual portion imprisoned within humans, animals, and even certain vegetables and fruits.[13]

Of foremost interest at present is the fact that three of the four homologies presented in this passage—flesh/earth, bone/mountains, and hair/plants—correspond closely to homologies given in texts I have considered above, while the fourth, skin/heaven, is a variation upon the equation of skull and heaven. Here, however, heaven is viewed not so much as a lofty sphere (and thus homologous to the skull), but as the outermost covering of the cosmos, so that the skin—the body's outermost shell—is taken to be its alloform.

Yet another text contains the story of the earth's origin from the body of a primordial man, although here it is not the entire earth that is created, but only a crucial portion thereof: the mountain that supports the heavens. Still, several of the homologies we have already encountered do recur. The text in question is Ovid's description of the transformation of Atlas, *Metamorphoses* 4.655–662:

> As large as he was, Atlas is made into a mountain; for his beard and hair
> Are changed into forests, his hands and arms are ridges.
> What had previously been his head is the utmost summit of the mountain,
> And his bones become stone. Then, grown great in all his parts,
> He grew to an immense size—thus you established it, O gods—and the sky
> With all the stars rested upon him.

While the transformation of hands and arms into ridges is unparalleled elsewhere, and results from Ovid's attempt to fit the entire body of Atlas into the image of a mountain, other transformations are quite familiar by now: hair/forests, bones/stones, and head/mountaintop, understanding that the summit of the peak (*summo . . . in monte cacumen*) here replaces the summit of the cosmos, the rim of heaven. In truth, this must be viewed as something of a cosmogonic account, for it recounts the separation of heaven and earth and the origins of the cosmic mountain—Mount Atlas had already been called the "pillar of heaven" (*ton kiona tou ouranou*) in Herodotos 4.184—that connects those realms.[14] Moreover, Greek and Roman antecedents for Ovid's story are hard to come by, *Aeneid* 4.246–251 being the sole source in which Atlas is similarly described, although there the language is metaphoric and no account of the man's transformation into the mountain is to be found. Whether such a story was known to Vergil or to Ovid is unclear; it also is possible that one or both of these poets reinterpreted pieces of an inherited cosmogonic tradition, making creative and poetic use of them in a new—and entirely appropriate—mythic context.

While the reflexes considered thus far mostly tell of the origin of the cosmos from a human body, others,—like section C of the "Poem on the Dove King," are more anthropogonic than cosmogonic in their orientation, telling of the creation of the first man from the elements of the cosmos. Often, such texts are all thought to derive from an apocryphal book of the Old Testament, the Book of the Secrets of Enoch (or, as it is usually cited, II Enoch, to differentiate it from the

Ethiopic text similar in name). This text—most probably written in Hellenistic Alexandria somewhere between 30 B.C. and A.D. 70 (and thus, perhaps subject to Greek or Iranian influence)—survives only in Slavic translation, in Russian, Bulgarian, and Serbian manuscripts of the sixteenth and seventeenth centuries.[15] In the crucial passage, II Enoch 30.8–9, God himself is speaking:

> And on the sixth day I ordered my Wisdom to make man out of seven elements put together: his flesh from the earth, his blood from dew and sun, his eyes from the abyss of the sea, his bones of stone, his thought from the speed of angels and from cloud, his nerves and hair from the grass of the earth, his soul from my spirit and from the wind. And I gave him seven faculties: hearing to the flesh, vision to the eyes, smell to the soul, touch to the nerves, taste to the blood, endurance to the bone, and sweetness to the thought.

Here are many of the same homologies found in the cosmogonic texts cited earlier. Clearest, perhaps, are flesh/earth, bones/stones, and hair/grass. To these may be added thought/cloud, recalling the homology of brain/cloud in *Grímnismál* 41. Again, the extension of the homology hair/grass to include nerves (thus one must here interpret the ambiguous term *žily* [which may also denote veins and sinew] given its association with the sense of touch in 30.9) may be understood as prompted by the morphologic resemblance between hair and nerves. The granting of smell to the soul (*ōbonĕnie duševno*) also informs us that the soul was understood as being, or at least involving, the breath, yielding the homology of breath and wind, to which God's spirit (*dux"*) is added as a secondary source. This also helps to clarify the homology of winds from the Holy Spirit (*Svjata Duxa*) in the "Dove King," where the spirit in question would appear to be a Christianized reinterpretation of the breath.

The derivation of blood "from dew and sun" (*ōt rosi i slnca*) is rather strange. Although blood is derived from dew rather than from the sea in certain other texts, and from fire in others still (usually with the explanation that this is why blood is warm and red),[16] nowhere else to my knowledge is blood ever said to be derived from the sun. Perhaps this may be the result of a textual corruption, for if one regards the phrase *ōt bezdny morsky* ("from the abyss of the sea") as an interpolation, then punctuates after *rosi* and again after *ōči ego*, one is left with *kr"v ego ōt rosi, i slnca ōči ego,* "his blood from the dew, and of the sun his eyes," which is more in keeping with the usual range of IE correspondences.

It is also worth noticing that within this text an attempt is made to build an expanded homologic set including not only items drawn from the microcosm and those from the macrocosm, but also the senses— that is, those faculties which mediate between macrocosm and microcosm, bringing knowledge of the former to the latter. This attempt, while conceptually bold, is not terribly successful, and many of the specific homologies—such as hearing/flesh/earth or sweetness/thought/ cloud—seem rather forced, being motivated by the desire to fill out a system rather than by any compelling internal logic.[17] It is nevertheless worth graphing the structure of this system, if only to see how creative minds could struggle to build ever more sophisticated systems starting from traditional homologies. If one accepts the emendations I have suggested, and removes the overtly Christian items ("speed of angels" as an alloform of thought, "spirit" as an alloform of soul), the following picture emerges:

Earth	:	Flesh	:	Hearing
Dew	:	Blood	:	Taste
Sun	:	Eyes	:	Vision
Stone	:	Bones	:	Endurance
Cloud	:	Thought	:	Sweetness
Grass	:	Nerves and Hair	:	Touch
Wind	:	Soul	:	Smell

That there are seven items listed in each of these series obviously presented certain problems when the analysis of the senses was attempted; "endurance" and "sweetness" were added to fill out the standard list of five sensory faculties. Use of a seven-part schema (following the theme of creation in seven stages from Genesis 1–2) was quite common in medieval texts describing the anthropogony, as was an octopartite pattern, the so-called Eight-Part Adam. But in both these forms, the description of how the first man's body was created from alloformic portions of the cosmos was an extremely popular *topos,* closely related versions being found in Latin, Celtic, Germanic, and Slavic sources dating from the ninth to the nineteenth centuries, only some of which can be cited here.[18] As I noted earlier, many authorities have viewed these as all ultimately derived from the lost Latin or Greek antecedent of II Enoch, although the evidence for this is less than overpowering, given how little we know of II Enoch prior to its sixteenth-century appearance in Slavic translations.[19] Even should the authorities be right in this hypothesis, one must still ask what it was that made these verses from a relatively obscure apocryphon so enduringly popular from one end of Europe to the other. What made the description of Adam's body being formed from the elements of the cosmos so tremendously appealing to Celts, Germans, and Slavs for a millennium or more? For my part, I believe that the most likely answer to such questions is that in such stories as that found in II Enoch 30.8–9, European peoples found a superficially Christianized—and thus acceptable—version of their own still familiar and fondly remembered pre-Christian creation accounts. They thus seized upon such reworkings of familiar themes, clung to them tenaciously, and circulated them widely. One could cite literally dozens of texts within this tradition, of which only a few must suffice here. Consider, for instance, an extract from the fifteenth-century Old Frisian Code of Emsig:

> God made the first man, that was Adam, from eight transformations: the bone from the stone, the flesh from the earth, the blood from the water, the heart from the wind, the thoughts from the clouds, the sweat from the dew, the locks (of hair) from the grass, the eyes from the sun, and then he blew in the holy breath (or: spirit), and then he made Eve, Adam's love, from his rib.[20]

Consider also an Irish extract of the thirteenth or fourteenth century (British Museum Additional MS. 4783, folio 7a):

> There is this to be known concerning the creation of Adam: (he was made) from seven parts. The first part is from the earth, the second part from the sea, the third part from the sun, the fourth part from the clouds, the fifth part from the wind, the sixth part from stones, the seventh part from the Holy Spirit [, the eighth part from the light in the deep].
>
> The part of earth, that is the body of a man. The part of the sea, that is the blood of a man. The part of the sun is his face and countenance; the part of cloud, his thought; the part of wind, the breath of a man; the part of stones, his bones; the part of the Holy Spirit, his soul. The part made from the light in the deep, that is his Christianity.
>
> If the earthliness should be dominant in a man, he is sluggish; if the sea, he is unsteady; if the sun, he is fair and lively; if the cloud, he is light and foolish; if the wind, he is renowned and hotheaded; if the stone, he is hard in discussions and greedy and a thief; if the Holy Spirit, he is lively, generous, and full of grace from the divine scriptures; if the light, he is a joyful and fortunate man.[21]

Like II Enoch, these two versions have been superficially Christianized, as is evident from the mention of Eve's creation (taken from Genesis 2.18–22) and the inspiration of Adam (taken from Genesis 2.7) in the Old Frisian account, and the derivation of Adam's soul from the Holy Spirit and his Christianity (a delightful anachronism) from the light in the deep according to the Middle Irish. These superficial additions notwithstanding, the ancient Indo-European homologies remain: flesh(or body)/earth, bone/stone, blood/water(or sea), and eyes(or face)/sun are found in both texts, while hair/plants is in the Old Frisian. Beyond this, breath/wind is stated explicitly in the Middle Irish and lies behind the derivation of heart from wind in the Old Frisian, where the heart is understood as the seat of life and thus replaces the life-breath. The Irish text also helps us to understand the logic behind the homology brain(or thought)/cloud. For when the homology is stated as brain/cloud (as in *Grímnismál* 41), its basis is the morphological resemblance between two crenulate entities. When it takes the form thought/cloud, the ground for comparison is the insubstantiality or fluffiness of the two alloforms. For as the Irish version tells us, when the proportion of cloud within an individual exceeds all other elements and thus dominates his constitution, "he is light and foolish."

This statement comes from the last paragraph of the Middle Irish text, which—like the treatment of the senses in II Enoch 30.9—is an expansion on the theme of the homologic relation of microcosm and macrocosm. In this passage it is also implied that the anthropogonic process is ongoing, such that each successive human being is created from the same elements of the cosmos as was Adam, going on to specify what the consequences should be if any single element were to preponderate over the others. As a result, we are told just what qualities accompany each material substance of which the body is constituted. Omitting the most fully Christianized items, the system is as follows:

Earth	:	Body	:	Sluggishness
Sea	:	Blood	:	Unsteadiness
Sun	:	Face	:	Fairness, Life
Cloud	:	Thought	:	Foolishness, Lightheartedness
Wind	:	Breath	:	Fame, Hotheadedness
Stones	:	Bones	:	Hardness, Greed, Thievery

A similar expansion is evident in an interpolation to a famous Old Russian text, the "Discourse of the Three Saints" (*Bes"da Trex" Svjatitelej*), in which is found another superficially Christianized reflex of these same basic homologies.[22] The Christianization, however, goes somewhat further here than in the Old Frisian and Middle Irish sources I have been considering. For not only are abstract qualities— usually Christian virtues and vices—associated to each homology, but a hierarchy is established in which the first group of alloforms (earth/ body) is most corporeal and thus "lowliest," while the last (Holy Spirit/ zeal and all that is good) is most fully spiritual (in a Christian sense) and is thus said to be "foremost."

> And thus he (i.e., God) made (Adam's) body out of eight parts com- posed in four. The first part is of the earth, which is the lowliest of all parts. The second is of the sea, which is blood and wisdom. The third is of the sun, which is beauty and eyes for him. The fourth is of the celestial clouds, which are thought and weakness. The fifth is of the wind—that is air—which is breath and envy. The sixth is of stones, that is firmness. The seventh is of the light of this world, which is made into flesh, that is humility and sweetness. The eighth part is of the Holy Spirit, placed in men for all that is good, full of zeal—that is the foremost part.[23]

The contents are by now so familiar that it is not difficult to restore the few pieces that are missing from the picture. Thus, a corporeal alloform for stones, which are only homologized here to "firmness" (*utvr'ždenije*), is obviously bones. Similarly, no corporeal alloform is given for earth because earth's normal homologue, flesh, has been pressed into service elsewhere in the system, as we are told that "the light of this world is made into flesh" (*svĕta sego mira, iže stvoren' pl'tnju*), an obvious allusion to the doctrine of Christ's incarnation.

Down into the nineteenth century, this anthropogony was still cir- culating, as evidenced by a Rumanian variant, part of a text entitled "Questions and Answers," dating to 1809:

> *Question:* "From how many parts did God make man?"
> *Answer:* "From eight parts: the body from soil; bones from stones; blood from dew; eyes from sun; thoughts from clouds; breath from wind; intellect from moon; the gift of prophecy from the Holy Spirit."[24]

Clearly, this is not an independent version, but most likely draws on earlier Slavic, Greek, and/or Latin traditions. Yet it is a testimony to the enduring attraction and power of this system of cosmogonic and anthropogonic mythology, for many of the same basic homologies keep recurring in sources the dates of which span three millennia or more. Perhaps it is worth summarizing the nature of those homologies at this point. Nine separate items recur with some degree of frequency.

1. Flesh/Earth. Occurring in all the texts cited except the *Puruṣasūkta* and Ovid's story of Atlas, the homology of earth and flesh—or, more broadly, the body—is one of those most firmly established. In certain Christianized versions of the anthropogony, this homology is denigrated to the advantage of other "loftier" or more spiritual homologies. Thus, the "Discourse of the Three Saints" calls the portion of the body formed from the earth the "lowliest" (*xužd'ši*) of all, and whereas most texts use a neutral term to denote the earth (ON *jǫrð*, OFris *erthe*, OE *fold*, OIr *talam*, ORuss *tělo*, Pahl *zamīg*, OCS and ORuss *zemlja*), certain others refer to "mud," "soil," "clay," or "loam," as the source of the base flesh (Lt *limus*, OE *lām*, MHG *leim*, Rum *pământu*). The basis for this homology is a substantive resemblance between the two materials compared, and also a positional relation within a homologic set that also involves the next set of alloforms.

2. Bone/Stone. Closely related to the homology of earth and flesh is that of bone and stone, for just as stones are the hard substance set inside the soft earth, so is the relation of bones to flesh. This powerful image is lost when the alloform of bone is defined as mountains, something that occurs in both the Eddic and Pahlavi accounts (ON *bjǫrg;* Pahl *kōf*). The chief characteristic of bones highlighted through this homology is their hardness, as is seen in II Enoch 30.9, where the faculty given to the bone is "endurance" or "firmness" *tr"pěnie*), and in the Middle Irish reflex, where one with an excess of bone is said to become "hard in discussions" (*cruaidh do trachtadh*). This homology occurs in all the sources we have considered thus far, with the exception of the *Puruṣasūkta*. A phonological as well as a semantic correspondence is evident in the terminology used for bones, Lt *os*, Pahl *ast*, ORuss and OCS *kost'* all being derived from PIE *H_2os-$t(H_2)$-.[25]

3. Hair/Plants. Somewhat less broad in its diffusion is the homology of plants and hair, which is lacking in the *Puruṣasūkta* and in the Middle Irish, Old Russian, and Rumanian reflexes. Other sources do consistently group hair and plants together, the plants in question regularly being inedible vegetation: trees (ON *baðmr*, Skt *vanaspatiḥ*), forest (Lt *silvas*), or grass (OCS *trava*, OFris *gerse*), although generic terms for "plants" also appear (Skt *oṣadhiḥ*, Pahl *urwar*). The grounds for comparison would seem to begin with the morphological resemblance of hair and grass, both being long, thin, and grouped in clumps, but they extend to other factors as well. The position of hair growing on top of the flesh (and not just the hair on the head) corresponds to that of plants growing on top of the earth. Further, hair and plants are characterized by incessant growth. This property of growth, as well as location on the extremity of the body atop the flesh, has led in some instances (see Chapter 4) to the extension of this homology to include nails as well as hair in the comparison to plants. When only morphological factors are taken into account, however, plants may also be homologized to sinews or nerves, as occurs in II Enoch.

4. *Blood(or other bodily fluids)/Water.* Considerable variation marks the homologies drawn between the fluid elements of microcosm and macrocosm. Some texts posit only one rather general set of allo-forms—most often that of blood and water—while others provide much more detailed analyses, comparing blood to riverine waters, urine to swamp waters, and so forth (implying here further homo-logies of blood vessels to riverbeds and bladder to swamps).[26] In two Old English texts, the *Rituale Ecclesiae Dunelmensis* and the *Dialogue of Solomon and Saturn,* a major divergence is apparent, blood being ho-mologized not to any fluid but to fire, normally taken as the opposite of all fluids. Perhaps this homology is intended to be surprising, for the texts go on to justify it, explaining that both blood and fire are red and hot, as evidence of (or better yet, *because* of) their alloformic relation.[27] Among peoples who live near the ocean, there is a tendency to homologize sweat and sea, based on the saline content of both fluids, as is seen in *Grímnismál* 40, where the term used is ON *sveiti,* which may denote either "sweat" or "blood," although its etymological con-nection to the former is unmistakable.[28] Other texts still relate tears to sea, blood to dew, sweat to sacrificial libations, or semen to water, in all instances the material resemblance of two fluids providing the fundamental ground for homologization. Beyond this, the specific properties of certain fluids help to refine the comparison; for instance, a common pattern of downward motion in droplets leads to the as-sociation of urine and rain, and the fact that both sweat and dew appear mysteriously and seemingly spontaneously on the surface of things leads to their being understood as alloforms of each other.[29]

5. *Eyes/Sun.* The two orbs that are involved in the act of vision—eye and sun—are consistently linked in the texts considered here, and in most other Indo-European discussions of microcosm and macro-cosm as well. So closely are the two associated that not only is it common in various Indo-European languages to refer to the sun as an "eye"[30] but in at least one stock the noun that denotes "eye" is actually derived from the word for "sun" (OIr *sūil* < *sūli,* a zero-grade form of PIE *sāwel-*).[31] Whereas we have only relatively recently come to understand the process of vision as one whereby light trans-mitted by the sun enters the eye, which acts as a receiver, so powerful was the homology of eye and sun throughout antiquity that the eye

was believed to be a source of light like its alloform the sun.[32] While
the terms for both items in this homology are quite consistently of
PIE origin—sun, from *sāwel:* Skt *sūryaḥ,* Pahl *xwar-šēd* (< Av *xᵛar-*
plus *xšaēta-*), ORuss and OCS *sl"n'ce,* Rum *soare,* OFris *sunna;* eyes,
from PIE *H_3ek^w-*: Skt *akṣiṇi,* ORuss and OCS *ōči,* Rum *ochĭ,* OFris
agene[33]—they do not agree in number, for while the sun is always
singular, the term for eyes almost always occurs in the plural or (in
those languages where the dual survived) in the dual. One must conclude that from the one sun, both eyes—indeed, all eyes—have their
origin. One might have expected the two eyes to be derived from the
two great celestial luminaries, sun and moon, but, as we have seen,
the moon was reserved for another use.

6. *Mind/Moon.* Of the various items of the macrocosm that recur
in different texts, the moon—somewhat surprisingly—is among the
rarer ones. The clearest sources in which it appears are those from
India, where the moon (*candra-māḥ* "shining moon") is said to come
from the mind (*manas*) of Puruṣa (*RV* 10.90.13, *AitUp* 1.4), a comparison that seems to be prompted by their phonological similarity.
Two other sources I have considered offer similar alloforms, although
there the phonological base has been lost: the Rumanian "Questions
and Answers," where the intellect (*înțelepciunea*) is formed from the
moon (*lună*), and the "Poem on the Dove King," where the moon is
homologized to the breast (ORuss *grud'*), the latter being understood
as the seat of the emotions, much as the mind is the seat of thought.
Again, in a text I will discuss shortly, the Pseudo-Hippokratic *Peri
Hebdomadōn* 6.1, it is said that "The place of the moon is where sense
prepares judgment" (*Lien* [= *lunae*] *locus sensus apparuit judicium*). And,
as has been demonstrated by Jacques Duchesne-Guillemin, the structure of this text strongly indicates that the "place where sense prepares
judgment" was the region of the chest or diaphragm.[34] But beyond
this there is no further evidence to offer. Perhaps there was no IE
homology of mind and moon, then—but if not, how can one explain
the appearance of this curious association in Slavic, Greek, and Indic
sources, not to mention the late Rumanian reflex? Moreover, how is
one to explain the omission of the moon from the eyes/sun homology,
where it might fit so well? On balance, I am inclined to believe that
the homology mind/moon was a part of the ancient system, but one
that was extremely fragile, resting as it did on a phonological resemblance rather than on substantive, morphologic, or positional bases,
as do the other traditional homologies. Thus, given normal processes
of semantic renewal, as other terms for mind and moon were intro-

duced lacking any phonologic similarity to one another, the homology tended to be abandoned.

7. *Brain(or thoughts)/Cloud.* Thoughts—which are differentiated from "mind" only by a subtle distinction—also show up in another homology, being denoted by a wide array of terms in different cosmogonic and anthropogonic texts (among them MIr *imrādud* "thought," MHG *muot* "mood," OFris *togt* "thought," MEng *wit*, Lt *cogitatio* and *mens*, Rum *cugetu* "cogitation," and OCS *pomysl'* "thought"). Yet all of these forms of mental activity are homologized to clouds, often with the specification that, like clouds, thoughts are weak (ORuss *m'kota*), light (MIr *etrom*), or unsteady (OE *unstaðelfæstnes*). In contrast, a morphological basis for the homology is provided when the microcosmic alloform has a more tangible nature, as in *Grímnismál* 40 where it is the brain—and not an abstraction like "thought"—that is homologized to the clouds. *Bundahišn* 28.4 also makes the brain (Pahl *mazg*) the starting point for its homology, although its alloform is presented as "(the realm of) endless light" (*asar rōšnīh*), one of the highest heavens in the Zoroastrian system, the result perhaps of the elevation of thought beyond the realm in which clouds are found.

8. *Head/Heaven.* Although most of the anthropogonic texts are silent regarding this homology, the Indic, Iranian, Germanic, and Latin cosmogonic sources consistently state that heaven—meaning here, no doubt, the rim of the celestial vault (ON *himinn*, Skt *dyauḥ*; Pahl *garōdman* is somewhat different in this regard)—was formed from the head or skull of a primordial being, its shape and location at the top of the body suggesting and sustaining the comparison. Ovid's story of Atlas presents an interesting reworking of this tradition, since given that Atlas becomes the cosmic mountain on which the heavens rest, his skull cannot possibly be said to become the heaven itself. Instead it is said to become the apex of the mountain (*summo . . . in monte cacumen*), that is, the very point where heaven and earth meet. Within certain other traditions, particularly those of Iran, the heavens were understood to be a shell that completely encased the earth, rather than a vault placed over the top of it, and consequently it is skin, the body's outermost covering, that appears as the alloform of heaven (*SGW* 16.10, *GBd* 28.4, *Peri Heb* 6.2).

9. *Breath/Wind.* One of the most consistent homologies is that of lifebreath and wind, the latter being interpreted as the respiratory process of the cosmos. Not only is this homology attested in virtually all the sources I have considered, save the Germanic and Iranian cosmogonic accounts, but the terms used to denote "wind" almost

invariably derive from the same PIE verb, $*H_3w(H_1)$- "to blow," although the nominal formations vary somewhat: Skt *vāyuḥ*, OCS *větr"*, ORuss *větra*, Lt *ventus*, Rum *vânt*, OE *wind*, and OFris *winde*.[35] In some of the later European reflexes, this comparison is Christianized, probably under the influence of Genesis 2.7, where God breathes life into Adam. Thus, in texts written within a Christian milieu the Holy Spirit often replaces the wind and the soul often replaces the breath.

These nine homologies are the basic building blocks in a system of natural philosophy, a system of stunning elegance and infinite subtlety. By identifying specific items in the cosmos as alloforms to corresponding parts of the human body, they form a major component of the creation mythology of virtually all peoples of antiquity who spoke Indo-European languages. Tables 3, 4, and 5 expand upon table 1, to lay out fuller evidence from all the texts I have considered thus far and a few to which I will shortly turn. The picture that emerges is one of a fairly consistent homologic system, in which there still existed some room for variation and innovation. I must emphasize, however, that building blocks are less interesting in themselves than the larger structures that can be constructed from them. The later chapters of this book will be devoted to those structures: the multiple applications of basic homologies to a variety of concerns.

There is a problem that remains to be addressed, one that two great scholars of generations past, Jacob Grimm and Hermann Güntert, worried over without resolving. Thus far, I have considered two different—but closely related—sets of materials. One is a cosmogonic tradition, in which it is told how the body of a primordial being served as the raw material from which the physical universe was made. The other is an anthropogonic tradition, in which—conversely—it is recounted how the elements of the physical universe served as the raw material from which the body of the first man (and thus, of humanity in general) was made. In the first instance, the process described is one of separation, (sacrificial) dismemberment; in the second, it is one of construction, putting together. The question that must be asked, then, is precisely how these two complementary traditions are related to one another. Both Grimm and Güntert considered this question within the context of the Germanic materials, where the issues are drawn with great clarity: how are the stories of Ymir's dismemberment and the Eight-Part Adam related?

For Grimm, the issue was rather simple, for he felt that the cosmogonic view, where "(one explains) the sun as a giant's eye," was "more congenial to the childhood of the world."[36] Thus, apparently Ymir was first, and the Eight-Part Adam was a later, more mature

Table 3. Semantic analysis of homologies: microcosm → macrocosm.

	Microcosmic alloforms								
Text	Flesh	Bone	Hair	Blood	Eyes	Mind	Brain	Head	Breath
					Macrocosmic alloforms				
Grímnismál 40–41	EARTH	MOUNT	TREES	SEA	—	—	CLOUD	HEAVEN	—
Rg Veda 10.90.13–14	—	—	—	—	SUN	MOON	—	HEAVEN	WIND
"Poem on the Dove King"	EARTH	STONE	—	—	DAWN	MOON	—	—	WIND
Škend Gumānīg Wizār 16.8–20	EARTH	MOUNT	PLANTS	—	—	—	—	HEAVEN	—
Metamorphoses 4.655–662	—	STONE	FOREST	—	—	—	—	TOP OF COSMIC MOUNT	—
II Enoch 30.8	EARTH	STONE	GRASS	DEW	SUN	—	CLOUD	—	WIND
Code of Emsig	EARTH	STONE	GRASS	WATER	SUN	—	CLOUD	—	WIND
British Museum MS. 4783 fol. 7a	EARTH	STONE	—	SEA	SUN	—	CLOUD	—	WIND
Discourse of Three Saints	light of world	STONE	—	SEA	SUN	—	CLOUD	—	WIND
Aitareya Upaniṣad 1–2	—	—	PLANTS	—	SUN	MOON	—	—	WIND
Greater Bundahišn 28	EARTH	MOUNT	PLANTS	SEA	SUN & moon	—	endless light	HEAVEN	WIND
Peri Hebdomadōn 6	CLAY	STONE	—	RIVER	—	MOON	warm soil	—	AIR
Empedokles	EARTH	STONE	LEAVES	—	—	—	—	—	AIR & aither

Note: Capital letters signify an item that falls within the general semantic range for the variants studied. Lower-case letters signify an item that falls beyond the general semantic range for the variants studied.

Table 4. Semantic analysis of homologies: macrocosm → microcosm.

Text	Macrocosmic alloforms								
	Earth	Stone	Plants	Water	Sun	Moon	Cloud	Heaven	Wind
	Microcosmic alloforms								
Grímnismál 40–41	FLESH	BONE	HAIR	SWEAT or BLOOD	—	—	BRAIN	SKULL	—
Ṛg Veda 10.90.13–14	feet	—	—	—	EYE	MIND	—	HEAD	BREATH
"Poem on the Dove King"	BODY	BONE	—	—	FACE	BREAST	—	—	HOLY SPIRIT
Škend Gumānīg Wizār 16.8–20	FLESH	BONE	HAIR	—	—	—	—	skin	—
Metamorphoses 4.655–662	—	BONE	HAIR	—	—	—	—	HEAD	—
II Enoch 30.8	FLESH	BONE	HAIR & nerves	BLOOD	EYES	—	THOUGHT	—	SOUL
Code of Emsig	FLESH	BONE	HAIR	BLOOD	EYES	—	THOUGHT	—	heart
British Museum MS. 4783 fol. 7a	BODY	BONE	—	BLOOD	FACE	—	THOUGHT	—	BREATH
Discourse of Three Saints	lowest part	FIRMNESS	—	BLOOD	EYES	—	THOUGHT	—	BREATH
Aitareya Upaniṣad 1–2	—	—	HAIR	SEMEN	EYES	MIND	—	—	BREATH
Greater *Bundahišn* 28	FLESH	BONE	HAIR	BLOOD	EYE	eye	BRAIN	HEAD	BREATH
Peri Hebdomadōn 6	FLESH	BONE	—	BLOOD & HUMORS	heat in viscera	SENSE	—	heat in skin	BREATH
Empedokles	FLESH	SHELL	HAIR	SWEAT	—	—	—	—	SOUL

Note: Capital letters signify an item that falls within the general semantic range for the variants studied. Lower-case letters signify an item that falls beyond the general semantic range for the variants studied.

Table 5. Etymological analysis of homologies.

Text				Microcosmic alloforms					
	Flesh	Bone	Hair	Blood	Eyes	Mind	Brain	Head	Breath
Grímnismál 40–41	hold	bein	hár	sveiti	—	—	heili	hauss	—
Ṛg Veda 10.90.13–14	(pad)	—	—	—	cakṣuḥ	MANAS	—	śiraḥ	pra-ANAH
"Poem on the Dove King"	tělo	KOST'	—	—	OČI	grud'	—	—	(svjata dux)
Škend Gumānīg Wizār 16.8–20	gōšt	AST	mōy	—	—	—	—	(pōst)	—
Metamorphoses 4.655–662	—	os	barba coma	—	—	—	—	caput	—
II Enoch 30.8	pl't'	KOST'	kosa	kr'v'	OČI	—	pomysl'	—	(duša)
Code of Emsig	flask	benete	lokkar	blod	AGENE	—	togt	—	(herte)
British Museum MS. 4783 fol. 7a	colaind	cnáimh	—	fuil	(drech)	—	imrádud	—	ANÁL
Discourse of Three Saints	pl't'	(utvr''ž-denije)	—	kr'v'	OČI	—	mysl'	—	v'zduxa
Aitareya Upaniṣad 1–2	—	—	loman	(retaḥ)	AKṢIṆI	MANAS	—	—	pra-ANAH
Greater Bundahišn 28	gōšt	ASTAG	mōy	xōn	cašm	—	mazg	sar	wēn
Peri Hebdomadōn 6	caro	os	—	sanguis	(calidum)	sensus	cerebrum	—	spiritus
Empedokles	—	(kogknē)	trikhes	hidrōs	—	—	—	—	pneuma
Posited PIE form	—	$*H_1OST(H_2)$-	—	—	$*H_3EK^w$-	*MENOS-	—	—	$*H_2ENH_2$-

Note: Capital letters signify a phonologic and semantic correspondence. Lower-case letters signify a semantic correspondence only. Lower-case letters in parentheses signify an item that falls beyond the general semantic range for the variants studied.

(*continued*)

Table 5 (*continued*)

Text	Earth	Stone	Plants	Water	Macrocosmic alloforms Sun	Moon	Cloud	Heaven	Wind
Grímnismál 40–41	jǫrð	bjǫrg	baðmr	sær	—	—	ský	himinn	—
Ŗg Veda 10.90.13–14	bhūmiḥ	—	—	—	SŪRYAḤ	candra-MĀḤ	—	dyauḥ	VĀYUḤ
"Poem on the Dove King"	ZEMLJA	kamen'	—	—	SOLNCE	MĔSJAC	—	—	VĔTRA
Škend Gumānīg Wizār 16.8–20	ZAMĪG	kōf	urwar	—	—	—	—	asmān	—
Metamorphoses 4.655–662	—	lapis	silvas	—	—	—	—	summo in monte	—
II Enoch 30.8	ZEMLJA	kamen'	trava	rosa	SL''N'CE	—	ōblak"	—	VĔTR"
Code of Emsig	erthe	stene	gerse	wetere	SUNNA	—	wolk	—	WINDE

Table 5 (continued)

British Museum MS. 4783 fol. 7a	talam	cloch	—	muir	grían	nél	—	—	gáeth
Discourse of Three Saints	ZEMLJA	kamen'	—	more	SLŬNCE	neves'n'	—	—	VĚTRA
Aitareya Upaniṣad 1–2	—	—	oṣadhi-vanaspatiḥ	āpaḥ	ādityaḥ	—	candra-MĀḤ	—	VĀYUḤ
Greater Bundahišn 28	ZAMĪG	kōf	urwar	zrēh	XWARŠĒD (& māh)	(asar rōšnīh)	—	garōdman	WĀD
Peri Heb-domadōn 6	quod circa ossa	lapis	—	aqua fluminem	sōl	(quod in terra calidum)	luna	jovem	aër
Empedokles	KHTHŌN	lithos	phylla	thalassa	—	—	—	—	aerōdos aitherōdos
Posited PIE form	$*GH^{z}DHOM$-	—	—	—	*SĀWEL-	—	*MĒ(N)S-	—	$*H_2W(H_1)$-

reworking of the cosmogonic tradition, just as Christianity was more mature than paganism. Güntert, for his part, wanted to keep the anthropogonic and cosmogonic traditions quite separate, seeing Ymir as the direct Germanic derivate of a PIE cosmogony, and the Eight-Part Adam as having entered Europe through a devious route, via II Enoch, which—being written in Hellenistic Alexandria—had acquired some passages, most notably 30.8–9, that showed the influence of Iranian speculation on the theme of microcosm and macrocosm.[37]

While both of these positions must now be rejected—Grimm's for its naiveté, Güntert's for its insupportable leaps[38]—the problem is made more vexing still by the existence of a third set of texts in which the basic building blocks of the system are arranged in a fashion that is neither straightforwardly cosmogonic nor anthropogonic, but simply homologic—stating the homologies without reference to the directionality of any transformations that may occur. Thus, for instance, is the famous chapter 28 of the *Greater Bundahišn*, which contains dozens of homologies, many of them quite novel—teeth/stars, mouth/gate of heaven, and so forth—but which also preserves the common Indo-European set with great fidelity. The chapter begins with the statement "It is said in the religion: 'Man's body is the measure of the material world'" (GBd 28.1, TD MS. 189.3–4), and the introductory phrase "It is said in the religion" (*pad dēn guft kū*) signals that a passage of the lost Avesta is being quoted, thus assuring us that the contents date at least to the Sassanid period (third to seventh centuries A.D.), and perhaps even earlier, the ninth-century date of the *Bundahišn*'s rescension notwithstanding. The passage goes on to state (*GBd* 28.4, TD MS. 189.8–190.5):

> (Each person has) skin like the sky, flesh like the earth, bone like the mountains, veins like rivers, blood in his body like water in the seas, and a belly like the ocean, and hair like plants—there where the hair grows more, like a thicket—the essence of the body (marrow) like metal, . . . breath drawn in and out like the wind . . . the peak of the head and the brain like (the realm of) endless light, the head like heaven, the two eyes like the sun and moon.

Most of these comparisons are now quite familiar. The homology of marrow and metal is of some interest for its novelty, the basis for this comparison perhaps being the location of strains of ore within rocks, just as marrow is found in streaks inside rock's alloform, bone. A certain expansion of the homologies is also evident, particularly with regard to the celestial and aquatic realms. Thus, in the regions above, three separate homologies are mentioned: (1) skin/sky, the sky seen as an external shell that encircles the cosmos; (2) skull and brain/ endless light (*asar rōšnih*), where the realm of endless light is one of the highest, but not the ultimate heavenly realm, reflecting the brain's position beneath the very top of the body (the "top of the head," *bālist ī sar*, does not properly belong here, but is apparently inserted because of the phonetic attraction of *sar* "head" and *asar* "endless"); and (3) head/heaven (*garōdman*), this heaven being the highest of all, the residence of Ohrmazd. Of the three, skin/sky seems to be a characteristically Iranian innovation, occurring also in *SGW* 16.10; brain/endless light, to be a variant upon from the older homology brain/cloud; and head/heaven preserves the same homology attested in Indic, Germanic, and Latin sources.

Turning to waters, we find the association of veins and rivers on the basis of their form and function, but somewhat surprisingly blood is homologized to sea water and not to fluvial water, which would be the logical continuation of the vein/river homology. A final fluid homology, belly/ocean, connects the two great reservoirs of fluid.

What is notable, quite apart from the relative novelty or conservatism of the specific homologies, is this text's noncommittal stance with regard to the directionality of the homologies. Far from stating that elements of the macrocosm became components of the microcosm at the time of creation, or vice versa, the *Bundahišn* merely claims that they are "like" (Pahl *ciyōn*) one another. The Pseudo-Hippokratic *Peri Hebdomadōn* 6.1–2, most likely written in the fifth century B.C., and once—but no longer, thanks to the brilliant analysis of Jacques Duchesne-Guillemin—thought to depend directly on the Avestan antecedent of *Greater Bundahišn* 28 (the lost *Damdād Nask*), also presents straightforward homologies, with no suggestion of either cosmogonic or anthropogonic slanting.[39] The introductory passage of *Peri Hebdomadōn* 6.1 is very cautious and tentative on this point:

> Those bodies and trees which are in the earth have a similar nature to the world, both the small and the great. For it is necessary that the parts of the world should all be similarly connected to the world, for they take their place in the world from parts (that are) equal and similar.[40]

The text then proceeds to the business at hand, which is organizing both body and cosmos in a system that has seven parts (the main

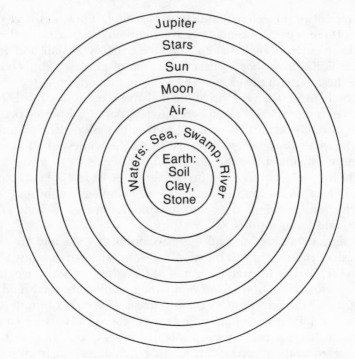

Figure 1a. The macrocosm according to Peri Hebdomadōn *6.1–2.*

theme of the *Peri Hebdomadōn* is the seven-partite structure of all things). This is not achieved without some difficulty, for of the seven items included, two—earth and water—are further subcategorized into three lesser groupings each (stone, clay, soil; rivers, swamps, seas). The resultant whole of eleven (expanded from seven) parts is then given an elegant organization as a system of concentric spheres, starting with the innermost (stone on the macrocosmic level, bone on the microcosmic) and working to the outermost limits (Jupiter and the bodily heat that resides in the skin).[41] The homologies presented may be listed as follows, moving from heights to depths or from periphery to core:

    7. Skin (i.e., the heat surrounding the flesh) : Jupiter
    6. Subcutaneous tissue (i.e., the heat underneath the skin) : Stars
    5. Heat in the viscera and veins : Sun
    4. Sense (located in the lungs and diaphragm) : Moon
    3. Breath : Air
    2. Bodily Fluids : Waters
        2c. Humors : Seas

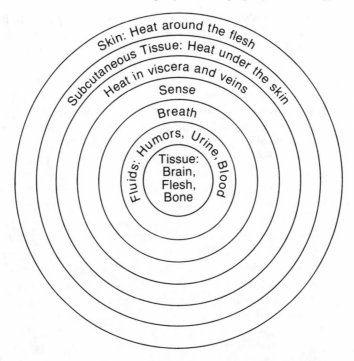

Figure 1b. The microcosm according to Peri Hebdomadōn *6.1–2.*

    2b. Bladder and Intestines (i.e., urine and feces) : Swamps
    2a. Blood : Rivers
  1. Tissues : Earth
    1c. Marrow, Brain, and Semen : Soil (i.e., soft earth)
    1b. Flesh : Clay (i.e., hard earth)
    1a. Bone : Stone

Alternatively, this system may be schematically represented as a set of concentric spheres, as in figure 1.

To be sure, this system is markedly different from any I have considered thus far. Its originality is striking and is one of the chief arguments for viewing it as independent of Iranian—or other—influence. Yet it would be an error to overestimate the originality of this text, for the same, highly traditional homologies are attested in other Greek sources, as for instance, in a famous fragment that survives from the work of the epic poet Khoirilos of Samos:

    Stones are the bones of the earth;
    Rivers are earth's veins.[42]

Yet whereas Khoirilos's use of the homologies is fairly traditional—the same kenning, "bones of the earth" *(hǫgna hreyrs)* occurs also in Old Norse *(Ynglingatal* 19.10)—the *Peri Hebdomadōn* rearranges them boldly, and the rearrangement makes certain adjustments necessary. Thus, hair—which could only go on top of the skin, resulting in the macrocosmic absurdity of plants growing beyond the outermost planetary sphere—has been dropped. Others have been given a new orientation, as for instance the homology of mind and moon, the organ of consciousness here being set in the lungs and diaphragm (presumably Gk *phrenes* in the antecedent Greek version) to reflect the moon's position as the central sphere of the system (the fourth in a set of seven), much as the diaphragm is the central arc in the body.[43] Others emerge more or less unscathed by the reworking, foremost among them bone/stone, flesh/clay, blood/rivers, and breath/air—that is, the lower items in the series. Beyond the realm of the diaphragm/moon homology, things become difficult, for the author of the text chooses to characterize the celestial spheres above all by their light and heat, and thus seeks spheres of heat within the body as their proper counterparts, settling on the heat in the viscera and veins for the sun, the heat in the flesh for the stars, and the heat in the skin for Jupiter. Yet nowhere does he say that one set of alloforms comes from the other. Rather, he refers only to bodily parts as being "imitations" of their macrocosmic homologues.[44]

If the novelty of the *Peri Hebdomadōn* presentation is remarkable, equally remarkable is the conservatism with which a source written some two thousand years later arranged the same basic building blocks. The source in question is Sir Walter Raleigh's *History of the World* 1.2.5, a section entitled "That Man is (as it were) a little world: with a digression touching our mortalities." The digression need not concern us here, but after quoting Gregory Nazianzus to the effect that in creating man God created "another world," a small one to go in the large, Raleigh proceeds to embellish this theme:

> For out of earth and dust was formed the flesh of man, and therefore heavie and lumpish; the bones of his body we may compare to the hard rockes and stones, and therefore strong and durable . . . His bloud, which disperseth it selfe by the branches of veines through all the bodie, may be resembled to those waters, which are carried by brookes and rivers over all the earth; his breath to the aire; his naturall heate to the inclosed warmth, which the Earth hath in it selfe, which stirred up by the heate of the Sunne, assisteth Nature in the speedier procreation of those varieties, which the Earth bringeth forth; Our radicall moisture, oile, or Balsamum (whereon the

naturall heat feedeth and is maintained) is resembled to the fat and fertilitie of the earth; the haires of mans body, which adornes or overshadowes it, to the grasse, which covereth the upper face and skin of the earth; our generative power, to Nature, which produceth all things; our determinations, to the light, wandring, and unstable clowds, carried every where with uncertaine winds; our eies, to the light of the Sunne and Moone, and the beauty of our youth, to the flowers of the Spring, which, either in a very short time, or with the Sunnes heat drie up, & wither away, or the fierce puffes of wind blow them from the stalks; the thoughts of our minde, to the motion of Angels; and our pure understanding (formerly called *Mens*, and that which alwaies looketh upwards) to those intellectuall natures, which are alwayes present with God; and lastly our immortal soules (while they are righteous) are by God himselfe beautified with the title of his own image and similitude.[45]

Here, the tradition is nearing its end, and one wonders to what extent Raleigh actually believed in the truth of this construction. Certainly he had other sources before him as he wrote, and his pompous verbosity hardly carries the force of conviction. In all likelihood, this passage is an antiquarian reminiscence on the theme of microcosm and macrocosm, but it does manage to preserve ancient content with staggering fidelity. Raleigh's skepticism is evident the moment he goes beyond what can be supported by the biblical account of creation, for having asserted that "out of earth and dust *was formed* the flesh of man" (as in Genesis 2.7), he becomes hesitant and hides behind the language of simile: "the bones . . . *we may compare* to the hard rockes," "his bloud . . . *may be resembled* to those waters." The result is neither cosmogony nor anthropogony, nor even really homology, but mere poetic fancy.

Not so in the *Aitareya Upaniṣad*, which presents the most daring and compelling of all the versions I have discussed. After telling how the original lone Self (*ātman*) created the levels of the universe (heaven, atmosphere, earth, and underworld), it goes on to tell that that Self produced the first man, here called Puruṣa ("Man") as in *RV* 10.90. The original Puruṣa seems to be an amorphous mass, however, for the primordial Self next works on him through heat (*abhi- tap-*), a process of transformation familiar from yoga, where ascetic heat (*tapas-*) is at once a mode and a sign of self-transformation. *AitUp* 1.4 describes the process:

(The Self) heated that one (i.e., Puruṣa, "Man"). When it was heated, its mouth broke off, like an egg. From the mouth, there was speech;

from speech, fire. Its nostrils broke off. From the nostrils there was breath; from breath, wind. Its eyes broke off. From the eyes, there was vision; from vision, the sun. Its ears broke off. From the ears, there was hearing; from hearing, the four quarters. Its skin broke off. From the skin, there was bodily hair; from the bodily hair, plants and trees. Its heart broke off. From the heart, there was mind; from mind, the moon. Its navel broke off. From the navel, there was the downward (anal) breath; from the downward breath, death. Its penis broke off. From the penis, there was semen; from semen, the waters.

Straightforwardly cosmogonic, this passage describes the transformation of the first man into the cosmos, and in this is quite like the *Puruṣasūkta* (on which it draws), the myths of Kūnī, Ymir, and Atlas, and the cosmogonic section of the "Poem on the Dove King." Unlike these, however, the *Aitareya Upaniṣad* posits intermediate steps between the microcosmic body and the macrocosmic universe. Thus, for instance, from the nose when first detached from the body there came breath, and thereafter from the breath came wind; likewise, from the eyes there was first vision, then the sun. Sometimes the traditional homologies are preserved in the first and third items of the expanded homologies (for example, *eyes*/vision/*sun*); sometimes in the second and third (for example, heart/*mind*/*moon*). These transformations may be graphed as in figure 2.

This expansion, while interesting, is not in itself remarkable. As we have seen, II Enoch 30.9 also expands upon the usual set of homologies to introduce seven sensory "faculties" or "natures" (*est'stv'*) placed within the bodily parts, which mediate between the body and the external world: vision between eyes and sun, smell between soul and wind, and so on. Here again, note the contrast of directionality: whereas II Enoch is anthropogonic, *AitUp* 1.4 is cosmogonic. The second

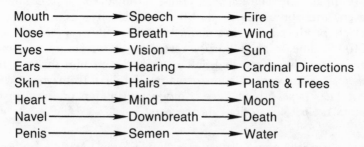

Figure 2. Microcosm to macrocosm according to Aitareya Upaniṣad *1.4.*

Khanda of the Upaniṣad pursues things further, however, adding an anthropogonic account as a counterpart to and reversal of the cosmogony:

> These deities (i.e., fire, wind, sun, etc.) that were thus emitted fell into the great sea. He (the primordial Self) afflicted it with hunger and thirst. They said to him, "Produce a resting place for us, where, being established, we may eat."
>
> He brought a cow to them. They said, "Truly, that's not enough for us." He brought a horse to them. They said, "Truly, that's not enough for us." He brought Puruṣa (i.e., a man) to them. They said, "Ah! Well done!" Truly, Puruṣa (or: man) is something that is well done. (The Self) said to them, "Enter into your respective resting places."
>
> Fire, having become speech, entered into the mouth. Wind, having become the breath, entered into the nostrils. The sun, having become vision, entered into the eyes. The four quarters, having become hearing, entered into the ears. Plants and trees, having become bodily hair, entered into the skin. The moon, having become the mind, entered into the heart. Death, having become the downward (anal) breath, entered into the navel. The waters, having become semen, entered into the penis.

The directionality of creation is thus reversed. A cosmogony becomes an anthropogony as the dismembered Puruṣa is reassembled. In truth, it is not so much a question of directionality as it is a much broader, more daring understanding of the nature of creation. For cosmogony and anthropogony are seen to be equally creative, each one being but a phase in an oscillating process whereby whenever the cosmos is created, the body is destroyed, and—conversely—whenever the body is created, the cosmos is destroyed. The material substances common to both microcosm and macrocosm thus pass from one set of alloforms to the other *and back again* as cosmogony and anthropogony endlessly alternate. To accommodate the full sweep of this construct, I must revise the diagram offered in figure 2, which shows only half of the process. In light of *AitUp* 2.1–4, the picture must appear as in figure 3.

Some of these cycles seem tighter in their logic than others. For instance, the cycle of breath works beautifully: as one exhales, breath leaves the body through the nose and enters the wind, leaving the wind and rejoining the body upon inhalation. The simple act of breathing thus alternately constructs the macrocosm (while deconstructing the microcosm), then constructs the microcosm (while de-

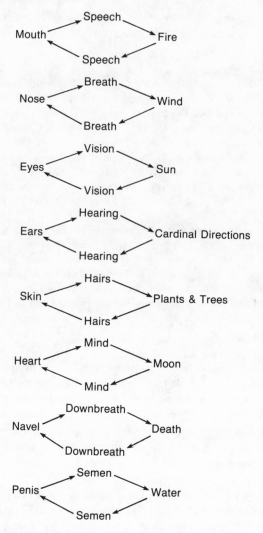

Figure 3. Microcosm and macrocosm according to Aitareya Upaniṣad *1.4–2.4.*

constructing the macrocosm). Similarly, as sound travels into the distance and ceases to be heard, the cardinal directions (the utmost statement of spatial distance) come into being as the sound enters them, while the ears fall apart, being no longer in use. But when sound travels from the distance and is heard by the ears, distance ceases to be, and the ears are reconstituted through the act of hearing.

Other cycles pose more difficulty, particularly those in which there is no mediation through the senses, as for instance the cycle of skin/hair/plants. Yet, as we shall see in Chapters 3 and 4, this cycle actually works admirably well, for it is the ingestion or absorption of plants that causes hair to grow from the skin, while the proper disposal of hair causes the growth of plants. In both instances, the material substance of one alloform is broken down and reconstituted as the matter characteristic of the other alloform, the two processes alternating in a never-ending cycle.

More important than the details of any individual cycle (or subcycle, perhaps) is the working of the entire system. For if we were to ask what sort of system might have given rise to the ideas contained in *both* the anthropogonic and the cosmogonic texts considered earlier, we might well posit one like that of the *Aitareya Upaniṣad,* in which cosmogony and anthropogony alike are but moments in an eternal alternation whereby matter passes from microcosm to macrocosm and back again. Moreover, this text is not alone in presenting such a view; it is found also at the very dawn of Greek philosophy, in the works of Anaximander[46] and more fully in those of Empedokles.

The basic outlines of Empedokles' system are well known, and a brief summary should suffice here. The cosmos is seen as consisting of the four elements he first grouped together: earth, air, fire, and water (fragments B21, B22, B38, and B71). The actions of these elements are governed by two eternal forces: Love, which acts to unite things, and Strife, which cuts them apart (B17, B20, B21, B26). Under the influence of these forces, the cosmos alternates between a stage of total Love, in which all elements are combined in a perfect, undifferentiated, spherical mass (B27, B27A, B28, B29), and a stage of total Strife, in which the elements are fully separated from one another, whirling at terrific speeds and struggling with one another (fragment B35; Aristotle, *Metaphysics* 985. 23–27). Between these two extremes there are a period of increasing Love and one of increasing Strife, during which time the elements exist in various compounds, the compounds growing larger under the influence of Love, and breaking into smaller units under the influence of Strife.[47]

Among the surviving fragments of Empedokles' writings, one of the most important is that which appears as B17 in the Diels-Kranz collection, a passage strongly reminiscent of *AitUp* 1.1–2.4. It opens with this statement:

> I tell (something) diploid: for at one time, the One grew to be one only
>
> Out of many, and at another time it separates again, to be Many out of one.

The One and the Many are thus placed in a relation of reciprocal alternation, each giving rise to the other in turn, as impermanent states of unity are produced by love, only to yield to equally temporary states of separation produced by strife. As Empedokles adds a bit later (B17.12–13), "Insofar as they never stop continuously alternating, thus they are ever motionless in the cycle." "One" and "Many" are thus but moments in an invariant cycle, while "Love" and "Strife" are the forces that produce change from one moment to another and back again, as in figure 4. In his poem *Peri Physeōs* ("On Nature"), Empedokles seems to have described the entire cycle, but from those fragments which have survived it is easiest to get a sense of how the transition from the One to the Many occurred under the force of increasing Strife.

Four separate fragments describe the nature of the One as a "perfectly rounded sphere" (*sphairos kukloterēs*),[48] firmly established in harmony, rejoicing in its solitary rotation.[49] Fragment B27A says of the

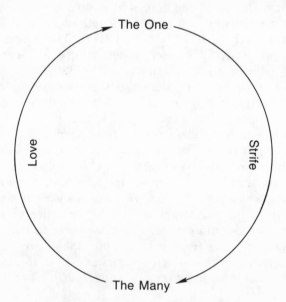

Figure 4. Empedokles' basic system.

sphere, "There was neither dissent nor unseemly battle in its limbs." This simple statement must be understood as a triple negation, for not only were there no dissent and no battle, but there also were *no limbs* in which these might occur, for limbs would only distort the perfect spherical shape of the One.[50] Fragment B29 makes this fully explicit, saying of the Sphere:

> Two branches (i.e., arms) did not shoot from its back,
> Nor feet, nor swift knees, nor generative members;
> But it was a sphere, and equal to itself on all sides.

The first evidence of Strife's activity, then, is the appearance of limbs upon the sphere, for as the first line of fragment B30 puts it, "Great Strife grew (lit 'curdled') within limbs," placing this event at the moment when the time alloted for Love's full rule had ended and the time for the increase of Strife's power had just begun. Strife thus initiates its work of separation by drawing out limbs from the previously limbless, undifferentiated sphere. That Strife will enact further violence upon the sphere and its new excrescences is abundantly clear from fragment B31, which tells us "All the god's (i.e., the sphere's) limbs trembled, one after another," using a verb (*pelemizō*) that is elsewhere employed to describe the trembling of fear prompted by a threatening and violent adversary.[51]

Apparently, the transition from One to Many, in Empedokles' view, took place quite literally through dismemberment, just as the transition from Many to One came as the result of reassembling scattered limbs (B20, B58, B59).[52] Disembodied limbs, however, are not the end point of the reign of Strife, but only a step along the course of increasing Strife. Limbs, too, may be further broken down by the action of separation, and Empedokles takes pains to tell us the precise composition of flesh, blood, and sinew (A78, B96, B98)—something he does for no other item in the entire universe, at least within the fragments of his work that survive.[53] It is worth citing in full the "formula" for the composition of bones: (B96):

> Earth dutifully received in her fair-breasted hollows (or: molds)
> Two of the eight portions of sparkling water
> And four of fire, and white bones came into being,
> Divinely fitted together with the glue of Harmony.

Bone is thus earth, water, and fire mixed together in a 1:1:2 ratio, just as flesh and blood, being lighter in weight and less dense than bone, contain air mixed in with the other three elements (B98). While both flesh and blood tend toward a 1:1:1:1 ratio of the elements, flesh deviates from this a bit, having slightly more earth than a perfectly balanced ratio would admit, being thus denser and less fluid than blood. It is blood, then, that is the perfect substance, containing all elements united in equal measure.[54]

Of equal importance to the details of these proportions is the specification in the last line of fragment B96, which finds an echo in B98, line 3, that these bodily parts are put together and held together by the power of Love and Harmony. Yet what Love puts together, Strife tears apart, and as the period of increasing Strife continues, these bodily parts are broken down, as are all things, until finally there is nothing left but the primal elements—earth, air, fire, and water—standing separate from one another and hostile to one another under the total rule of Strife. This stage is but a moment, however, after which Love's powers begin to increase. And as they increase, the elements are fused together again, forming first tissues, then limbs, then bodies, then larger agglomerations still, until finally the perfect unity of the Sphere is restored—only to be broken down again.

To be sure, Empedokles' Sphere is not a man, yet in all other respects what is said of it is startlingly similar to what we are told of Puruṣa in the *Aitareya Upaniṣad*. Dismembered, they both give rise to the elements of the world, out of which elements they are again reassembled—presumably, only to be dismembered again. Regarding the homologies, however, the two sources differ, for whereas the Upaniṣad preserves such one-to-one equations as those of hair/plants, eyes/sun, and breath/wind, Empedokles views things differently, interpreting all organic matter—as, indeed, all matter of any sort—as compounds of varying proportions of earth, air, fire, and water.

This quadripartite elemental system appears to have been Empedokles' own creation, and it was enormously influential on the history of western philosophy down to modern times. Elegant in its simplicity and its flexibility alike, it is one of the hallmarks of his genius. Yet there persists evidence, in the fragments of his *Peri Physeōs* and in testimonia regarding his work, of an older system with which he was familiar: the system I have explored in this chapter. Five separate instances may be cited.

In one of the briefest of the surviving fragments, B55, Empedokles speaks of "sea, the sweat of earth" (*gēs hidrōta thalasson*). Aristotle contemptuously dismissed this phrase (*Meteorologica* 357a24) as mere poetry, contributing nothing to a true knowledge of nature. Yet within Empedokles' statement is not only the explicit homology of sea and sweat but also an implicit homology between earth and flesh, based on material and positional resemblances. For if sea is the saline fluid that runs off of earth when the earth is warmed—and this, Theophrastos reported, was the sense of Empedokles' comparison—sweat is the saline fluid that runs off of flesh when the flesh is warmed.[55] This homology of earth and flesh is further implied in another brief fragment, B148, where the soft tissue that encases living creatures— that is, the flesh—is described, perhaps poetically and perhaps more seriously, as a type of earth: "mortal-surrounding earth" (*amphibrotēn khthona*). The four-part homologic set apparent in these fragments, then, is as follows:

> Earth : Flesh
> Sweat : Sea

Another traditional homology is attested, not in an actual fragment of Empedokles' writings but in an ancient summary of his ideas prepared by Aetius, who tells us that Empedokles declared the soul to be a mixture primarily consisting of air and aither, the latter being that rarefied, fiery element which filled the uppermost heavens.[56]

The fullest and most fascinating treatment of any homology appears in Fragment B82:

> The same hairs and leaves and thick feathers of birds
> And scales (of fish) come into being on sturdy limbs.

Here Empedokles expands upon the simple alloformic pair hair/leaves, adding feathers and scales to build a larger set. His expansion is not simply random, for his additions are intended to call our attention to his system of the four elements: earth (represented by plants), air (represented by birds), water (represented by fish), and fire (somewhat surprisingly, represented by humans).[57] The result is an elegant twelve-part homologic set:

> Earth : Plants : Leaves
> Air : Birds : Feathers
> Water : Fish : Scales
> Fire : Humans : Hair

So sophisticated is this construction that one of the most serious recent interpreters of Empedokles has claimed that here we may perhaps see "the first awareness of biological analogy and homology."[58] But in light of the other sources I have treated, one can hardly attribute such radical novelty to a Greek philosopher of the Fifth century B.C. Genius he was, but he was working with a set of building blocks already several millennia old.

A novel twist on the old system is also apparent in Empedokles' discussion of crustacea, tortoises, and other animals characterized by exoskeletons, which he contrasts to organisms "dense inside and rarefied on the outside" (B75). Tortoises and others of their ilk he describes in B76 as "stone-skinned" (*lithorrhinos*), by which he means that their bones are on the outside, where their skins ought to be.[59] Yet he refers to these external bones as "stones" (*lithos*). A mere poetic metaphor? Perhaps, but a metaphor that rests upon the ancient homology of bone/stone. Given the presence of four other traditional homologies within the extant Empedoklean corpus, plus the correspondence of Empedokles' alternation between One and Many to the cosmogonic/anthropogonic cycle, I am inclined to view Empedokles as a creative—but faithful—heir to the Indo-European body of thought on the themes of creation and destruction.

Within that system, anthropogony and cosmogony were both described, the two being complementary halves of one cyclical process, a process whereby matter was recurrently transubstantiated from a microcosmic form to a macrocosmic form and thence back again, bones becoming stones becoming bones becoming stones . . . world without end. The body and the universe are alloforms of each other, their respective component parts subtly interrelated along the lines of the homologies I have detailed in this chapter. As will become clear, I have only begun to convey just how subtle this homologic system could be.

© 2

Sacrifice

One of the most obvious practical applications of a myth describing creation through bodily dismemberment is ritual sacrifice. Sacrifice is, in fact, the most prominent of all Indo-European rituals, attested in a stunning variety of forms among the various Indo-European groups.[1] Offerings included human victims;[2] domestic animals, including horses (use of which was limited to royal sacrifices),[3] and more commonly oxen, sheep, pigs, and goats;[4] milk products; agricultural products; and intoxicants such as mead, wine, and the pressed drink the Indo-Iranians called *sauma (Skt soma-, Av haoma-, OPers hauma-).[5]

Even in its most abbreviated forms, sacrifice is a rich, complex, polyphonic act, open to a variety of interpretations by practicants and analysts—the latter indigenous and foreign—alike. It has been viewed as a gift exchange, an act of communion, commensality, or other means of bridging the chasm that separates the sacred from the profane. Alternatively, attention has been called to the fact that in sacrifice killing of animals for food is made a legitimate act instead of a sinful one, and the meat obtained is thereby made sanctified instead of suspect. Yet again, the social functions of sacrifice have been emphasized, for joint participation in acts of prayer, killing, butchering, and eating serves to bind the participants in a cohesive community.[6] Each of these interpretations has a degree of validity, and they are not mutually exclusive. Within the sacrificial practices of any given culture, it is likely that one or more of them will be most prominent, while others will also be evident, although proportionately deemphasized.

Within the sacrifices of the Indo-Europeans, another aspect of sacrifice seems to have been foremost, that which has been studied most fully by Adolf Jensen, Mircea Eliade, and more recently by Cristiano Grottanelli: sacrifice as the repetition of cosmogonic action.[7] As we shall see, each performance of sacrifice was felt to re-create the world, dispersing material substance from its microcosmic form to the macrocosm, and thus sustaining creation. In order to demonstrate this, I shall consider a number of the oldest and best-attested sacrifices as conceived and practiced by the Romans, Germans, Greeks, Iranians, Indians, and Celts, studying their connections to cosmogonic mythology, implicit and explicit, as well as the correspondences among them, common points that are best understood as part of a common tradition.

Let us begin with Rome. There, as Walter Burkert and Jaan Puhvel have recognized, the story of creation through dismemberment was told in connection with the primordial king of Roman myth: Romulus, of whose death two conflicting accounts were given.[8] The first of these is a stereotyped apotheosis legend, in which the great king was said to be lifted up into the skies, where he assumed a divine mode of existence.[9] The other version, which seems to have circulated widely,[10] is quite different. Plutarch, in his *Life of Romulus,* chapter 27, having cited the apotheosis legend, continues: "But others conjecture that the senators rose up against him and dismembered him in the temple of Hephaistos, distributing his body (among themselves), and each one putting a piece in the folds of his robes in order to carry them away." Numerous other sources give the same account, and the dismemberment is consistently reported in unflinching terms. Thus, as Plutarch here uses the graphic verb *diaphtheirantas,* Valerius Maximus 5.3.1 has *laceravit,* while in the latter source and in Florus 1.1.17 the body of Rome's first king is described as *discerptum* "cut into pieces." Most of the sources provide no explanation of the senators' motive in choosing this gruesome mode of doing away with their sovereign. Dionysius of Halicarnassus 2.56 perhaps goes furthest, saying that after the body had been cut apart "they distributed the body in pieces, in order that his corpse not be seen, and they marched out, each one hiding his part under his robes, and afterwards he buried that (piece) in the earth, unseen."

Were the story of Rome's founding cast in the form of a murder mystery, such an explanation might have some merit, and one can appreciate that in the transition from myth to (pseudo)history, Dionysius and others might have felt the need to posit a plausible motive— the need to dispose of their victim's body in secret—for the senators' cruel act. But Walter Burkert has made a convincing case for quite another explanation,[11] and we must consider both the hidden cosmogonic and the sociogonic significance of this story. First, on the cosmogonic side, note that Romulus's body was finally placed in the earth, which is to say that (by virtue of bodily decomposition, if nothing else), his body *became* the earth, just as the flesh of the primordial victim in the cosmogonic accounts I considered in Chapter 1 was said to have become the earth and his bones the stones.

On the sociogonic side, two facts are worth noting. First, the family of Romulus played no appreciable role in the later legends of Rome. Second, it was the first senators who were regarded as the primordial ancestors and founders of the patrician families that forever after constituted the city of Rome; the senators were regularly referred to as the city's *patres,* its "fathers," even within accounts of their murder of the city's single *pater,* Romulus (for example, Livy 1.16.4; Dion Hal 2.56). Given these data, Burkert has convincingly argued that while Romulus lived he alone incarnated Rome in its totality. Upon his death that totality was shattered, and individual families assumed roles as limbs of the state, quite literally speaking. Rome now existed as the sum of these families or *gentes,* and the gentes existed as mutually supporting and interdependent parts of Rome. The distribution of Romulus's bodily parts is thus a mythic sociogony, describing the creation of a differentiated social order in which no *gens* could claim totality or absolute supremacy, but in which each had a role to play in the functioning of the city. Every meeting of the senate, therefore, was nothingless than a reassembling of the primordial totality, that is to say, a convocation of all the Roman gentes reunified the pieces of Romulus's dismembered body. At all other times, however, as the gentes carried on their separate existence, Romulus's body remaining scattered, and each adjournment of the senate repeated the dispersion of his bodily parts.[12]

So much for myth. Burkert's analysis goes further, comparing the story of Romulus's dismemberment to one of the oldest and most important of all Italic sacrifices, the Feriæ Latinæ, a festival originally celebrated by the Latin peoples under the leadership of Alba Longa before the emergence of Rome as a major power, and later taken over by the Romans after their destruction of the Albans in the seventh century B.C.[13] After the Roman takeover, one of the first duties each year for newly elected consuls was to fix the date for celebrating the Feriæ Latinæ, at which time delegates from all Latin cities would assemble at the Alban Mount, the highest point of the Latin countryside, for a common sacrifice to Jupiter Latiaris, "Jupiter of the Latin Peoples," whom Servius (Commentary on *Aeneid* 12.135) calls *deus antiquissimus* "most ancient god." All warfare ceased for the per-

formance of this ritual, in which all the Latin peoples celebrated their
common brotherhood. The fullest account of the ceremony is found
in Dionysius of Halicarnassus 4.49; he, however, wrongly calls it an
innovation of Tarquin designed to cement relations with the Latin
cities after the fall of Alba Longa.[14]

> Planning for the agreements with these cities to stand firm for all
> time, Tarquin thought to designate a common temple for the Ro-
> mans, the Latins, the Hernicians, and those Volscians who had en-
> tered the alliance, in order that they might come together each year
> at the appointed place to congregate, feast together, and take part
> in common rituals.
>
> When all had accepted this happily, he designated the place where
> they would make the assembly; a high mountain, lying just about
> in the middle of the peoples, overlooking the city of the Albans.
> And he set down laws that they would hold assemblies here each
> year, while there would be truces among all of them, and they would
> jointly perform common sacrifices to that deity called Jupiter La-
> tiaris, and they would feast together. And he ranked what each city
> needed to provide for the rites, and the portion that each one ought
> to receive.
>
> The cities taking part in the festival and the sacrifices were forty-
> seven in number. And the Romans celebrate these festivals and these
> sacrifices down to this day, calling them the *Latinæ* ("the Latin rites").
> And of the cities that share in these rites, some bring lambs, some
> cheeses, some a portion of milk, some anything similar, like a sac-
> rificial cake *(pelanos)*. And each receives its ranked portion of the
> one bull that is sacrificed by all in common. And they sacrifice for
> all, and the Romans possess hegemony over the rites.

The culminating act was thus the sacrifice of a bull, a white bull
according to other sources (Arnobius, *Adversus Nationes* 2.68), offered
"by all in common" *(koinōs hypo pasōn)*. This victim was dismembered,
and its meat was distributed to the groups that assembled for the
ceremony, a share in the ox being the concrete sign of their mem-
bership in the federation of Latin peoples. Moreover, the distribution
of meat was highly formalized, coded along hierarchic lines. Large,
powerful cities received large, prestigious cuts of meat, while small
portions were alloted to the lesser members of the federation, even
to the point that when a city shrunk to insignificance it was denied
any portion at all.[15] Given its sociopolitical importance, the distribution
of meat was carefully watched and regulated, and any mistake in the
assignment of portions could result in a pontifical decree that the

entire ritual be repeated, as could the failure of any participant to pray for the welfare of the whole Roman people.[16]

That these two specific ritual errors were taken so seriously confirms much of what I have said thus far, and much of what Dionysius said in his description of the ceremony's purposes. For the first of these errors—improper division of meat—must be understood as constituting a breach of the social hierarchy, a hierarchy that is confirmed and reestablished each year through the *proper* division and distribution of meat. Similarly, the second error—failure to pray for the common good—constitutes a breach of social solidarity (albeit solidarity under Roman domination), which is confirmed and reestablished each year through these very prayers.

Proper performance of the sacrifice is thus seen to be a creative act—more sociogonic than cosmogonic—in which the dual nature characteristic of a segmentary society is created, such a society existing both as a set of separate, hierarchically ranked subunits and as the cohesive totality that incorporates all of those subunits. Within this sociogonic rite, such a cohesive totality appears both in the assembly of representatives from all cities and in the victim before it is sacrificed, while hierarchic separation appears in the scattered cities to which representatives return and in the various cuts of meat taken from the victim's dismembered body. The structure is the same as that in the myth of Romulus's dismemberment; social solidarity is again represented in the form of an intact body (in the myth, human; in the rite, bovine), and social separation and/or hierarchy in the form of flesh distributed from a dismembered corpse. The relations between myth and ritual can be graphed as in table 6.

There is no explicit Roman testimony linking the myth of Romulus's death to the bull sacrifice of the Feriæ Latinæ, however much they both describe the creation of social groupings from the dismembered body of a focal victim.[17] The connection between the two remains a scholar's construct, resting on the similarities adduced in table 6. Such is not the case, however, with one of the earliest, most famous, and best-described Germanic sacrifices—that performed by the Semnones, as reported by Tacitus, *Germania* 39.[18]

This fascinating text is one of the few parts of the *Germania* for which Tacitus made use of direct Germanic informants, who seem to have been none other than Masyos, king of the Semnones, and his seeress Ganna, who visited Rome during the reign of Domitian (A.D. 81–96), shortly before the writing of the *Germania*.[19] The account of the Semnones' sacrifice is thus one of the rarest and most precious items encountered within ancient ethnography, an authoritative sum-

Table 6. Roman mythico-ritual patterns: Feriæ Latinæ and the dismemberment of Romulus.

	Social totality and solidarity	Social segmentation and hierarchy
Ritual		
Relevant group	Latin League	Latin cities
Spatiotemporal expression	Assembly on Alban Mount	Dispersion from Alban Mount
Representative form	Whole ox	Cuts of meat
Myth		
Relevant group	City of Rome	Roman *gentes*
Spatiotemporal expression	Convocation of Senate	Adjournment of Senate
Representative form	Romulus	Romulus's dismembered body

mary of a functioning cult; moreover, it is the earliest and most thorough description of pre-Christian Germanic sacrifice to be found anywhere.[20]

This is not to say that there are no difficulties in the interpretation of the text. Tacitus has condensed a great deal of information into a very brief description, and his language conveys a wealth of detail in each short phrase. At points, important grammatical constructions are ambiguous, and scholars have often selected the more obvious readings rather than the more fully expressive ones. Most of the thorniest issues of grammar and content were resolved however in a landmark article by L. L. Hammerich, whose arguments have since won considerable support among Germanists.[21] Following Hammerich, I translate as follows:

> They say that the Semnones are the oldest and most noble of the Suebi. This belief is confirmed in a religious ceremony of ancient times. At a fixed time, all the people of the same blood come together by legations in a wood that is consecrated by the signs of their (ancestral) fathers and by an ancient dread. Barbaric rites celebrate the horrific origins, through the sacrifice (*caeso*, lit "dismemberment") of a man for the public good (or: "in public") . . .
>
> There the belief (*superstitio*) of all looks backward (to the primordial past), as if from that spot there were the origins of the race. The

god who is ruler of all things is there. Others are inferior and subservient.

The good fortune of the Semnones adds to their authority. One hundred cantons are inhabited for them, and this great body causes them to believe themselves to be the head of the Suebi.

The Semnones are thus said to be a part of the Suebian confederation, or amphictyony, which is described by Tacitus in *Germania* 38 as being divided into numerous tribes, each with its own name, all of whom consider themselves part of a larger entity, referring to themselves collectively as Suebi.[22] The bond that connects them is one of (fictive) kinship, derived from a (mythic) genealogy, for we are told that "all the people of the same blood" (*omnes eiusdem sanguinis populi*) come together to a place consecrated by the signs of their common ancestors (*auguriis patrum . . . sacram*). Although we are not given the details of the genealogy that connects all the various Suebian peoples, it is undoubtedly a continuation of the mythic genealogy of the Germanic peoples given by Tacitus in *Germania* 2, for we are told elsewhere (Pliny, *NH* 4.99), that the Suebi were part of the Irminones or Herminones, one of the three groups named in Tacitus's account:

> (The Germans) celebrate in ancient songs—which are their only means of remembrance or recording the past—an earth-born god, Tuisto (or: Tuisco). His son Mannus was the origin of their race and their founder. They assign three sons to Mannus, and from their names they call those close to the ocean Ingaevones; those in the middle, Herminones; and all the rest, Istaevones.

Each of these three groupings thus has a tribal ancestor from whom they take their name: the Ingaevones from Ing, who corresponds to the Old Norse god Yngvi (Freyr); the Herminones from Irmin, the national god of the Saxons according to Widukind of Corvey and others (who may also correspond to ON Jǫrmunr, a by-name of Óðinn); and the Istaevones from *Ist, who is unknown elsewhere.[23] This brief account—taken from the ancient songs of the Germans themselves, as Felix Genzmer convincingly showed[24]—must also be seen as preserving cosmogonic lore. For as I have argued in the past, following Hermann Güntert, the names of the first ancestors that are given here—Tuisto (< PIE *dwis-to-* "the doubled one, the twin") and Mannus (< PIE *manu-* "man")—preserve those usually given to the actors in IE myths of creation, in which "Twin" most often is the sacrificial victim and "Man" performs the offering.[25]

Tuisto—whose name is synonymous with that of Old Norse Ymir, from whose body the world is made in the Eddic accounts[26]—is thus seen to be the ancestor of the whole universe, as well as all humanity. Mannus, his son, is presumably the ancestor of the Germans, and Mannus's three sons are the eponymous ancestors of the three major branches of the Germanic people. Presumably the lineage continued, supplying a founding father for the Suebi (said in *Germania* 38 to be the largest of all Germanic tribes) and others, with the eldest son of the Suebian ancestor being cast as the founding father of the Semnones, who are "the oldest and most noble" (*vetustissimos se nobilissimosque*) of the Suebi. Germanic sociopolitical organization and mythic genealogy are thus intimately correlated, as shown in figure 5. What is evidenced here is a classic segmentary system, in which separate subgroups form ever larger social aggregates on the strength of their perceived common kinship.

In order to do this, they must actually *feel* their common origins: they must actively remember their bond of kinship. Such sentiments are reaffirmed and reestablished in and through the regular repetition of the Semnones' sacrifice, in which "all the people of the same blood" (*omnes eiusdem sanguinis populi*) reunite at a cultic place that not only is "consecrated by the signs of their fathers" but is the very spot where their people had their origins (*inde initia gentis*), which is to say the very spot where Tuisto—the "earth-born deity" (*deum terra editum*)— came into being, lived, and died. Not only solidarity and common kinship are celebrated in the Semnones' cult, but also hierarchy. Tacitus states in the opening words of his description: "They say that the Semnones are the oldest and most noble of the Suebi. This belief is confirmed in a religious ceremony of ancient times." The ritual thus not only brought all the Suebi together but also reasserted the position of the Semnones at their head. As a sacrifice that served to establish both social solidarity (among the Suebi as a whole) and hierarchic segmentation (among the various Suebian tribes), the Semnones' cult is strongly reminiscent of the Feriæ Latinæ, and the ritual acts performed in each ceremony are quite similar as well.

As to what was actually done within the Semnones' cult, Tacitus is brief but highly expressive. A human victim was dismembered: on this the terminology is clear. Not only is the participle *caesus* (from *caedere* "to cut, hew, cut to pieces") used to denote the manner in which the victim was offered, but the ritual is also said to be "barbaric" (*barbari ritus*). This is not simply a condemnation of human sacrifice per se, for Tacitus elsewhere (*Germania* 9; *Annals* 13.57) discusses the human offerings of the Germans without such language.

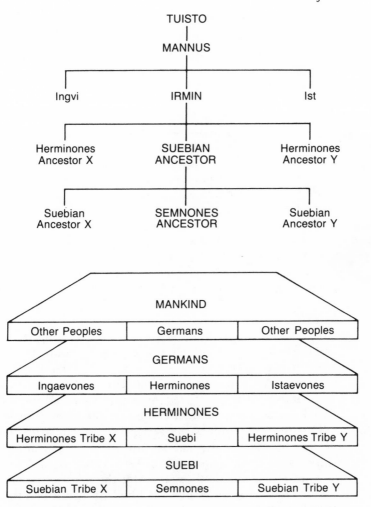

Figure 5. Germanic mythic genealogy and segmentary social organization.

Rather, there was something specific within the Semnones' practices that he found particularly offensive, and Hammerich has persuasively argued that this was dismemberment of the victim, perhaps performed in full public view (*caesoque publice homine*). Archaeological evidence may now provide grisly corroboration of these practices.[27]

Finally, we are told precisely why the Semnones perpetrated such an act, for the "barbaric rites" are said to "celebrate the horrific origins" (*celebrant barbari ritus horrenda primordia*). And what origins are these that could be so horrific? Given the context—a sacrificial cultus that consciously hearkened back to the first beings, "Man" and "Twin"— it seems most likely that the reference is to a Germanic variant of the mythic theme of creation through sacrifice, with the physical and social universe alike being formed from the victim's dismembered body.[28]

Each time the Semnones performed sacrifice, they thus repeated acts of creation: "horrific origins," as it were.[29] Each victim re-presented Tuisto, the "Twin," and was dismembered at the very spot where the original Tuisto first appeared and was carved up to form the various peoples of the world, of whom the Semnones were—in their own view, of course—the most important.

We are not told in any detail what became of the victim's dismembered body, whether it was distributed to the participants in the rite like the bull in the Feriæ Latinæ and Romulus's corpse, scattered to the elements like Ymir's body in the Old Norse accounts, or disposed of in other ways. It is possible that Tacitus gives us a hint in the final sentence of his account, where he tells us that the Semnones "believe themselves to be the head of the Suebi" (se Sueborum caput credant), a phrase that may be no metaphor, but may perhaps reflect their share in the bloody offering.[30]

The two rituals I have considered thus far are among the most ancient and the best attested within their respective culture areas, and they also resemble each other closely in detail and general structure. Both are celebrations of sociopolitical solidarity and segmentation, in which large national or tribal aggregations are assembled, reminded of their common bonds, and then dispersed into their constituent subunits. This process parallels the sacrificial dismemberment of a central victim—bovine for the Latins, human for the Semnones— which reappears each year, whole, only to be torn apart again.[31] Finally, these processes repeat the acts described in the myth of creation— explicitly so for the Semnones—in which the first man is said to have been dismembered in order to create the cosmos and/or the social groups that inhabit it.

Certain authors, most notably Kasten Rönnow, have sought to find a similar pattern within the myths and rituals of the Greek Orphics, and have called attention to numerous fascinating pieces of evidence.[32] Yet as with all of the "Orphic" materials, scholarly controversy abounds, and the data are seldom sufficient to argue to solid, tenable conclusions.[33] The Greeks seem to have had multiple myths of the first sacrifice—that of Prometheus, that of Deukalion, that of the Bouphonia, for instance, in addition to that in which Dionysos-Zagreus was the victim—most of which preserve only faint traces of the Indo-

European pattern.[34] There is one ancient Greek author who discussed sacrifice in considerable detail, however, explicitly relating it to a cosmogonic pattern, and speaking of both sacrifice and cosmogony in terms that correspond closely to those we have encountered among the Latins and Germans. He is an author whose cosmogonic theories I considered in Chapter 1: Empedokles, who in addition to his work on the nature of the universe (the *Peri Physeōs*) wrote another treatise, the *Katharmoi* ("Purifications"), which has sacrifice as one of its central topics.[35]

There are a few differences between Empedokles' view of sacrifice and that which is present in the rituals I have discussed, quite apart from the obvious fact that Empedokles was a philosopher speculating critically upon the nature of sacrifice, rather than a priest performing the ritual. First, he focused more on the cosmogonic side of sacrifice than on the sociogonic, as seems only appropriate in light of his other interests. Yet paradoxically, given his cosmic focus, he considered most deeply the effect of sacrifice on the individual sacrificer, rather than on the cosmos, thus adding a powerful ethical dimension to his analysis. Finally, what was most shocking to his contemporaries, Empedokles was opposed to sacrifice. Günther Zuntz, in the most thorough recent study of the *Katharmoi*, has gone so far as to call the rejection of sacrifice the very center of Empedokles' life and thought,[36] stating that it was his program "to controvert the accepted traditions of public and private worship. No revaluation more fundamental could be contemplated; he purport[ed] to denounce the current rites and the gods demanding them . . ."[37]

The reasons for this become clear when we recognize—as is now the general trend in Empedoklean scholarship—that the *Peri Physeōs* and the *Katharmoi* consciously and meticulously mirror each other, the former describing the cyclical existence of the macrocosm, and the latter that of the microcosm.[38] This microcosm, however, is not defined simply as man, but rather as *daimōn*, the immortal soul, which passes through a whole series of bodies, of which the human is only one. And just as in the *Peri Physeōs* it is the forces of Love (which unifies all things) and Strife (which separates or cuts apart) that drive the universe through its multiple forms, so in the *Katharmoi* these same forces drive the daimōn through its various incarnations.

As we saw in Chapter 1, Empedokles took the sphere as the starting point for his discussion of the macrocosm, the point in space and time wherein the cosmic elements are all united in love and harmony. To this, on the microcosmic scale, corresponds the reign of Aphrodite, goddess of love, which, shockingly to a Greek audience, he places

prior to the reign of any of the deities mentioned in Hesiod's *Theogony*.
In fragment B128, Empedokles describes this paradisal reign, particularly stressing the form of cult addressed to Aphrodite, that is, to
Love enthroned as queen of the universe: a cult in which the offerings
entailed no death and no dismemberment.

> Ares was not any god for them, nor was Kudoimos ("Battle-din"),
> Nor was Zeus king, nor Kronos, nor Poseidon,
> But Kypris (= Aphrodite) was queen.
> They appeased her with pious gifts:
> With painted animal (figures), with perfumes of artificial fragrance,
> With sacrifices of unmixed myrrh and of fragrant frankincense,
> Pouring libations of golden honey to the ground.
> The altar was not smeared with the unmixed (or: "unceasing") gore
>   of bulls.
> Rather, that was the greatest defilement for men:
> Taking away the life-force in order to eat the noble limbs.

In this golden age, humans, gods, plants, and animals were all united
in love, with no violence among them.[39] And what disrupts this golden
age is nothing other than the introduction of animal sacrifice, specific
stress here being laid on the shedding of blood—the perfect element
in Empedokles' system (fragment B98)—and the dismemberment of
the victim's corpse. The latter is particularly significant, since, as Empedokles made clear in his work on the nature of the cosmos (see
especially frament B20), he saw dismemberment as the act of Strife
par excellence: the violent tearing apart of those things which Love
brings together. The breakdown of the cosmos from the perfect Sphere
to the scattered elements began with the Sphere's dismemberment
B27, B30, B31), just as we are told that the reign of Aphrodite ended
with the dismemberment of the first sacrificial victim.

What is more, whenever an individual daimōn performs sacrifice,
this act of Strife has catastrophic effects for him (or her). The perfect
state for a daimōn is existence as a god, from which one is expelled
upon performance of sacrificial dismemberment, separated from his
or her prior perfect existence by the very Strife he or she has un-
leashed. The process is described in some detail in fragment B115, a
passage that draws on *Theogony* 793–805 but goes considerably beyond
it in its premises and conclusions:

> There is a proclamation of Necessity, an ancient decree of the gods,
> An eternal one, secured by broad oaths.

Whenever some one of those daimōns who were apportioned long-
lasting life
Should defile his dear limbs with gore [. . .]
He will wander for three thousand years away from the blessed ones,
Springing forth in manifold forms of mortal bodies through time,
Exchanging one painful path of life for another.
For the force of air drives him to the sea
And the sea spits him onto the surface of the land; Earth (sends him)
to the beams
Of the radiant sun, which toss him to the eddies of air.
One receives him from the other, and all abhor him.
I am now one of those: a wanderer, having fled from the gods,
Trusting to raging Strife.[40]

The long cycle of rebirths in various forms—Empedokles tells us
elsewhere that he has been a boy and a girl, a bush, a bird, and a fish
(fragment B117)—is thus a set of purifications (*Katharmoi*), atone-
ments for the crime of having performed the classic act of Strife:
sacrificial dismemberment.

We must stress, however, that these rebirths are not random, but
follow a clear structure, whereby the daimōn is reborn within each of
the four cosmic elements. "The force of air drives him to the sea and
the sea spits him onto the surface of the land; earth to the beams of
the radiant sun, which toss him to the eddies of air" (B115, ll. 9–11).
Again, the births Empedokles relates in B117 are coded to this same
system: birth as a fish representing water, as a bird representing air,
as a bush representing earth, and as a human representing fire, the
last perhaps because of the fiery human soul.[41]

Each sacrifice is thus seen to repeat the cosmogony, although somewhat ironically it is the sacrificer, not the victim, who is scattered to
the macrocosmic elements as a consequence of the act of dismemberment. In Empedokles' view, sacrifice and creation are alike tragic
events: regrettable falls from a perfect state, born of Strife alone. This
novel line of thought notwithstanding, the basic ideas are tremendously ancient, preserving highly traditional themes and details with
considerable fidelity. Within an antisacrificial polemic, the older, Indo-
European sacrificial ideology remains clear.

The same pattern, in which sacrifice is seen to repeat the cosmogony,
was also prevalent in ancient Iran. In his brilliant researches, Marijan
Molé clearly demonstrated how cosmogony and eschatology lie at the
heart of every Zoroastrian sacrifice, repeating creation at the same
time that they anticipate the final "Renovation" (*Frašagird*) wherein
the universe will be restored to its original perfection.[42] But the Ira-

nian datum with the strongest correspondences to the materials I have considered from Greece, Rome, and Germany is not drawn form the Zoroastrian cultus, but is a description of animal sacrifice as performed by the Magi of Asia Minor in the fifth century B.C., which Herodotos—himself a Persian citizen, with ready access to knowledgeable informants—presents in his *History* 1.131–32.[43]

> I know the customs used by the Persians to be these. It is not their custom to establish statues, temples, and altars, and they hold those who build them to be foolish, I suppose, because they never believed the gods to be ones whose nature is like that of a man (*anthrōpophueas*), as do the Greeks. They do honor to Zeus on the highest of mountains, ascending them to offer sacrifice, and calling the entire rim of heaven "Zeus." They sacrifice to the sun, and also to the moon, and to earth and to fire and to water and to the winds . . .
>
> And this is the sacrifice of these Persians with regard to the aforesaid gods. They build no altars, and kindle no fires when thinking to sacrifice, nor do they indulge in libations, flutes, fillets, or barley. And whoever wishes to sacrifice to one (of the gods), he leads the victim to a purified place, and he calls the god, being wreathed with a tiara chiefly of myrtle. Now in truth, they do not pray for blessings for the sacrificer himself, but pray for good to come to all Persians and to the King, for (the sacrificer) thinks himself to be among all the Persians. Then, having cut the victim into pieces limb from limb, boiled the flesh, and strewn the softest grass, particularly clover, he then places all the flesh on top of this. When he has arranged (the pieces), a man—a Magus—standing beside him, sings a theogony, as it is not their custom to perform sacrifices without a Magus. Having waited a little while, the sacrificer carries away the flesh, and uses it as he pleases.

Numerous details within this account merit and have received close attention: the mountaintop locus (as with the Feriæ Latinæ), the strew of clover (like the Indian *barhiṣ*), the prayer for general well-being (perhaps even cosmic renewal) rather than personal prosperity, the absence of fire or libation (in contrast to Zoroastrian practice), to name but a few. Beyond these details, a correct interpretation of the text as a whole rests on understanding three key terms within it: *theogoniē* ("theogony"), *theos* ("god"), and *dia-tithēmi* ("to arrange").

A theogony is literally an account of "the birth of the gods," but whenever it was used after Hesiod, it could not fail to evoke that author's great *Theogony*, the closest thing to a systematic and authoritative account of creation that the Greeks possessed. In Hesiod, the

births of the gods are hardly related for their own sake, but cumu-
latively are portrayed as being tantamount to the emergence of the
universe from primordial chaos to its present state. In stating that the
presiding Magus chanted a "theogony" within the course of the sacrifice, Herodotos meant to denote nothing less than a hymn of creation, and not merely a praise-song to one god or another, as some
have maintained.[44]

Analysis of the use of the noun *theos* in this passage leads to the
same conclusion, for Herodotos employs it quite strangely here. In
spite of all evidence to the contrary—which is abundant, and must
have been so in his time also—Herodotos asserts that the "gods" (*tous
theous*) of the Persians were not worshipped in anthropomorphic form
(*ouk anthrōpophueas*). This is not an error on his part, for he presents
us with a list of the deities he has in mind, none of which is anthropomorphic: Heaven, Sun, Moon, Earth, Fire, Water, and the Winds.[45]
Rather, these are the constituent parts of the macrocosm, and the
birth of such "gods" as these would amount to nothing less than a
cosmogony.

The intimate connection of cosmogony and sacrifice is thus asserted
through the creation hymn chanted by the officiating priest, and this
connection is further evidenced in the sacrificial acts. At the center
of the sacrifice lay the dismemberment of an animal victim, that victim
being offered to the abovementioned "gods." The verb used to describe the deposition of the victim's flesh on the strewn clover under-
lines the importance of dismemberment, for Herodotos does not use
the simple verb *tithēmi* "to place, set down," but instead chooses a
compound form, *dia-tithēmi* "to arrange each of several items in their
separate places, to distribute."[46] The Magus thus must have carefully
laid out each piece of meat in its own special place, perhaps—as Cristiano Grottanelli, who first recognized the significance of this verb,
suggested to me—reconstructing the victim and/or the cosmos in the
process.[47]

Further, we must recognize that, in Herodotos's account, it is those
parts of the cosmos which commonly appear as alloforms of bodily
members—heaven (the alloform of the head, or sometimes of the
skin), sun (the alloform of the eyes), moon (mind), earth (flesh),
water (blood), and wind (breath) that are said to be the "gods" who
receive sacrifice. Only the "god" fire is an innovation on the traditional pattern, and fire in India and Iran seems to have had a special
connection to the omentum, the fattiest piece of visceral tissue, which
burned brightest and thus may have been seen as the microcosmic
incarnation of fire.[48] The fact that the dismembered victim is exposed

for only a short time and is then carried off—presumably to be eaten—should not deter us from concluding that the sacrifice had as its purpose the dispersion of the victim's bodily members from microcosm to macrocosm in repetition of the cosmogony. For as Strabo, who followed Herodotos closely but added certain information drawn from his own first-hand observation of Magi in Cappadocia, tells us (15.3.13): "(The Magi) say that the god requires the victim's soul, and nothing else."

This view of sacrifice as a ritual of cosmic maintenance that (1) repeats the cosmogony, and (2) translates matter from the microcosm to the macrocosm via a system of homologic alloforms, is well attested in India. A full study of Indic sacrificial thought and praxis is a topic for several volumes, at the very least,[49] and I will thus focus on only a small fraction of the available evidence. To begin, let me cite the opening paragraph of one of the oldest and most famous of the Upaniṣads, the *Bṛhadāraṇyaka* which presents an analysis of the macrocosmic alloforms of the sacrificial victim, here a horse.

> Om. Truly, the head of the sacrificial horse is the dawn. His eye is the sun; his breath is the wind; the fire is his open mouth. The body of the sacrificial horse is the year. His back is heaven; his innards are the atmosphere; his underside is the earth; his sides are the four cardinal directions; and his ribs are the intermediate directions. His limbs are the seasons; his joints are the months and fortnights. His feet are the days and nights. His bones are the stars; his flesh the clouds; the sands are his undigested food. His intestines are the rivers; the hills are his liver and lungs. His hair is the plants and trees. His front half is the rising sun; his rear half is the setting sun. When he yawns, there is lightning; when he shakes, it thunders; when he urinates, then it rains.

Here, three common IE homologies persist—eye/sun, breath/wind, and hair/plants—alongside others that are less broadly attested. Thus, the passage contains an attempt to homologize the three levels of cosmic space (heaven, atmosphere, earth) to three horizontal planes found within a quadruped victim: heaven being associated with the animal's back, atmosphere with its body cavity, and earth with its underbelly. This set of homologies, found also in Iran, is, in all likelihood, of Indo-Iranian date.[50]

A specifically Indian innovation is the attempt to describe the storm as alloforms of certain bodily parts or processes of the sacrificial victim. Here, speaking of a horse, the lightning is compared to its yawn, the thunder to its shaking, and the rain to its urine. Elsewhere, in a text of considerably earlier date used in the sacrifice of a cow, the rain is homologized to her udders and the lightning to her teats.[51] Details were obviously flexible, but the intent was the same in both instances.

Most daring of all is the Indic homology of time and the sacrificial victim.[52] Thus, the four limbs of the horse are presented as alloforms of the four seasons, while the subdivisions of those limbs—the joints—become subdivisions of the seasons: months and fortnights. Finally, the base on which the joints and limbs rest—the feet—becomes the base of fortnights, months, and seasons: the days and nights. As a result of these homologies, all time—as well as all space and matter—is seen to have its source in the sacrificial victim, and it is the proper and fully knowledgeable performance of sacrifice that serves to create time and the cosmos.

Although ever open to speculative reworking and specific innovations, the system of cosmic homologies and its application to sacrifice is of great antiquity in India, well attested in the *Saṃhitas* and *Brāhmaṇas* written centuries before the *Bṛhadāraṇyaka Upaniṣad*. Perhaps the oldest evidence is found in the sole hymn of the *Ṛg Veda* given over to consideration of the horse sacrifice, itself the starting point for *BṛhadUp* 1.1. There we read (*RV* 1.162.18):

> The ax comes together with the thirty-four ribs of the steed which is bound to the gods.
> You must make the unsevered limbs into works of art: having named (them) aloud, joint by joint, you must dismember (them).

And again, (RV 1.162.19cd–20):

> However many (pieces) I make of your limbs, so many lumps I pour forth into the fire.
> Do not burn your own body, which is entering (the other world): may the ax not injure your corpse!
> May a hasty, incompetent dismemberer not ruin your severed limbs with a sword, having proceeded incorrectly.[53]

The text is extremely difficult to translate and to interpret, in part because of the many *hapax legomena* that occur, and in part because the *Ṛg Veda*, being a liturgical text rather than a ritualist's manual, does not spell out for us the actions alluded to here. Three points, however, may be made with certainty: (1) the victim is being dismembered; (2) precise rules govern the procedures for dismemberment:

and (3) dismemberment and burning of either the bodily parts themselves or representatives (the "lumps" of RV 1.162.19d) of them play important roles affecting the entry of the victim into another world or another mode of existence.

Fortunately, we possess the ritualist's manuals that accompany the hymns of the *Ṛg Veda*, the most important of which is the *Aitareya Brāhmaṇa,* and *AB* 2.6 gives a precise account of what is to be said and done when an animal victim is dismembered. The slaughterers (*śamitāra*) are brought forward, the victim is consecrated, a fire is set in front of its body, and sacred grass (*barhiṣ*) is strewn on the earth.[54] Next, the assent of the victim's relatives is invoked before the dismemberment begins. Finally, we are given the sacred formulas that accompany the dismemberment itself:

> "Lay its feet down to the north. Cause its eye to go to the sun; send forth its breath to the wind; its life-force to the atmosphere; its ear to the cardinal points; its flesh to the earth." Thus, (the dismemberer) places this (animal) in these worlds.

Clearly this process of dispersing the victim's bodily parts to the macrocosm is felt to repeat the cosmogonic events described in *RV* 10.90.13–14:

> The moon was born of his mind; of his eye, the sun was born;
> From his mouth, Indra and fire; from his breath, wind was born.
> From his navel there was the atmosphere; from his head, heaven was rolled together;
> From his feet, the earth; from his ear, the cardinal directions.
> Thus they cause the world to be created.

Of the five homologies presented in *AB* 2.6, three are taken directly from these verses—eye/sun, breath/wind, and ear/cardinal directions.[55] A fourth—life-force/atmosphere—seems to be a conscious modification of a homology offered in *RV* 10.90.14, navel/atmosphere, specifying just what is contained in or behind the navel that makes it similar to the atmosphere.[56] But the fifth homology found in *AB* 2.6 is perhaps the most interesting and important of all, for it is well attested elsewhere in the IE world, but not in any Indian text prior to this one—that of flesh and earth—clearly indicating that this is not simply a Brāhmaṇic reworking of materials from the *Puruṣasūkta* but, at least to a certain extent, an independent tradition, in which a common IE pattern of speculation regarding sacrifice and creation is faithfully preserved.

Here, as elsewhere, sacrifice was considered to be a repetition of creation, which could have cosmogonic and/or sogiogonic dimensions. The former of these was stressed in the Indo-Iranian tradition and in the writings of Empedokles, the latter in the Italic Feriæ Latinæ. The Semnones' sacrifice, as described in *Germania* 39, seems to have spanned both. An alternation is also evident between the use of human and animal victims, the former being attested among the Germans, the latter among the Italians, Indians, and Iranians. Here, it is Empedokles who seems to have spanned both practices, for while in the passages I have considered he mentions only an animal victim, in another celebrated fragment (B137) he argues that each animal victim is really a human (or better yet, a daimōn) in another bodily form, and he goes on to denounce sacrifice as a form of murder, indeed of unwitting patricide, matricide, and infanticide.[57]

The picture of IE sacrificial practice and ideology that emerges is this: human and/or animal victims were offered—animals perhaps serving in some sense (and at some times) as substitutes for human offerings. In any event, a central feature of the ritual was dismemberment of the victim's corpse. Various bodily members were then distributed to participants in the sacrifice, in repetition of the sociogonic parts of the creation myth, while other portions were dispersed to the cosmos, either "in spirit" or through the medium of fire, in repetition of the cosmogonic parts of the same myth. Table 7 summarizes the relevant evidence.

Indic analysis of the sacrifice did not stop here, but moved to even more daring conclusions. Recognizing the cyclicity of anthropogony and cosmogony, the Indian sages looked for a similar cyclicity within the sacrificial rites. The question which they seemed to pose was this: if the body of a sacrificial victim contains the potential to re-create the cosmos, how came such potential to reside in this body? As early as *Atharva Veda* 9.5.20–21, a solution was offered:

> Truly, the (sacrificial) goat strode through this world in the beginning. This (earth) became its breast, heaven (became) its back.
> The atmosphere (became) its middle; the cardinal points, its sides; the oceans, its bellies.
> Truth and Right (became) its eyes; all truth and faith, its breath; the Virāj (meter), its head.
> This truly is a sacrifice without limits: the goat accompanied by five grain-offerings!

The solution is as stunning as it is simple: the victim can become the cosmos because earlier the cosmos had become the victim. Such logic

Table 7. Patterns of sacrifice among the Indo-Europeans.

	Dionysius of Halicarnassus 4.49	Tacitus, Germania 39	Empedokles	Herodotos 1.131 f.	Aitareya Brāhmaṇa
Human victim		X	X		
Animal victim	X		X	X	X
Dismembered	X	X	X	X	X
Distribution to participants	X	*		*	
Repeats sociogony	*	X			
Dispersion to cosmos		*	X	X	X
Repeats cosmogony		X	X	X	X

X = explicitly attested
* = implicit in accounts

may be pursued in infinite regress and progress alike, stretching out to an eternal cycle of sacrifice and creation, matter ever flowing from microcosm to macrocosm and back again.

This view of sacrifice becomes the central theme of the *Brāhmaṇas*, which never tire of telling the story how the first victim—now called Prajāpati ("Lord of Creatures") more often than Puruṣa ("Man"), although the latter name does persist in places[58]—was taken apart to create the world, only to be put back together again so that the sacrifice might be performed and the world re-created.[59] The great sacrifices of the later Vedic period are also structured around this theme, with as much attention being given to the symbolic re-creation of the primordial victim as to the sacrificial repetition of his dismemberment. Thus, for instance, in the Agnicayana, an entire year is devoted to the construction of a fire altar, the five levels of which are explicitly said to correspond to the five bodily layers of Prajāpati (marrow, bone, flesh, skin, hair) at the same time that they correspond to the cosmic levels of earth, atmosphere, and heaven together with two intermediate zones.[60] Matter is drawn from all creation in the building of the fire altar—earth and water to make the bricks, grass (= Prajāpati's hair) to place on top, and so on—only to be dispersed again when the altar is torn down upon completion of the offering.[61] Once again, in the Pravargya, an offering of milk that has been heated in a clay pot, the ritual comes to center less on the offering itself than on the construction of a *Mahāvīra,* a "Great Man," in which the clay pot is set out as the "head" of a human figure, with the other ritual implements being used to form legs, arms, torso, and so forth. In the course of this ritual, the body of the primordial victim, "Man" (here, *vīra-*), is thus reconstructed, only to be torn apart again.[62]

Such elaborate rituals as these probably belong to the later development of sacrifice in India, in which the IE ideology of sacrifice was applied on a scale unrealized anywhere else.[63]

The fire altar of the Agnicayana and the "Great Man" of the Pravargya are strongly reminiscent of another form of sacrifice attested from the opposite end of the Indo-European world. Unfortunately, we know relatively little about Celtic sacrifice, in comparison to what is attested for its Indic, Iranian, Greek, Roman, and Germanic counterparts. All accounts of sacrifice among the insular Celts are found in sources written well after the conversion to Christianity, while the only descriptions of sacrifice among the continental Celts that have come down to us are those of Greco-Roman authors horrified at such practices. Of the Greco-Roman accounts, undoubtedly the most important was that contained in the twenty-third book of the lost ethnography of Poseidonios, portions of which have survived in the writings of Athenaios, Julius Caesar, Diodoros Sikelos, Strabo, and later authors.[64] Valuable though these sources are, they rarely provide us with sufficient data to venture interpretations with any real certainty. The following remarks on Celtic sacrifice are thus considerably more tentative than those which have gone before. It is my hope, however, that the other IE materials I have discussed may shed some light on a well-known Celtic ritual that has heretofore baffled most authorities.[65] Let us take as a starting point Strabo 4.4.5, in which a brief summary of Poseidonios's discussion of human sacrifice among the Celts is given. After describing the practice of divination from the death throes of a human victim, Strabo goes on to say:

> They did not sacrifice without the Druids. Other forms of human sacrifice are told, for some (victims) they shot with arrows, some they impaled in sacred places, and constructing a *kolossos* of wood and straw, into which they threw fatted livestock and all sorts of wild animals and men, they burnt this all up as an offering.

This last sacrifice, often referred to as that of the "Wickerman," is also described in Caesar's *De Bello Gallico* 6.16:

> Others have effigies (*simulacra*) that are monstrous in size, the limbs of which—these being interwoven with withes—they fill with live men. When these are set afire, the men are deprived of life, encircled by flames.

The victims were human and animal alike, as Strabo tells us, although Caesar does not mention animals. Together, they were gathered within an enormous construction, a "colossus," which took the form of a human figure, complete with bodily limbs, the whole structure being flammable in the extreme. Diodoros Sikelos does not give a description of the Wickerman itself, but he does seem to be describing this same sacrificial practice in the following passage (5.32.6), from which we learn that the human victims were criminals or prisoners of war and that agricultural offerings (firstfruits) accompanied the humans and animals.

> In accordance with their savagery, they act with extraordinary impiety concerning sacrifices. For having guarded evildoers for five years, they impale them for the gods, and offer them with many other firstfruits (*aparkhōn*), kindling immense fires. And they use spear-won captives thus as sacrificial victims for the honor of the gods, and some of them put the animals taken in battle to death along with the men, or burn them or do away with them by some other means of punishment.

Returning to the Wickerman, we must note that this humanoid figure (*simulacrum*, according to Caesar), while larger than any man, is still much smaller than the cosmos. Neither microcosm nor macrocosm, the Wickerman is perhaps best described as a form of "mesocosm," a mediating form between individual and universe. Drawing together all forms of life—human, animal, vegetative—it is offered as a sacrificial victim, its constituent members being consumed by fire and thus, perhaps, dispersed to the macrocosm. Far from being a mere instrument of barbaric sadism, the Wickerman might then be seen as a device that reveals how man is a part of a larger whole, a totality that has his very shape, while also revealing that all such beings are ultimately destined for destruction and dispersion into the larger cosmos beyond. Supervision of this process rests with the Druids, who presided over every sacrifice and are described as being natural philosophers (*physiologoi*) and theologians.[66] As Diodoros Sikelos 5.31.4 has it, "It is not their custom to make a sacrifice without a philosopher, for they say that thank-offerings to the gods ought to be offered by those who are acquainted with the divine nature, as it were, speaking the same language as the gods." Moreover, according to one extremely conservative Old Irish text, (*Senchus Mór* I, 22), the Druids "claimed that they made the sky and earth and sea and so forth, the sun and moon and so forth."[67]

That the Druids could be involved in both the practice of philosophy and that of human sacrifice has struck most scholarly authorities as an inconceivable paradox. Thus, in one of the most learned works on the Druids to be written in recent decades we find their claims to higher intellectual activity minimized and ridiculed, while in another work of equal seriousness and erudition the attempt is make to argue away all the considerable evidence connecting the Druids to sacrificial ritual.[68] Yet far from being antithetical, among the Indo-European peoples, sacrifice and philosophy were inseparable, one being *fons et origo* of the other. This was evident even to an author such as Pomponius Mela, writing in a period when the Druids had been subjected to Roman repression and the old ways were dying out. He writes of the conquered Gauls (*De Chorographia* 3.2.18–19):

> These people are arrogant and superstitious, and at one time they were so savage that they believed a man to be the best and most pleasing sacrificial victim for the gods. Vestiges of their past ferocity remain, so that while they refrain from the final dismemberment (*ultimis caedibus*), nonetheless they take away a little portion (from the victim) when leading the consecrated ones to the altars. Still, they have their own eloquence and their masters of wisdom, the Druids. These ones profess to know the size and form of the universe and of earth, the motion of sky and stars, and what the gods desire.[69]

From what we have seen before, there should be nothing here to surprise us. That someone who knows "the size and form of the universe and of earth" (*terraque mundique magnitudinem et formam*) should also perform sacrifice is only natural, for the universe and the earth— in the Indo-European view—are only the sacrificial victim writ large, as is also reflected in several important verbs for the action of sacrifice: Skt *tanoti, tanute* "to spread out, stretch forth, expand";[70] Gmc **blōtan* (Goth and OE *blōtan*, ON *blōta*, OHG *bluozan*), "to inflate, swell up, expand";[71] and Latin *mactare* "to magnify, increase, make great."[72] The action of sacrifice is thus seen to be one of expansion or amplification, taking matter from the microcosm of the victim's body, and expanding it to macrocosmic form and dimensions. Not merely a consecrated slaughter, it is understood as the maintenance of the cosmos, the repetition of creation, and the celebration of the indestructibility and infinite mutability of all matter.

3

The Origin of Food and the Nature of Nutrition

One item of the macrocosm often had a separate section of the creation account allocated to it alone. This was food, the nature and origin of which were treated in what I will call a *sitiogony* (from Gk *sitos* "food, bread, grain"), that is, a myth of the creation of food. Consideration of the sitiogony also permits us to pick up on variants of the basic mythic structure in which a primordial animal, usually domestic, plays an important role, either alongside a human companion or by itself.

Within certain variants, most notably the Old Norse Story of Ymir's cow Auðhumla as told in *Gylfaginning* 6 and the various accounts of the she-wolf that suckled Romulus and Remus,[1] nothing terribly dramatic occurs. The animal provides food for the first man or men in the form of milk, then disappears from the story. Elsewhere, things are not so simple, for the animal—now usually specified as an ox or a bull[2]—shares the man's sacrificial fate, being killed and dismembered at the dawn of creation. The animal's body, however, is treated differently from that of the human victim in the world's first sacrifice. For whereas the human body is transformed into the constituent elements of the macrocosm, the body of the bovine is transformed into one macrocosmic element only: food, in its liquid and solid components. Specifically, the first bovine at death becomes fluids, most often milk, butter, and/or water, and edible plants, especially grain.[3]

Iranian sources offer us some of the clearest examples of a sitiogonic account. Certain sections of the Younger Avesta, which probably date to the Parthian period, allude to it clearly,[4] and according to the Pahlavi texts it was recounted at length in the *Cihrdād, Varštmānser, Hūspāram*, and *Bāg Nasks* of the lost Sassanid Avesta.[5] The fullest versions are now to be found in the *Greater Bundahišn* 13.0–9 (TD MS. 93.8–94.15) and *Zad Spram* 3.42–51, but the contents are obviously much older than the date at which these texts were compiled (ninth century A.D.). Both sources, following the general Zoroastrian rejection of cattle sacrifice, treat the death and transfiguration of the primordial ox, *Ēvagdād* ("Created Alone" or "First Created") as an act of aggression, a murder that was part of the Evil Spirit Ahriman's assault against the good creation of Ohrmazd at the dawn of time. This murder proved creative, however, as Ahriman's aggression inevitably back-fires. *Zad Spram* 3.42–47 tells the story as follows:

> Fifth, Ahriman came to the cattle (*gōspand*).[6] He struggled against the cattle. As the ox Ēvagdād died, because it possessed the nature and form of plants, fifty-seven species of grain and twelve species of healing plants came into being. From every bodily member they grew, just as the details of every one that came from those bodily members are revealed in the *Dāmdād Nask*.
>
> And every plant that grew from a bodily member causes the growth of that bodily member. As it says there (in the *Dāmdād Nask*): "The ox scattered its marrow to the earth. Then grain grew up, with sesame, vine, and vetch. Because sesame has its origin in marrow and is itself marrow, it is an increaser of marrow. And this too is said: "From blood is the action of the vine." Since the vine [and by extension, wine] is itself blood, it is of a plant's nature and is a helper for the healthy nature of the blood. And likewise it is said: "From the nose is the species that is called vetch, and that species came to be another name for the nose."

The text continues, giving similar analyses of the origin, nature, and salubrious effects of various plants, usually based on their physical properties or wordplay deriving from their names (*ZS* 3.48–49; see also *GBd* 13.1–2), but here we see the essential features of the myth: from the ox's body are formed fluids—marrow, especially, but also blood[7] (a later section adds a lengthy treatment of the ox's semen, a *topos* peculiar to Iranian variants of the myth)[8]—and edible plants, here subcategorized as grains and healing herbs, both of which have the power to restore the specific bodily parts from which they had their origin.[9]

Mithraic reliefs—which have now been shown to be best understood as preserving Old Iranian sacrificial ideology, and not Zoroastrian theology as was once believed[10]—also preserve details of an ancient sitiogony. For there, as can plainly be seen in the drawing reproduced in figure 6, along with numerous other examples that might be cited,[11]

ALCIMVS·TI·C·L·LIVIANI·SER·VILC·SOL·M·V·D·

Figure 6. Grain springs from the body of the bull slain by Mithras. Line drawing of Roman marble statue dating from the second century A.D. *From Franz Cumont,* The Mysteries of Mithra, *rpt. ed. (New York: Dover, 1956), p. 39.*

grain sprouts from the body of the dying bull. Mithras thus performs an act of creation, a sacrifice in which food is created from a (primordial) bovine victim.[12]

India also preserves numerous variants on the sitiogonic pattern. The *Śatapatha Brāhmaṇa* contains at least three different variants of the myth, as follows:

Variant I: Vṛtra and the Kuśa Grass
Indra slew Vṛtra. He, being slain, putrefied and flowed forth in all directions toward the waters, for truly the ocean is in all directions. Therefore, truly, the waters became disgusted. They fled far, far away. From them, the (Kuśa) grasses came into being, for these truly are the unputrefied waters. But there is mingled in the other water that matter which the putrid Vṛtra poured forth. The priest destroys this putrefaction in the polluted waters by these two purifiers (i.e., the Kuśa grass and the purified water). Then he consecrates with the waters that have been made fit for sacrifice. Therefore he deputrefies with these two purifiers. (*SB* 1.1.3.5)

Variant II: Soma, the Sacrificial Horse, and Barley
The sacrificer mixes the soma-libation with barley meal. He mixes it with barley meal, because truly Varuṇa crushed the eye of King

Soma. That eye swelled up (*aśvayan*); from that, a horse (*aśvaḥ*) came into being. Since it came into being from a swollen spot (*śvayathāt*), therefore its name is "horse" (*aśva*). A tear gushed forth from that horse. From that tear, grain came into being. Therefore they say that grain belongs to Varuṇa. That which was destroyed of Soma's eye—with this grain, one causes it to be well: one makes it whole. Therefore, the sacrificer mixes the soma libation with barley meal. (*SB* 4.2.1.11)

Variant III: Prajāpati and the Fire; Libations and Plants
(After Prajāpati had created Fire [*Agni*] from his mouth as the first of beings), Prajāpati thought: "Truly, this Fire is an eater-of-food, which I have given birth to from myself. But there is no food here other than me. Truly, however, I am not-to-be-eaten." Indeed, at that time the earth was bald: there were neither plants nor trees. This was on his mind.

Now Fire turned round toward Prajāpati, as if to eat him, and— being frightened—his greatness fled. His voice, truly, is his greatness: his voice fled. He strove to obtain a libation from himself. He rubbed his hands together. Because he rubbed, therefore (his palms) are hairless. From this he obtained a ghee libation or a milk libation, but truly both consist of milk.

This offering did not propitiate Fire, for it had hair mixed in it. He burnt it, saying: "Absorb this, O Burning One (*oṣa dhaya*)!" From that, plants (*oṣadhayaḥ*) came into being. Therefore, they are named "plants." He rubbed his hands a second time, and he obtained another libation, a ghee libation or a milk libation, but truly both consist of milk. Truly, this offering propitiated the Fire. (*SB* 2.2.4.3–5)

In these three variants, for all their fascinating lines of idiosyncratic development, the core narrative remains the same and can be summarized in the following formula: victim → food (= fluid + edible plants). In variant I, the victim appears as a monster, vanquished in the most celebrated combat of Indian myth.[13] In variant II, Soma (the celebrated ritual intoxicant) and the sacrificial horse appear. In variant III, Prajāpati himself—who inherits Puruṣa's role in the *Brāhmaṇas* and *Upaniṣads*—is the central character.[14]

Once again, certain variations are apparent in the means whereby each of these creatures was transformed into food. A sacrificial context is clearest in variant III, where Prajāpati is threatened by the ravenous fire that was his initial creation. This fire, moreover—as is clear from numerous other texts—is the sacrificial fire, the mouth of the gods and the universe, into which all offerings are placed. Prajāpati's problem is thus to create something that will satisfy the fire's hunger, lest it otherwise consume him. His task is all the more difficult because he is frightened speechless, and cannot call on the creative power of ritual formulas (*mantras*). He thus takes a part of his own body—one might almost say that he dismembers himself in the most minimal way—rubbing the palms of his hands bare, and creates milk and ghee from the hair and other detritus he thus obtains.

An underlying sacrificial context is also apparent in variant II, which begins with the ritual pressing of soma. From the soma plant, partially crushed with the sacred mortar and pestle, a horse is created, which is itself also injured—again, one could say partially dismembered—in the same spot as was the soma, and from this, a drop of fluid in the form of a tear comes into being. Certain details of the text are the result of the wordplay characteristic of the *Brāhmaṇas*, for the action of "swelling" is introduced only because the verb *śvi-* yields forms like the third person singular perfect *aśvayan*, which closely resemble the Sanskrit term for horse, *aśva-*.[15]

Whereas in these two versions a sacrificial background remains fairly obvious, a martial context figures in variant I, in which Indra kills Vṛtra in battle.[16] Yet while the "sacrificial" variants retain the motif of dismemberment in only the most abbreviated form, here Vṛtra falls apart totally, his whole body turning into fluid. The fluids thus produced, however, are as tainted as the monster from which they flowed, and they are described as being the fluids of bodily corruption and decay, which contaminate all the waters with which they mingle.

In all three variants, the fluids that flow from the victims' bodies—putrid waters, tears, or libations of milk and ghee—cause the creation of plants, although once again each variant adapts this basic construct (fluids → plants) to its own particular narrative constraints and ritual context. Thus, in variant I, the sacred Kuśa grass from which purifying filters are made cannot itself be created from Vṛtra's impure fluids of decay. In fact, the Kuśa filters are the very antithesis of corrupt fluids, being used to purify—literally, to "deputrefy" (Skt *utpunāti*) all contaminated waters. Thus, the Kuśa grass is said to grow from the pure waters only, those which withdrew when threatened by Vṛtra's corruption.

Variant III, for its part, makes use of wordplay to account for the production of plants from fluids, for as Prajāpati pours out his libations of milk and ghee he recites a mantra, having by this time recovered his voice. The mantra he chooses commands the fire, "Absorb this, O Burning One," which in Sanskrit sounds almost identical to the word for "plants" (*oṣa dhaya* is the mantra; *oṣadhayaḥ* the name for plants). Mantras being possessed of inherent creative force, plants then appear.[17]

The creation of plants from fluid is fairly simple only in variant II, in which grain springs directly from the horse's tear. Yet this version is more complex than it appears at first, for it has an elegant cyclicity absent from the other two variants. Thus, it begins with a plant—Soma, the very king of plants—from which an animal is created. From the animal, a fluid is created; and from the fluid, yet another plant. Moreover, this second plant (unspecified "grain," but no doubt the barley mixed into the soma libation) has the ability to restore both Soma and the horse to their initial state of wholeness, healing their injured eyes. This cyclical structure is laid out graphically in figure 7.

While variants I and III lack such a neatly cyclical construction, they do nevertheless voice similar claims for the restorative properties of the plants whose origins they describe. Thus, in the former, the Kuśa grass is said to be able to deputrefy all polluted waters, as we have seen, while the plants Prajāpati created according to variant III came to serve as fuel for the sacrificial fire, thus appeasing the fire and obviating the threat that it would consume Prajāpati, which is to say, restoring Prajāpati to his former state of security.

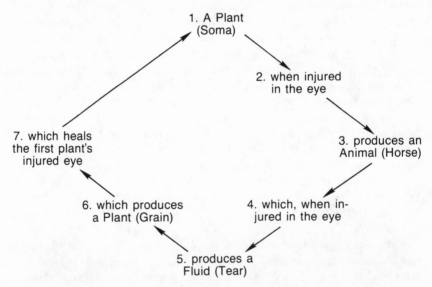

Figure 7. The cyclical structure of the sitiogony in Śatapatha Brāhmaṇa 4.2.1.11.

With one exception, the underlying context behind all these examples is sacrifice. In order to appreciate this more fully, it is helpful to recall a crucial passage I considered in the previous chapter, *Aitareya Brāhmaṇa* 2.6, wherein the instructions are given for the ritual dismemberment of the sacrificial victim:

> "Lay its feet down to the north. Cause its eye to go to the sun; send forth its breath to the wind; its life-force to the atmosphere; its ears to the cardinal points; its flesh to the earth." Thus, the sacrificer places this (animal) in these worlds.

As we saw, this passage describes how the performance of sacrifice repeats the cosmogonic dispersion of the victim's body to its macrocosmic alloforms. Yet there is a slight problem in this line of analysis. For in Indic cosmogonies such as the *Puruṣasūkta* (*RV* 10.90), the universe is created from the body of a human victim, not an animal, and in this sacrifice the animal victim merely does service for its human counterpart. This emerges clearly from a section of *AB* 2.6 that is usually overlooked. It comes shortly before the section just quoted, and is associated with the strewing of the sacred grass (*barhiṣ*) on which the dismembered pieces of the victim will be placed:

> "Strew the *barhiṣ*." Truly, the animal is one who has plants as its body. Thus one makes the animal one who has all as its body.

With this gesture and formula, immediately prior to the immolation and dismemberment of the victim, a crucial transformation is ritually accomplished. The animal is effectively lifted out of its normal state and changed into a grander, more elevated being. Initially, the animal is "one who has plants as its body" (*oṣadhyātmā*), following the alloform cattle/food(= fluids + edible plants), and the sacrifice of such a one might ordinarily be expected to produce only food or plants. Yet in order to (re-)create the entire universe, one must first secure a victim "who has all as its body" (*sarvātman*-): a human, like Puruṣa-Prajāpati, or an animal that has been "made" into such a creature. The text here states that the sacrificer "makes the animal one who has all as its body" (*paśum eva tat sarvātmānaṃ karoti*), and this makes the cosmogonic dispersal of the victim's body possible. Were the animal not remade thus, it would remain "one who has plants as its body," and sacrifice would be a repetition of the sitiogony only, producing food and not the entire universe. In fact, the cosmogonic treatment of the sacrificial animal outlined in *AB* 2.6 is rather unusual; the more regular treatment of an animal victim's body is that given in *Śatapatha Brāhmaṇa* 3.7.4.4 and elsewhere:

> The sacrificer consecrates the victim, saying: "To the waters, thou, to the plants." Insofar as the victim exists, thus far he makes it fit for sacrifice. Truly, when it rains, then plants are born. Having eaten plants and having drunk water, thence sap exists. From sap there is semen, and from semen, cattle. Insofar as the victim exists, and insofar as it is born, thus far he makes it fit for sacrifice.[18]

The logic here rests on the alloform cattle/food(= fluids + edible plants). Once sacrificed, the animal victim becomes first water—particularly in the form of rain—then plants, as the rain causes plants to grow. Water and plants become cattle again, as male animals eat and drink, then they refine the consumed water and plants into semen, from which new cattle are born. The sacrifice described in this passage thus repeats the sitiogony, while the events that follow (eating and drinking, production of semen, and so on) reverse the sitiogony, converting fluids and plants back into cattle again.

In the clearest European variant of the sitiogonic myth I have been able to locate,[19] the sacrificial background is absent. Rather, in this Old Irish narrative, *Adaigh ConRói* 7, the creation of food is presented as part of the lore of cattle raiding. Here are described certain events that transpired after the great hero of the Érainn people, Cu Roi, carried off the cattle and the daughter of Echde Echbel:[20]

> Then Cu Roi bore off the cows and the maiden, and they came to Castle Cu Roi, between that place and the sea to the west. Then the cows let flow (their milk), for they had been driven without having been milked. And there grew a plant from that. Its name is Bo-eirne ("Cattle of the Erainn"), for Cu Roi was of the Erainn.

Here we find no ritual death and dismemberment of the animal victim; rather, food—again defined as fluid plus plants—results from the relatively minor injury inflicted on cattle that are driven across Ireland with their udders swollen. The pain they suffered is relieved when they halt, in the spontaneous flow of milk, which gives rise to the Bo-eirne plant. Finally—what is most striking in this account— the very name of the plant that is created identifies it as the alloform of cattle, for OIr *Bó-eirne* contains the normal name of cattle, *bó* < PIE *g^wou-, just as Gk *botanē* (> Eng *botany*) is derived from a cognate term for cattle, Gk *bous*, and marks vegetation in its relation to cattle.[21]

In all, we are not so far from the Old Norse cow Auðhumla of *Gylfaginning* 6 or the she-wolf that suckled Romulus and Remus, for these primordial animals—like the ox Ēvagdād; Vṛtra, the sacrificial horse, and Prajāpati in the *SB* texts I have discussed; and the cows of Cu Roi—created food from their bodies and came into existence primarily for the creation of food.[22] It would seem that the sitiogonic account circulated in two different but closely related forms. The first of these is considerably simpler, and might be called the lactational pattern, for here the first bovine produces the first food in the form of milk, and then disappears from the story. Within the sacrificial pattern, however, as shown in table 8, things are more complex.

The main thrust of this myth is to establish the alloform of cattle/ food, in which cattle are understood as all domestic livestock, but above all bovines,[23] while food appears in two forms: fluids—especially milk and milk products, but also water—and edible plants.[24] This corresponds fairly closely to what we know of the IE diet, which included primarily meat, milk products, and agricultural products, chiefly grain.[25] The homology cattle/food thus links together two different forms of food, and might also be expressed as a homology of meat food/non-meat food, with meat remaining a category unto itself,

Table 8. Sitiogonic narratives of the sacrificial type.

	Zad Spram 3.42 ff.	Śatapatha Brāhmaṇa 1.1.3	Śatapatha Brāhmaṇa 4.2.1	Śatapatha Brāhmaṇa 2.2.4	Adaigh ConRói 7
Animal victim	Ox: Ēvagdād	Monster: Vṛtra	Sacrificial horse	Prajāpati	Stolen cows
Injury	Killed in cosmogonic assault	Killed in battle	Eye injured by ritual pestle	Threatened to be consumed by fire	Driven unmilked
Creates fluid	Marrow and blood	Putrid waters	Tear	Milk and ghee libations	Milk
Fluid creates plants	57 grains 12 herbs	Kuśa grass	Grain (Barley)	Plants	Bo-eirne plant ("Cattle of the Érainn")
Plants cause restoration	Provide food and healing	Purifies putrid waters	Heals injured eyes	Feeds and appeases sacrificial fire	Relieves swollen udders

while non-meat food was subject to further subcategorization. A full taxonomy of food might thus be constructed, as in figure 8. Of the two main categories, meat ever remained the most prestigious, but also the most dangerous, being consumed only on ritual occasions, while the slaughter of animals was considered rightful only within sacrifice, where it was hedged by a host of sacred precautions. The marked ambivalence with which meat-eating was regarded is evident in a great many texts and practices throughout the Indo-European world,[26] as for instance, in a brief passage from the *Śatapatha Brāhmaṇa* (3.1.2.21):

> The Adhvaryu Priest causes the sacrificial patron to enter the hall. He should not eat of a cow or an ox. "Truly, the cow and the ox bear all this world. Come, let us give the energy of (all) other foods to the cow and the ox." The energy which was of (all) other foods— that they gave to the cow and the ox. Therefore, the cow and the ox eat most. Truly, he who would eat the cow and the ox, he is like one who eats all things. He is like one who goes to his end. Truly, he will be (re-)born as something awful—an abortionist or evildoer. Therefore, one should not eat of a cow or an ox. But Yajñavalkya [one of the greatest Vedic sages] said, truly, "I eat (beef), if it is tender."[27]

Alloformic logic, however, provides a means for dealing with the thorny problems posed by the eating of meat. For if—as the text

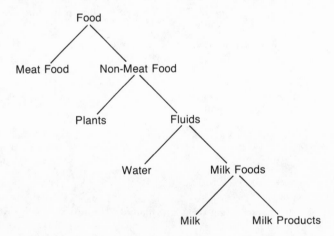

Figure 8. The general IE taxonomy of food.

asserts—meat contains the essence of all foods, and if one who eats meat is thus "one who eats all things" (*sarvāśyam*), then one may escape the evils of meat-eating while still reaping the same benefits as if one had eaten meat, if only one eats all other things besides meat. That is to say, by consuming the alloforms of cattle—food, in its twin forms of fluids plus edible plants—one is in effect eating cattle, or to put it differently again, eating all things.

That cattle should be seen as the alloform of fluids plus plants no doubt strikes us as strange. Yet within the normal experience of pastoral peoples, there are tangible signs that support such a homology. Thus, on the one hand cattle do produce food from their bodies, in the forms of fluids—most notably milk, but also blood, which is sometimes drunk, and urine (= water), which is used in the making of certain cheeses and as a general disinfectant—and also plants, for the way manure stimulates the growth of grasses and grains is quite obvious to anyone who grazes cattle over any length of time.[28] Similarly, it is quite evident that cattle are produced from—that is, thrive and grow as the result of consuming—fluids (water and milk) and the plants on which they graze. The same material content thus may be seen to circulate from cattle to food (= fluids + plants) and from food to cattle in a never-ending cycle: microcosm to macrocosm, macrocosm to microcosm, ad infinitum, the former motion repeating and the latter reversing the events described in the sitiogonic myth.

In addition to providing the means for understanding the nature of food, this myth also provided the means for understanding the entire nutritional process. More precisely, it answered the question of how and why food has the ability to build and nourish the bodies of animals and humans alike.

The starting point for this flight of speculative thought lies in the recognition that cattle and humans are built of the same organic tissues and bodily parts, both containing flesh, bone, blood, hair, eyes, brains, breath, and the like. Yet this isomorphism notwithstanding, different alloforms existed for the bodily parts of humans and animals: different not only in their specific identities but also in their overarching structure. For whereas in cosmogonic accounts, the various Indo-European peoples took pains to establish precise individual alloforms for each of the significant bodily parts of the first man (see Chapter 1), their sitiogonic narratives posited one alloform only (albeit with a bipartite nature) for all the bodily parts of the first bovine: that alloform is food.

The crucial distinction is that whereas the body of the first man (and every human thereafter) is *dispersed* throughout the cosmos, following the cosmogonic pattern, the body of the first bovine (and all cattle thereafter) is *concentrated* in food, following the sitiogonic pattern.[29] Food thus has a curiously ambiguous nature. For while on the one hand it is an important, in truth an indispensable item of the macrocosm, it may also be understood as nothing less than a microcosm of the microcosm. That is, within food—indeed, within a single drop of water or kernel of grain—are found all the essential bodily parts of the primordial ox, or, for that matter, of any human or animal: flesh, bones, blood, and all the rest.

The nutritive process must thus be understood from several interlocking perspectives. First, it is the continual re-creation of human and animal organisms from the food they ingest. Second, it is the translation of material substance from its food alloform to its human or animal alloform. Third, it is a reversal of the sitiogony. For whereas food was initially created from a body that fell apart—the body of a primordial animal—eating restores to wholeness bodies that would otherwise fall apart, through malnutrition, disease, old age, and ultimately death.[30]

Explicit and detailed theories of how the nutritional process works are to be found in ancient Greek, Indic, and Iranian sources. The three bodies of data differ in many ways—so many that any direct transmission of ideas or texts from one area to another seems highly unlikely[31]—but they exhibit quite a similar general understanding of what food is and how it nourishes the body, an understanding that is also closely related to the sitiogonic myths. Given this, I consider it most likely that these accounts draw on a traditional theory of nutrition and sitiogony.[32] Although other texts might be profitably examined,[33] it will suffice here to take up three examples in detail. The first of these is a summary of Anaxagoras's theories of nutrition, contained in Simplicius, *Physics* 460.10 (Diels-Kranz A45).

> ... from the same food that is set before one—such as bread—many dissimilar things come into being: flesh, bones, veins, sinews, hair, nails, and perhaps also feathers and horns. The like (substance) is augmented by like. Therefore, Anaxagoras understood these things to be in food and in water—(for) if trees are nourished by water, (water must contain) wood and bark and fruit. Therefore, he said that all is mixed in all, and coming-to-be comes about through (a process of) separation.

The topic of nutrition seems to have played an important role in Anaxagoras's thought. At least two other detailed summaries of his theories have survived in the ancient doxographical sources,[34] and most scholars now agree that his analyses of such biological processes as nutrition and embryology provided the starting point for his broader theories of the nature of the universe.[35] An important fragment preserving his own words (Diels-Kranz B10) poses Anaxagoras's central concern quite succinctly: "How can hair come into being from that which is not hair, and flesh from that which is not flesh?" The implicit answer is that they cannot, and bodily growth—either *in utero* or as the result of eating—thus became for Anaxagoras a key example of the Parmenidean universe in which all change and becoming were to be understood as matters of appearances only, superficial shiftings of form that left the true underlying being unchanged.

Thus—to pursue Anaxagoras's favorite example—bread can never truly become flesh or hair, nor do flesh and hair come into being from any substance other than flesh and hair. If it appears that bread turns into flesh or hair, this is only because flesh, hair, and all the other bodily parts were already present within the bread (or any other food, for that matter), albeit in invisible particles. The apparent change whereby bread appears to become bodily parts is best understood as a process of separation and redistribution effected by eating and digestion, whereby the invisible particles of flesh, hair, and so on are detached from their temporary location within bread, sorted out, and joined to the part of the body to which they properly correspond: particles of hair going to hair, particles of flesh going to flesh, and so forth.[36] The particles thus become visible, and the bodily parts to which they are joined, grow. As Simplicius put it, "the like (substance) is augmented by like," and the term rendered "like" for the sake of simplicity (Gk *homoion*) could just as properly—perhaps even more so—be translated "homologous."

Food, for Anaxagoras, was thus nothing other than a microcosm of the microcosm, containing all parts of the human—or animal, or (in the case of water) even plant—body within it. Nor is this all, for his thought ultimately leads to an infinite regression of worlds within worlds, microcosms within microcosms. While all of the body is present within a bite of bread, all of bread (and all that bread contains) is present within a kernel of grain, and all of grain (plus all that grain contains: bread, bodies, and the rest) is present within a drop of water. As Anaxagoras repeatedly proclaimed, all is present in all (fragments B4, B6, B11, B12), every piece of matter being infinitely divisible, and the most infinitesimal pieces of matter still containing portions of all things (B3, B6).

On the question of how all things come to be within all things, or to refer the question to the immediate topic at hand, how pieces of flesh, hair, and the like come to be present within food and drink, the remaining fragments and testimonia of Anaxagoras have relatively little to say. This is only to be expected, for his Parmenidean stance prohibits any suggestion except that things have always been thus, the universe being fundamentally changeless. There is one testimonium, however, Aristotle's *Physics* 187b (Diels-Kranz A52), that presents a rather different view, that of an endless cycle in which "Anything comes into being from anything else, like water separating out from flesh, and flesh (separating out) from water . . ."

Water thus seems to be but a temporary residence for particles of flesh and other bodily matter, particles that had earlier been present in fully constituted organisms, and that will return to those organisms which drink water. Similar conclusions, no doubt, could be posited regarding food. Hair, flesh, and so forth move from a bodily incarnation to an incarnation in food and drink, whence they move back to other bodily incarnations. Within food and bodies there is the same material substance, matter moving from one form to the other in eternal alternation. The two incarnations are nothing other than alloforms of each other.

Similar concepts are found within *Śatapatha Brāhmaṇa* 7.1.2.1–6, although in a style of presentation radically different from Anaxagorean philosophical thought. Here the same basic understanding of the nature of food and the nutritional process is laid out within an aetiological myth that has as its primary concern establishing the central importance of the fire in sacrificial ritual, pursuing the subtle implications of an India-specific identification of the fire as mouth of the gods, or even mouth of the universe, since it is through the fire that all sacrificial offerings are "eaten."[37] The text reads as follows:

> Prajāpati emitted progeny. Having emitted progeny, having run the whole race, he fell apart. When he fell apart, his vital breaths left him. Then his semen left him. When these had left, he collapsed, and when he collapsed, food flowed forth from him. Food flowed forth from the eye on which he lay. Truly, there was then no foundation whatever.
>
> The gods said, "Truly, there is no other foundation here than this one. Let us put Father Prajāpati back together. Truly, he will become a foundation for us." They said to Fire (Agni), "Truly, there is no other foundation here. Let us put Father Prajāpati back together in you. Truly, he will become our foundation."
>
> (Fire answered:) "What's in it for me?"
>
> They said, "Truly, this food is Prajāpati. We will eat this with you as our mouth. This will be our food, we who will have you for our mouth."

"Agreed," (said Fire). Therefore, the gods—who have Fire for their mouth—eat food. Truly, no matter to what deity one pours an offering, one always pours it into Fire. Truly, the gods take food with Fire as their mouth.

The breath that had left Prajāpati, truly that is the wind that goes about. And the semen that left him, that is the sun. And the food that flowed forth from him, truly that is all the different food (one eats) in a year.

The gods heat this in the Fire. Then the Fire mounts up on that which has been heated. And because of this, the breath that left Prajāpati returns, and they place it inside him. And the semen that left him, they place inside him. And the food that flowed forth from him, they place inside him. And having put him together again, all whole, they raised him upright, and that one whom they raised up, he is (all) these worlds.

Here, as usual in India, cosmogony is portrayed as resulting from the dismemberment or dissolution of Puruṣa-Prajāpati, the first man. In this account, three specific items are considered, each of which correlates to one of the three vertical levels of the Indian cosmos: earth, atmosphere, and heaven. Thus, Prajāpati's semen (or, less concretely, his "virility" or "energy," Skt *vīryam*) becomes the sun, located in the distant above; his breath becomes the wind, located in the intermediate atmosphere; and the rest of his body becomes food, scattered across the surface of the earth.[38] This process of bodily dispersal (or dismemberment, broadly construed) is diagrammed in figure 9.

The text does not stop with the dissolution and dispersion of Prajāpati, however, for it goes on to describe just how his body is per-

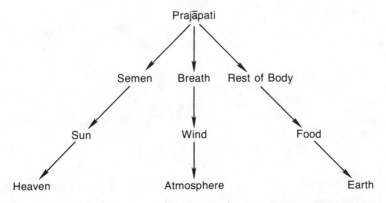

Figure 9. Prajāpati's dissolution according to Śatapatha Brāhmaṇa *7.1.2.1.*

petually being reassembled, through the mediating agency of the sacrificial fire (Agni), "the mouth of the gods." Now, three items are necessary for the production of fire: heat, oxygen, and fuel. What is more, in the analysis offered by this text, these three items are drawn from the three levels of the universe: heat from the sun, oxygen from the atmosphere, and fuel (the food of the fire, in the expected dual form of plants [wood] plus fluids [libations]) from the earth. These three items in a broader sense constitute the fire's sustenance, the things it consumes and on which its life depends. Finally, the text asserts that when the fire eats these items, Prajāpati is restored to wholeness, for through the action of the sacrificial fire, the sun is changed back into Prajāpati's semen, the wind into his breath, and the food or fuel drawn from the earth into the rest of his body. The process is as diagrammed in figure 10.

Whereas Anaxagoras discusses what happens when an individual organism eats—even going so far as to consider what happens when a plant consumes water[39]—this Brāhmaṇic passage proceeds at a totally different level. For what is described here is a cosmic act of eating, many times larger than ordinary life. In place of the normal eater of

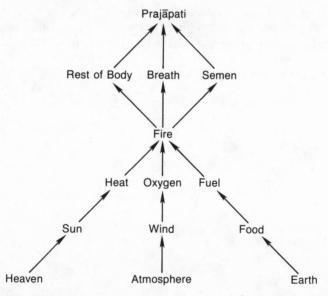

Figure 10. Prajāpati's restoration according to Śatapatha Brāhmaṇa 7.1.2.2–6.

food, it focuses on the sacrificial fire. In addition to more ordinary foods, air and heat are also consumed. And the end result of this super-normal eating is the restoration or reconstruction of the body of Prajāpati, the primordial man. Yet the theory presented is much the same as that of Anaxagoras: eating is the reappropriation of bodily parts from foodstuffs in the external universe, where those bodily parts have temporarily come to reside. An important Iranian text, *Dēnkart* 3.157.18 (Dresden ed., 129.7–16), presents this same basic understanding, again in a highly idiosyncratic fashion.

> The preservation of the body is for its assistance against oppression and for the hindrance of the Adversary. That preservation is food and water, in order to join the strength that is within food to the strength that is in the elements that constitute the body. For instance, the moisture that is within food is joined to the elemental moisture in the body, such that the elemental (bodily) moisture does not acquire dryness, which is a result of Ahriman's onslaught. The fire that is within food is joined to the elemental fire in the body, such that the elemental fire does not cool off and acquire cold, which is a result of Ahriman's onslaught. The wind (*wād*) that is within food is joined to the elemental wind (or: breath) in the body, such that the elemental wind does not acquire weakness. The clay that is within food is joined to the elemental clay in the body such that the elemental clay does not dissolve into laziness of deeds. All this is so that the body, from the oppression and onrush that come from Ahriman's onslaught, becomes established as incorruptible. And human life is established with food that is fitting and moderate.

Here, as elsewhere in Middle Persian literature, the nutritional process is placed in a thoroughly dualistic context.[40] The purpose of eating is to give the body strength, strength that is necessary to withstand the assaults of the evil spirit, Ahriman. Four forces that Ahriman brings against the body are mentioned: dryness, cold, weakness, and dissolution into "laziness of deeds," the last of which perhaps represents obesity or loss of all muscle tone. Yet proper food provides defenses against these ills, rendering the body capable of resisting Ahriman's attack. Against dryness, food provides moisture; against cold, fire; against weakness, wind; against "the dissolution into laziness of deeds," clay. Moreover, each of these basic substances—moisture, fire, wind, and clay—possesses a bodily counterpart, as expressed in the formulaic statement "The X that is within food is joined to the elemental X in the body." Precisely what these elemental X's in the body are, we are not told, with the exception of the elemental bodily wind, which must be identified with the breath, for the same Pahlavi

Table 9. The effects of food according to *Dēnkart* 3.157.18.

Food element	Bodily element	Ahriman's threat	Body's defense
Moisture	(Blood)	Dryness	Moisture
Fire	(Body Heat)	Cold	Heat
Wind	Breath	Weakness	Vitality
Clay	(Flesh)	Dissolution, Lassitude	Firmness

term, *wād* (< Av *vāta-*) denotes "breath" and "wind" alike. In similar fashion, the other elemental X's in the body must be understood as the bodily alloforms of the macrocosmic X's present in food. Thus, to the moisture within food probably corresponds blood, "the elemental moisture in the body," and moisture—conveyed from food to blood—enables the body to ward off the dryness and desiccation brought on by Ahriman. To the fire within food corresponds bodily heat, "the elemental fire in the body," and heat—conveyed from food to the body's warmth—makes possible resistance to Ahriman's cold— cold, like desiccation, being a characteristic property of a body that is no longer living, a corpse. "The elemental wind in the body," as we have seen, is the breath, and the vitality the wind inspires to the breath makes possible resistance to weakness. Finally, to clay corresponds flesh, "the elemental clay in the body," which is made firm by the clay conveyed from food to flesh, and thus made proof against dissolution and lassitude. The full system is laid out in table 9.

These three texts—Simplicius's summary of Anaxagoras's theories, *SB* 7.1.2.1–6, and *Dk* 3.157.18—agree in that all posit a homologic relation between food and the bodily parts present within eaters of food. They differ in the precise way they describe this homologic relation. The *Dēnkart* speaks only of elements (moisture, fire, wind, and clay) that are present in food and body alike, while Anaxagoras speaks only of bodily parts ("flesh, bones, veins, sinews, hair, nails, and perhaps also feathers and horns"), which are also present in food and body alike. On the one hand, this is quite a significant difference, for whereas in the formulation of the *Dēnkart*, food and human (or animal) bodies are parallel microcosms, both containing within themselves the same basic elements that, when writ large, constitute the full cosmos,[41] in Anaxagoras's view, food is a micro- cosm of the microcosm, containing within it the parts of the body, the body itself being a microcosm of the universe at large.[42] On the other hand, this difference is only a superficial one, for both Iranian and Greek sources agree that the elements present within food, however they might be described, are readily transmutable into the elements of the body, this transmutation of matter from a food alloform to a bodily alloform being the essence of the nutritional process. With this the Indic passage agrees fully, going further to spell out the ideas that were established in the sitiogonic myths: transmutation from food to body is only half of the process, and is possible only because the body itself is also transformable into food, as described in the sitiogony.

Vaguer traces of these theories are found in a famous Roman story, usually referred to as the Apologue of Menenius Agrippa, variants of which are preserved in Livy 2.32.9–11, Dionysius of Halicarnassus 6.86, and Zonaras, *Epitomē Historiōn* 7.14.[43] This parable is said to have been related at the time of the (mythic) first secession of the plebes, when the lower orders of Roman society threatened to make themselves independent of their patrician superiors. Facing this crisis, the patricians sent a messenger to the plebes, Menenius Agrippa, who (in Livy's version) told them the following fable:

> At the time when in man, all (the bodily parts) did not agree in unity, as they do now, but individual limbs had their own opinions and their own powers of speech, the other parts were outraged at having to procure all things for the belly by their own care, work, and service, while the belly rested in their midst, doing nothing other than to savor their delightful gifts. Therefore, they conspired that the hands would not bear food to the mouth, the mouth would not accept that which was given, and the teeth would not chew. As a result of this rage, wishing to overcome the belly by hunger, all the bodily members together, and the body as a whole wasted away terribly. From this it became apparent that the belly is by no means lazy in its service (to the rest of the body), and just as others nourish it, so it gives back to all parts of the body that whereby we live and flourish: blood, which is perfected by the food that is brought together (in it), and also parceled out in the veins.

This attempt at persuasion—so we are told—succeeded, and the plebes returned to their accustomed place within society, convinced that their revolt could not succeed and that the patricians were not the parasites they had previously seemed to be. It is not possible to go into the fascinating political and social content of this story here;[44] rather, I am concerned here with the view of digestion and the nutritive process that provided the basis for this tendentious little fable.

For although this is only indicated in passing, it is clear that digestion was viewed as a process whereby food is taken into the body, broken down, and distributed to the various bodily parts via the blood, so that each member might be individually sustained. In this, it is extremely similar to the Greek, Iranian, and Indic materials I have discussed,[45] although it lacks a thorough analysis of how the material substances present in food are homologous to the organic tissues they nourish.

Their differences of detail notwithstanding, such theories of nutrition stood in the closest possible relation to the sitiogonic myths, the two being in effect alternate halves of a cyclical process. In sitiogony the various items of food (with the exception of meat, a special case) are created from a bodily organism—usually cattle, following the pattern of the primordial bovine. In nutrition this is reversed, as bodies (animal and human) are created out of food.

Going further, it is also evident that nutrition reverses sacrifice, just as it reverses sitiogony, the initial sitiogony being said in most mythic accounts to have resulted from the first animal sacrifice. And since, as we saw in Chapter 2, sacrifice is the ritual process whereby matter is translated from the body to the external cosmos, nutrition, conversely, is the process whereby matter is returned from the cosmos to the body via the medium of food.

Nor is this all. We have also seen that cosmogony and anthropogony alternate in cyclical fashion, much as do nutrition and sitiogony or nutrition and sacrifice, for in practice, every sacrifice is followed by a meal. Moreover, having established that sacrifice is a repetition of the cosmogony, we may begin to suspect that nutrition is similarly related to the anthropogony. Such a suspicion is supported by many anthropogonic accounts such as *Gylfaginning* 5–6, *Timaios* 76E–77A, *Greater Bundahišn* 14.17–31 and 34.1, or the many versions of the Eight-Part Adam story that appear in the texts generally known as *L'Enfant Sage*,[46] in which the very first question asked, either implicitly or explicitly, after the creation of the first humans is "What did they eat?" To cite but one example, consider an Old Irish anthropogonic account, *Lebor Gabála Érenn* 1.24:

> Thus, God made man: his body from earth—his head from the land of Garad, his chest and middle from the land of Arabia, his belly from Lodain, his legs from the land of Agoiria—his blood from the water, his breath from the air, his warmth from the fire, and his soul from the breath of God. Thus it is that the four elements are in every man.

He created man and woman, truly in God's image. He created them and blessed them and said: "Increase: you must multiply and fill the earth. Subjugate it to you, and rule over the fish in the sea and the birds in the sky and all the animals upon the earth."

And God said: "I have given to you all the grass that proffers seed upon the earth, and all the trees that possess the seeds of their own species within themselves, that they will grow for your food and nourishment."

Although the anthropogonic account proper contains a number of interesting features—the introduction of earth from different locales to show that all space contributed in the making of the first man; the reduction of eight homologies to four, based on the classic elements earth, air, fire, and water; the treatment of the creation of the soul as separate from that of the body; the subtle introduction of the first woman—the chief point of interest at present is the direct association of nutrition with anthropogony.[47] Such an association, of course, is perfectly logical. For whereas anthropogony is the initial process whereby human beings are created, nutrition is nothing less than the continual repetition of that process, the means whereby the body is constantly re-created and preserved. In children, and particularly in infants (the latter's food being entirely fluid, just as fluids were the first food created in most sitiogonic myths), food produces growth, adding new material substance to the body, quite literally creating more of the body than previously existed. In adults, the effects of food are less dramatic, but when one is deprived of food for any length of time the sustaining creativity of food becomes readily apparent, for without constant re-creation of the body thrugh nutrition, bodily matter visibly withers away.

Nutrition also works upon the very same principle as does anthropogony, for in both processes matter is translated from the macrocosm to the microcosm, that is, from the world to the body. The sole difference between them on this score is that whereas in the initial anthropogony matter was gathered from all the various parts of the cosmos—stones, earth, sea, clouds, and so on—nutrition is a good deal simpler, making use of a highly specialized single item in which all these different forms of matter are concentrated. That item is food, divided into the two subclasses of fluids and edible plants.

At this point it is possible to perceive some relations between the Indo-European myths of the first man and those of the first ox; between sacrifice and nutrition; among cosmogony, anthropogony, and sitiogony. To begin, we must recognize that cosmogony and sitiogony

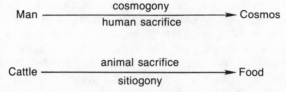

Figure 11. Cosmic processes: cosmogony, sitiogony, and sacrifice.

are parallel processes, described respectively in myths of the first man and those of the first ox. Both, moreover, are repeated in the performance of sacrifice, sacrifice ideally containing both a human and an animal victim, although in practice an animal often did service for both. These relations may be graphed as in figure 11.

Anthropogony, however, reverses cosmogony and sitiogony alike, shifting matter from the macrocosm to the microcosm. Similarly, nutrition reverses sacrifice, perpetually re-creating the body, while de-creating food. When we add these processes to our consideration, the relations of figure 11 become those of figure 12, and the dynamism of the cosmos becomes more apparent. This dynamism will become more apparent still when I consider theories of death, resurrection, and cosmic catastrophe in Chapter 6, but before I do so, it will be useful to explore certain other particular applications of this general system of homologic thought.

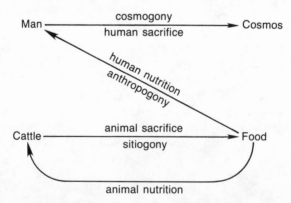

Figure 12. Cosmic processes: cosmogony, sitiogony, anthropogony, sacrifice, and nutrition.

4

Cures for Baldness, Disposal of Hair

The materials considered thus far have contained two related but nevertheless quite distinct traditions regarding the origin of plants. Thus, in Chapter 1, focusing on cosmogonic accounts common among the Indo-European peoples, we saw that plants were formed from the hair of a primordial man, giant, god, or demon, hair and plants thus being established as alloforms of each other. Yet in Chapter 3, focusing on sitiogonic accounts, we found that plants, together with milk and/ or water, were formed from the entire body of a primordial animal, most often a bovine. Livestock and food were thus established as alloforms, proper food being defined as fluids plus plants.

There is no contradiction in this state of affairs. Rather, this is an instance of the well-known redundancy of myth, whereby multiple different versions of the same basic story may appear, each variant working out some fine detail of logical content that others leave unresolved. Here the existence of these two variants derives from a fundamental distinction between two different kinds of plants. One story, the origin of plants from the bovine, treats only of edible plants—cereals primarily, but also vegetables and herbs—as the terminology consistently employed clearly shows.[1] The other narrative (the origin of plants from the hair of a humanoid being), in contrast, is concerned only with inedible plants—primarily grasses, but also occasionally trees—as the terminology employed displays with equal clarity.[2] The homologies that are established also underscore this point, for edible plants are associated with another edible item—livestock—while inedible plants are associated with something equally inedible—hair.

Beyond the fact that they both consist of matter (the same matter, given their relation as alloforms) that is inherently unappetizing, hair and grass resemble each other closely in three different ways: physical form, positional relation to other items within the full system of homologies, and internal dynamism or growth pattern. With regard to formal resemblance, it is immediately apparent that an individual hair is like a blade of grass, both being long, slender, pliant threads that attain mass only in larger clumps. Second, whereas plants always grow upon the earth, hair always grows upon flesh, flesh and earth themselves being homologized. Consideration of the relations among these four items yields a four-member homologic set:

> Hair : Plants
> Flesh : Earth

Finally, plants and hair seem to have an inner dynamism exceeding that of any other object within the microcosm or macrocosm, for both are characterized by incessant growth, unlike flesh, earth, bones, stones, blood, sea, eyes, sun, and the like.

Linguistic evidence shows the same close association between hair and vegetation. Of particular interest are two sets of nouns formed from the verbal root *wel- "to cover," by the addition of common suffixes. Were there a simple bifurcation of meaning, whereby one noun denoted "hair" while another closely related noun denoted "plants," that alone would be significant, but the evidence is stronger still, for both words seem to have signified hair and plants alike, or better yet "hair/plant matter." Thus, from PIE *wol-k̂o- we have as reflexes Av *varəsa-, OCS *vlas"*, and Russ *volos,* all of which mean "hair," but also Skt *valśa-,* which denotes a sprout, shoot, or twig.[3] Similarly, from PIE *wol-to- are derived OIr *folt,* W *gwallt,* OCS *vlad',* and ORuss *volod',* all meaning "hair," alongside Corn *gwels* "grass," OHG and OE *wald* "woods, forest," ON *vǫllr* "meadow," and OPruss *wolti* "ear of grain."[4]

The consistent association of hair and vegetation is also apparent in the customs that surrounded the disposal of hair clippings among many of the Indo-European peoples, whereby shorn hair regularly was buried in the earth, in mounds of grasses, or under trees. As early as 1893, Johann Kirste, writing on the ceremonies of the first tonsure as performed in ancient India and among the highly conservative southern Slavic peoples, came to this conclusion.[5] Although Kirste was subjected to immediate criticism[6] and his essay has long been ignored in the scholarly literature, his insight was fundamentally correct. And, while the relatively recent date of the Slavic evidence,[7] upon which he relied heavily, made it easy to dismiss his conclusions, other data not subject to such objections confirm his position.[8]

The Indic Cūḍākarman, the ceremony for a child's first tonsure described in the *Saṅkhāyana Gṛhya Sūtra* 1.28 and elsewhere, affords invaluable evidence.[9] It is performed for a child of the priestly class at the age of one or three years, for a child of the warrior class at five years, and for a child of the commoner (*vaiśya*) class at seven years. The child's hair is untangled and anointed, and a young kuśa shoot (a sacred grass) is placed in it. Next, the child's hair, together with the kuśa shoot, is shaved off with a copper razor—a consciously archaic ritual implement, copper technology having long since been replaced by iron. The shorn hair is then placed in a specially constructed mound of bull dung mixed with kuśa grass. Finally, "they bury the hairs to the northeast, in a place abounding with plants or close to water."

What is most striking in this description, as Kirste recognized, is the constant association of the child's hair with vegetation. This is accomplished first through the insertion of the kuśa shoot in the child's hair, next through the placement of the shorn hair on the mound of grass plus a fertilizing medium, and finally through burial of the hair in the earth "in a place abounding with plants" (*diśi bahvauṣadhike*). Quite similar in many ways are some of the rites performed by the chief priest of Jupiter at Rome, the Flamen Dialis, and by his wife, the Flaminica, as described in Aulus Gellius, *Attic Nights* 10.15:

> The ceremonies placed upon the Flamen Dialis are many, and the forbearances are also numerous . . . No one should cut the hair of the Dialis except a free man . . .
> The cuttings of the nails and hair of the Dialis are buried in the earth under a fruitful tree . . . There are almost the same ceremonies for the Flaminica Dialis, and they say that other different ones are to be observed. For instance, she is covered with a dyed gown, and in her veil she has the shoot of a fruitful tree.[10]

In the past, scholars often treated these observances as "taboos," but the text allows considerable doubt on this point. Gellius specifically states that he is discussing the rituals (*caerimoniae*) of the Flamen Dialis as well as the avoidances (*castus*) this priest had to observe, and the question is whether these practices fall in the first or the second category. Recently, W. Pötscher has shown that much of what had been assumed to be simply taboo or superstitious avoidance on the part of the Flamen Dialis is best understood as ritual with a profoundly creative and positive significance.[11] That the rules surrounding the treatment of the Flamen Dialis's hair are not banal superstition may also be perceived from the parallel observances of the Vestal Virgins. As Pliny reported in *Natural History* 16.235, "Truly, there is a lotus tree in Rome, in the area of Lucina . . . Now, this tree is about five hundred years old or older—its age is uncertain—and it is called "the hairy one" (*capillata*) because the hair of the Vestal Virgins is brought to it." In this passage, we begin to sense the rationale for disposing of hair in association with plants. For the lotus is no mere tree; as Pliny states in *Natural History* 22.55, citing the authority of Homer,[12] it is "the most delightful among the plants that grow up beneath the gods." And this particular lotus—nourished, as it were, upon the hair of the Vestal Virgins—had reached the inconceivable age of five hundred years or more. Truly, it was the oldest and best of trees, having been sustained by the hair repeatedly offered by the best and most sacred of women.

The treatment of hair taken from the Flamen Dialis and the Flaminica Dialis shows detailed correspondences to procedures in the Indic *Cūḍākarman*. Thus, a shoot is stuck in the hair of the Flaminica Dialis, just as a shoot is placed in the hair of the young Indian boy, and the hair and nails of the Flamen Dialis (presumably also those of the Flaminica) are buried in the earth, as is done in India.

Within the Slavic ceremonies Kirste considered, shorn hair is also buried in the earth, usually beneath a tree, and such a mode of disposal for hair clippings was commonly noted by folklorists of the eighteenth and nineteenth centuries throughout Germany,[13] Rumania,[14] and Ireland. In the last instance, a particularly interesting explanation was given by some informants, who stated that one's hair had to be buried in the earth and not burned, so that it could be restored to its owner at the Resurrection.[15]

Examples like these could easily be multiplied, but doing so would add rather little to the study of ancient IE themes. While collectively they may tend to corroborate a general picture arrived at independently from consideration of ancient sources, authoritative texts, and select sorts of folkloric evidence (see note 8 to this chapter), generalized folklore, for all its admitted conservatism, is still too subject to change, too difficult of verification and secure interpretation, and too chronologically recent to be of great assistance.

Of much surer value is the evidence of an important Avestan text that describes the proper treatment of shorn hair: *Vīdēvdāt* 17.1–6.[16] Here, Zarathuštra is said to have asked Ahura Mazdā: "For what (act) would the demon Aoša ("Destruction") punish (lit "sacrifice") mortals with the most violent death?" And the Wise Lord responds:

Truly, that (is the act for which one is so punished), O Righteous Zarathuštra, when one arranges and cuts one's hair and clips one's nails, and then lets them fall into holes in the earth or into furrows. For by these improprieties, demons (*daēvas*) come forth, and from these improprieties, noxious creatures (*xrafstras*) come forth from the earth, which mortals call lice and which devour the grain in the fields and the clothes in the closets. Now when you must arrange and cut your hair and clip your nails in this world, Zarathuštra, hereafter you should bear it ten steps from righteous men, twenty steps from the fire, thirty steps from the water, and fifty steps from the *barəsman* (bundle of sacred twigs) when it is laid out. Then you should dig a pit here, ten fingers deep in hard soil and twelve fingers deep in soft soil. To that pit you should bear the cuttings. Then you should pronounce these words, victorious Zarathuštra: "Now for this one may Mazdā make the plants grow by means of Aša ('Right')." You should plow three or six or nine furrows for Xšaθra Vairya ("Good Dominion"), and you should recite the Ahuna Vairya prayer three or six or nine times.

There is much that is fascinating in this text: the need to carry potentially impure matter away from sources of purification (righteous men, fire, water and *barəsman*); the use of troughs to mark off sacred space; and the spontaneous production of monsters from hair and nails that are improperly disposed of—a point to which I shall return. But the heart of this passage lies in the sacred formula, recitation of which is prescribed for the moment at which the hair and nail clippings are placed in the ground: "Now for this one may Mazdā make the plants grow by means of Aša." This statement is a *mąθra* (= Skt *mantra-*), a ritual formula filled with efficacy and magicoreligious force. This *mąθra* is taken from one of Zarathuštra's own hymns (*Yasna* 48.6c), and put to a creative new use quite outside its original context. In its original setting, this line refers to the creation of cattle at the beginning of the world, and the demonstrative pronoun *ahyāi* "for this one," refers to the cow. Thus, Mazdā is said to have created the plants for the well-being of the cattle.[17] But here, isolated from its initial context, the pronoun lacks a referent of any sort and might thus be assumed to refer back to the speaker himself: "for this one (standing here)," that is, "for me." Whether cattle or humans are the intended beneficiaries, in its new setting the Gāthic quotation has become a spell, a ritual by which the proper disposal of hair and nails leads to the production of vegetation. Again we encounter the association of hair and nails with the plant world, along with the ritual prescription to dispose of hair and nails by burying them in the earth.

This Avestan passage goes further than the other sources I have considered in explicating the reasons for such treatment of hair and nails (the latter seem to be added as something of an afterthought).[18] For alongside the specification that proper disposal of hair and nails will produce vegetation, we are told that improper disposal will produce vermin, lice (Av *spiš*)[19] "which devour the grain in the fields" (*yaom yavohva nižgənhənti*); that is, such clippings become the destruction of vegetation, or better yet, *antivegetation*, the antithesis of vegetation.[20] Proper disposal of hair is thus established as a ritual in which a portion of the cosmogony is repeated, each individual's shorn locks becoming plants just as did those of the primordial victim from whose body the world was made. Should this ritual be botched, the effects are catastrophic, turning a normally creative act to destruction. That the ritual burial of hair and nails is here to be understood as a repetition of the cosmogony is underscored by recitation of the Ahuna Vairya prayer, the prayer the Wise Lord chanted when he first began the work of creation.[21]

Vīdēvdāt 17, like Pliny's description of the "hairy" lotus, merely makes explicit what is implicit in the Indic *Cūḍākarman*, the Slavic ceremonies of the first tonsure, the treatment of hair and nails cut from the Flamen Dialis and the Flaminica, and in all probability the folk customs of Germany, Rumania, and Ireland regarding shorn hair. In all cases, hair cuttings are buried in the ground—planted, as it were—most often in close conjunction with shoots, grass, plants, or trees. The purpose of this is to effect the transformation of hair into vegetation, shifting material substance from its microcosmic to its macrocosmic alloform, along the lines laid out by cosmogonic myth and the sacrificial ritual.

Sacrifice was the preeminent ritual form of the Proto-Indo-European people: most dramatic, most expensive, most solemn, and most all-encompassing. As we saw in Chapter 2, sacrifice was nothing less than the reenactment of the cosmogony on a *total* scale. Yet at the level of a single homology, the proper disposal of cut hair is no less a repetition of the cosmogony, whereby matter was transferred from the body to the cosmos. Far from being a trivial, mundane, or banal activity, the disposal of hair was an important ritual, a sacrifice on a small scale, which—when properly performed—helped to sustain the very universe.

While most often it is alleged that proper disposal of shorn hair sustains the life of vegetation, a slightly different formulation is found in a Middle High German charm recorded in chapter 87 of the *Phi-*

losophia Colus, a text published in Leipzig in 1662. Given in verse form, the charm describes how to procure luxuriant hair:

> The old women say:
> "If young people secretly wish to acquire long hair,
> They must first cut off some hair in their youth.
> Then they lay this in the earth together with hops tendrils
> So that thereafter they grow together to the same length."[22]

Another Middle High German text, a Breslau manuscript of 1568, describes the procedure favored by "some magicians" (*etzliche Magi*) for attaining the same result. After boring a hole in a young willow tree, they place some of their client's hair inside it, claiming "as the tree grows up quickly, so also grows one's hair, if no one cuts down the tree."[23]

Although these charms are quite similar to the materials I considered earlier, they also differ from them in important ways. For while elsewhere interest centered on the question of what would happen to the shorn bits of hair—furthering the growth of the "hairy" lotus tree in Pliny *NH* 16.235, or of all vegetation in *Vīdēvdāt* 17.5—these medieval German practices shift the focus to the question of what will happen to the hair that remains on the subject's head. No longer is disposal of hair cuttings in association with the earth or vegetation intended to make the hair grow *into plants*; rather, the goal here is to make the hair grow *like the plants*. In these charms, hair and vegetation almost fuse into one entity, the growth of either one being tantamount to the growth of both, while conversely the nongrowth of one also produces the nongrowth of the other: if the willow tree mentioned in the Breslau manuscript were to be cut down, the client presumably would go bald. It thus is unclear whether these charms work on the cosmogonic pattern, whereby matter is shifted from microcosm to macrocosm (hair becoming plants), or on the anthropogonic pattern, plants becoming hair.[24]

Other Germanic data are less ambiguous, being clearly anthropogonic. Among these, the most important are the numerous folk remedies for baldness in which vegetable matter is applied to the scalp in order to restore lost hair. Decoctions of burdock root (*Klettenwurzel*) and fireweed (*Brennessel*) are thus used in many regions of Germany, as are onion juice, water from the roots of wintergreen, and numerous others.[25] In all cases, the intent is the same: to transmit needed material substance from the plant world to the hair. The only significant difference among these various remedies is that each one resolves the practical problem of how to place essential vegetable matter within the hair by way of a slightly different modus operandi. Moreover, the same general practice is attested in the oldest Indo-European charms for hair loss that have come down to us: *Atharva Veda* 6.136 and 6.137, dating from about 800 B.C. The first of these opens with an apostrophe to an unnamed plant to be recited while it is gathered from the soil:

> You are a goddess, born upon the divine earth, O Plant!
> We dig you now, you who stretch downward, in order to make the hairs firm.
> Make the old ones firm; cause to be born those which are (still) unborn; make those which have been born (grow) longer!

In the third and final verse, the Atharvan priest addresses his client, as he applies the healing substance:

> That hair of yours which falls out, and that which is cut off with its roots (still) attached—
> This now I sprinkle with the all-healing herb!

Nowhere is this "all-healing herb" identified, although from this hymn we can discern its most important physical property. Apparently it is possessed of long, firm roots, for it is called "you who stretch downward" (*nitanti*, the singular vocative feminine of the present participle from *ni-tan-*). The cure is thus a homeopathic one, in which a plant with strong roots is sprinkled over the head of one whose hair falls out. The goal, obviously, is to produce hair that resembles the plant. This same intention—causing hair to acquire the properties of a select species of its macrocosmic alloform—is explicitly stated in the refrain to *AV* 6.137. 2, 3: "The black hairs must grow on your head like reeds." It is a mistake to view this as nothing more than "sympathetic magic." Rather, it is a sophisticated application of the anthropogonic side of creation mythology, having much in common with the theories of the nutritional process discussed in Chapter 3, and the healing rituals to be discussed in Chapter 5.

An amusing passage from the Irish epic *Táin Bó Cúailnge* also preserves the basic motif of curing baldness by the application of plant matter. The baldness in question, however, is of the chin and not the scalp, for we are told that the young hero Cú Chulainn wished to appear old enough to attract worthy opponents in battle. In the version of the *Lebor na hUidre* (ll.6125–6132), the story is as follows.[26]

> It was then that the women said to Cú Chulainn that he was mocked
> in the encampment because there was not a beard on him, and the
> best warriors would not go to meet him, but only rogues. It would
> be easier for him (they said) to make himself a beard with mulberry
> juice. And he did this last-named thing, because he sought battle
> with a man, Lóch Mór mac Mo Febais. Cú Chulainn then took a
> fistful of grass and chanted over it, so that everyone now thought
> that a beard was on him.

What Cú Chulainn chanted, we are not told, nor how the mulberry
juice and the grass combined to give the impression of a beard, although one may suppose that the former was for color and the latter
for texture. But one ought not pursue the matter too earnestly. Far
from being a serious account of a magicomedical remedy that was
actually employed, this is a parody or burlesque constructed upon an
older tradition of such cures.

Within the Greco-Roman world, it is clear that baldness was treated
with therapies based upon the homology of hair and plants. One such
treatment employed an aromatic substance, *ladanum*, secreted by different varieties of the plant species *Cistus*.[27] Pliny describes its working
in *Natural History* 26.30, listing its use as a hair restorer along with
numerous other properties and applications:

> (Diarrhea) is checked with both kinds of ladanum, that which comes
> forth from the crops when crushed and sifted. It is drunk in honeyed
> water, and also in good wine. The herb is called *ledon*, which in Cyprus
> adheres to the beards of goats. The better kind is in Arabia. That
> which is now produced in Syria and Africa they call *toxicus* [playing
> on the senses of both "toxic" and "pertaining to the bow" (Gk *toxeus*)],
> for they extract it with a bow, the strings of which are surrounded
> with wool, so that the dewy substance (of the plant) adheres to the
> woolly substance. We have said more on this under "Unguents." It
> is extremely heavy in odor, and extremely rough in touch, for it
> collects a great deal of earth. When it is judged to be most pure, it
> is fragrant, pliant, green, and resinous. Its nature is softening, drying,
> promotive of good digestion, and conducive to sleep. *It stops hair
> from falling out and preserves its black color.* With mead or rose oil, it
> is poured into the ears. Added to salt, it cures scales of the skin and
> oozing ulcers. Taken with styrax for a lingering cough. Most effective
> for belching.

Given the wide variety of ailments which might be treated with ladanum, it may seem a bit arbitrary to stress the inclusion of hair loss

in such a list. That the snake oil of the ancient world would keep one looking young, as well as cure scales, sores, coughs, insomnia, and digestive troubles, seems quite unremarkable on first inspection. Yet when we uncover the precise reason why ladanum was favored for hair loss, a profound logic emerges. In another passage (*NH* 12.37) Pliny describes in fuller detail the nature of ladanum and the way it was collected.

> Even now Arabia glories in its ladanum. Many record that this is owing to chance and accident, caused by the injury done to aromatic plants by goats—animals injurious to other foliage as well, but hungriest for fragrant shrubs, as if they can perceive the (great) value of these. (Goats) graze on stalks that are swollen with sweet fluid, and they brush off the sap that trickles (from the cut stalks) with the rough shag of their beards, accidentally producing an intermingling (of beard and sap). This (mixture) forms a pellet, together with dust, and this is colored by the sun. Therefore, there are goat hairs in ladanum.

Ladanum is thus seen to have been an oleoresin formed from the sap of aromatic plants, dust, and goat hair. Laboriously collected—the preferred method was by combing the pellets out of goats' pelts—it was imported to Greece and Rome from Arabia or from Cyprus and North Africa. Mixed with various substances, it was used medicinally.

Of greatest interest to us is the ingestion of ladanum dissolved in wine or in honeyed water to keep hair from falling out, and we may now perceive just what rationale lay behind this practice. In ladanum, animal hair and vegetable matter were thoroughly intermingled: its hallmark was the presence of goat hair within the resin, and counterfeiters even attempted to produce a similar effect by mixing myrtle berries with "other dirt of animals."[28] Ladanum must thus have appeared to be a kind of *Urstoffe,* primordial undifferentiated matter in which the homological alloforms hair and plants had not yet been separated. Rather than being either hair or plants, ladanum was both and neither: more precisely, it was that substance which contained within it the potential for hair and plants alike. Taken into the human body, it was pressed into anthropogonic service and sprung forth as a new, full, young, and black head of hair. Recall Anaxagoras's rhetorical question (fragment B10): "How can hair come into being from that which is not hair, and flesh from that which is not flesh? The use of ladanum provides a suitably subtle answer to this challenging question. Hair is here born from a substance that both *is* and *is not* hair, ladanum being prehair matter, or hair *in potentio*.

Ladanum, however, in addition to being prehair, is also prevegetation, having its source in plants (the sap of aromatics) and hair (goats' beards) alike. It is thus perfectly intermediate to hair and plants. Appropriated anthropogonically, it becomes the former; cosmogonically, the latter. Understood most deeply, ladanum is merely a moment in an ongoing process, that process being the eternal cyclical alternation between plants and hair, matter ever passing from one to the other and moving through ladanum as an intermediate stage.

Based on the Germanic, Indic, and Greco-Roman data I have considered, it would thus seem that there existed a broad tradition of cures for baldness and hair loss among the Indo-European peoples, in which anthropogonic processes were manipulated for this practical end: matter was taken from the macrocosm (plants) and translated into its microcosmic alloform (hair). And just as in nutrition the anthropogony is repeated on a total scale, so the cure of baldness seems to be the nutrition of one microcosmic element alone, or anthropogony on a small scale. Further, just an anthropogony complements cosmogony and nutrition complements sacrifice, so also the cure of baldness complements the disposal of shorn hair.[29] Together the two processes alternate endlessly, hair becoming vegetation and vegetation becoming hair, as represented in figure 13.

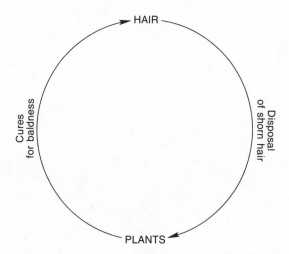

Figure 13. Practical applications of the homology hair/plants.

For us, such matters as haircuts and hair restoration have become thoroughly secularized and trivialized, while the nature of the universe has become a recondite and thoroughly impractical matter, consideration of which flourishes only among astrophysicists, theologians, and children. Yet within traditional Indo-European lore, it would seem, a different state of affairs prevailed: cosmological wisdom informed virtually all practical concerns, and nothing was too small or too mundane to be considered apart from the total cosmic process.

5

Magical Healing

The curing of baldness, like the digestion of food, is a process whereby restoration of the body is effected. It is a universal fact of existence that the passage of time poses various threats to the human body, as connoted in the semantics of the IE verb *ĝer-*, which combines the senses of "to grow old" and "to be worn down," depicting the aging process as one of gradual erosion.[1] In part, nutrition combats such erosion, as food replenishes bodily matter that would otherwise be lost. Similarly, the loss of hair, one of the most obvious signs of advancing age, constitutes an attrition or erosion of bodily matter. And just as the incorporation of macrocosmic substance through eating wards off the bodily attrition evident in malnutrition and starvation, so the incorporation of one specific macrocosmic substance—plants, via cures for baldness—wards off the bodily attrition evident in hair loss.

Beyond the threats posed to the body by the normal aging process, there exist other, less predictable threats, such as those of injury and disease. The same resources were mobilized against such threats as against baldness and malnutrition. A system of magical healing was thus constructed from the homological building blocks of creation mythology. Within this system, methods were developed whereby matter could be shifted from the macrocosm to the microcosm and back again, as necessary, to counter the threats to the wholeness and well-being of the body posed by injury and disease.

Specialists in the art of healing were regularly given titles formed from the verbal root *med-*. Thus, Av *vī-mad-* denotes a physician, as does Lt *medicus* (with secondary formation in *-icus* from an original substantive *mēd-*). Greek also retains this title in several proper names given to prominent healers, such as *Mēdos, Mēdē, Agamēdē* ("Great healer," < **Mga-mēdē*), *Mēdeia, Perimēdē,* and so on, while Latin contains numerous terms related to the medical art that are derived from the same root, such as *medeor, -ērī* "to heal," alongside *medicīna* and *remedium,* with their obvious English cognates.[2] Moreover, as Emile Benveniste demonstrated, use of the root **med-* to denote one who works cures tells us a great deal about the nature of that process, for this is a specialized use of a root that had a more general sense: the imposition of proper order on things or people by one possessed of knowledge and authority.[3]

The nature of the order a healer established is also spelled out in the semantics of another verb applied to the art of healing, particularly within the Germanic languages: IE **kai-lo-,* which occurs in Goth *hailjan,* OE *hǣlan,* OHG *heilen,* and OBulg *cěljǫ,* all of which mean "to heal." What is expressed most directly through these terms, however, is not just the establishment of a vague state of "health" or "well-being" but more precisely a state of "wholeness, totality, completion," as shown in the nominal and adjectival formations from this root, such as Goth *hails,* ON *heill,* OHG *heil,* and OBulg *cel",* all of which mean both "healthy" and "whole"; OE *hāl,* which occurs in the latter sense only; or OPruss *kailūstiskan* (singular accusative) "health, wholeness."[4]

So desirable was this state of wholeness thought to be that two common IE formulaic greetings and toasts express the wish that the one addressed may be "whole."[5] Such a state of well-being and wholeness might be lost through injury or disease, whereupon the healer's task was to restore it.

We are able to recognize something of the medical system whereby Indo-European healers sought to restore wholeness, thanks to a correspondence first adduced by James Darmesteter in the last century and since studied in some detail by Benveniste and by Jaan Puhvel.[6] The starting point for the comparison is Pindar's Third Pythian Ode, ll. 46–55, in which the poet recounts the nature of Asklepios's training in the medical arts by the centaur Kheirōn:

> They came—those possessing sores
> which had sprung up by themselves; those whose limbs were
>   wounded by the gray spear
> or by a boulder thrown from afar;
> and those whose bodies were wasted by the summer's fire
>   or the winter's (cold)—and he rescued each
> from his own grief, tending some with soft incantations;

some by giving them soothing potions
   to drink or by tying drugs round their limbs
on all sides; and some he set straight by cutting (i.e., surgery).

To this must be compared a text from the Younger Avesta, *Vidēvdāt* 7.44, in which the Wise Lord instructs his prophet, Zarathuštra:

> When those who possess many cures come together, O Spitama Zarathuštra, when he who cures with the knife, he who cures with plants, and he who cures with sacred formulas come together here . . . truly he who cures with the beneficent sacred formula is the most curing of curers.

As Benveniste and Puhvel have rightly stressed, these three modes of healing, together with the three ailments mentioned in the Pindaric ode, correspond to the three characteristic social classes of Indo-European societies, healing by words (incantations or formulas) being the therapy characteristic of priests, suitable for the almost magically appearing ulcers in *Pythian* 3.46f.; healing by surgery being characteristic of the warrior class, suitable for wounds suffered in battle; and healing by herbs or plants being characteristic of the food-producing commoners, suitable for emaciation from tuberculosis or malnutrition.[7]

Healing by acts of magical speech is the highest form of healing. This is made explicit in the Avestan text and is also implied in *Pythia* 3, both by its primary position in the list and by its association with the highest social class, the priests. "He who cures with the beneficent sacred formula is the most curing of curers (*baēšazanąm baēšazyōtəmō*)." Yet another example of this same medical taxonomy, noted first by Arthur Christensen,[8] supports this interpretation, albeit in a backhanded way. The source in question is the Hippokratic *Aphorism* 7.87: "Whatever drugs do not heal, the knife heals. Whatever the knife does not heal, fire heals. And whatever fire does not heal must be considered incurable." Here, the modes of healing are ranked in reverse order, from lowliest and least effective (healing by plants) to the next higher rank (surgery) to the highest, but in this final rank we find healing by fire rather than the expected healing by charms, prayers, or incantations. What this healing by fire was exactly is hard to tell—cauterization, perhaps. But the substitution of fire for charms in the top position is an innovation that results from the Hippokratic campaign to rationalize medical practice, to rid it of "magical" or "superstitious" elements. What is remarkable here is that in locating something to take the place of unacceptable "spells" the text has recourse to an item with priestly associations no weaker than those of spells: fire, which, as a purifying agent and sacrificial medium, was central to both the Greek and Indo-European public and domestic cults.[9]

Notwithstanding the importance of the Hippokratic school in our own medical tradition, adopting its disparaging attitude toward earlier medical practice can be limiting. For "magic," as sensitive anthropologists have increasingly realized, is most often nothing more than a non-Aristotelian view of causality, an analogic system in which items that have some perceived relation may act upon one another, even if separate in time and space. In this there is nothing superstitious or ignorant. Rather, he who would heal by "magical" means must possess profound knowledge of the subtle similarities that join ostensibly foreign objects to the patient's body, for it is through the manipulation of those objects by word and gesture that analogic, homeopathic, or "sympathetic" cures are effected.

Such a view, I believe, is tremendously helpful in understanding the workings of "magical" healing as attested in certain spells that circulated widely among Germans, Celts, Slavs, Greeks, and Indo-Iranians. Systematic comparison of these spells began with a brilliant essay by Adalbert Kuhn,[10] which appeared in 1864 and took as its starting point a spell for injury to limbs found in the second Merseburg Charm, which was written in Old High German early in the tenth century A.D., but which preserves contents far more ancient in their origin:

> Fol and Wodan   rode to the wood
> When Balder's stallion   injured its foot.
> Then chanted Sinthgunt,   sister of Sunna (the sun),
> Then chanted Friia,   sister of Folla,
> Then chanted Wodan,   as was well-known to him:
> "Be it bone-injury,   be it blood-injury,
>   be it limb-injury—
> Bone to bone;   blood to blood;
> Limb to limb,   thus be fastened together!"[11]

As has been generally recognized, this text falls into two distinct parts: a mythic frame-story, which establishes a sacred precedent for use of the charm that follows, and the charm itself. Although the frame story contains numerous points of interest,[11] it is of less importance for a comparative inquiry than is the charm, for in various forms this charm remained extremely popular and was widely diffused throughout the Germanic world and also among the neighboring Finno-Ugrians,[12] continuing to be used in both cultures into modern times. Kuhn, pursuing work begun by Jacob Grimm, assembled a great number of more recent Germanic reflexes, including the following Norwegian version (p. 51), in which—as in many other instances—Jesus replaces Wodan in the story:

> Jesus himself rode to the heath,
> And as he rode, his horse's bone was broken.
> Jesus dismounted and healed that:
> Jesus laid marrow to marrow,
> Bone to bone, flesh to flesh.
> Jesus thereafter laid a leaf (on it)
> So that these should stay in their place.

Again, a version from Devonshire (p. 54) replaces Wodan with Christ and accordingly transforms the ride into the wood into the most famous ride of the later god: that into Jerusalem.[13]

> For a sprain: As our blessed Lord and Saviour Jesus Christ was riding into Jerusalem, His horse tripped and sprained its leg. Our Blessed Lord and Saviour blessed it, and said:
>
> > Bone to bone and vein to vein,
> > O vein turn to thy rest again!
> > N.N. so shall thine in the Name, etc.

Although this type of charm is most often used by Germanic peoples for the healing of sprained or broken limbs among horses, occasionally it is applied to humans, in which case a different mythic precedent is provided. The most striking instance of this is a Middle High German text, *Codex Vaticanus* 4395 bl. 83a (Kuhn, pp. 56f.):

> God had four nails driven into his hands and feet, from which he had four wounds when he was on the holy cross. The fifth wound, Longinus gave him, and this was not avenged . . . On the third day (after the crucifixion), God commanded the corpse, which had lain in the earth: "Flesh to flesh, blood to blood, vein to vein, bone to bone, limb to limb, be right in its place." By this same command I bid you: "Flesh to flesh . . ."[14]

The same basic form of charm was current in Russia in the early nineteenth century, having reached the Slavs most probably by diffusion from the Germans or Finns, although independent preservation of common IE materials cannot be ruled out.[15] The text that most forcefully indicates a broad tradition of charms that might be called "For Injury to Limbs" however, is the one that made Kuhn's treatment a classic: the Indic spell contained in *Atharva Veda* 4.12, which should probably be dated no later than 800 B.C. The hymn begins with wordplay on the two names of an herb to be used for the healing of broken limbs—the *Arundhati*, also know as *Rohaṇi* ("Growing"), the latter name formed as the feminine present participle of the verb *ruh-* "to grow."[16] After this introductory passage, the hymn is strikingly similar to the Merseburg Charm:

> Rohaṇī, you are "Growing"—growing the broken bone.
> Cause this to grow, O Arundhati!
> What of you (i.e., the patient) is injured, what of you is broken, is
>   crushed—
> By healing this, may the creator put together again joint with joint.
> May your marrow with marrow come together; together, your joint
>   with joint.
> Together, that of your flesh which has slipped apart; grow together
>   your bones!
> Marrow with marrow, be put together; pelt with pelt, grow.
> Your blood, grow on the bone; flesh with flesh, grow.
> Hair with hair, be united; skin, be united with skin.
> Your blood, grow on the bone; put together that which
>   is broken, O plant!
> Stand up, go forth, run forward, (like) a chariot whose
>   wheel is good, whose felly is good, whose nave is good:
> Stand upright!!! (*AV* 4.12.1–6)

Formally, syntactically, and semantically, this is quite close to the Second Merseburg Charm, and most scholars have agreed with Kuhn's conclusion that both are independent variants of a common IE prototype.[17] In both texts, the speaker commands bones, blood, and limbs or joints to come together, with the Atharvan charm adding to the list marrow, flesh, bodily hair, and skin. In none of these instances, however, is there a phonological correspondence, with the exception of the phrase "marrow to marrow" in the Norwegian variant and in *AV* 4.12, where Norwegian *marv* and Sanskrit *majjan-* both derive from PIE **moz-g-*, with endings in *-o-* and *-en-* respectively.[18]

That the Germanic and Indic variants are part of a common tradition is made more probable by the existence of a Celtic version of the same charm, first recognized by Wolfgang Krause in 1929.[19] This occurs in the mythic account of the healing of the severed hand of Nuada, king of the Tuatha Dé Danaan, which is briefly described in the *Lebor Gabála Érenn* 7.329:

> Dian Cecht [the usual physician among the Tuatha Dé] set a silver hand (on Nuada), with full motion in every finger and in each joint, and Credne the artisan stood by him. Miach, the son of Dian Cecht, set joint to joint and sinew (or: vein, or nerve) to sinew (or: vein, or nerve) of his arm, and healed him in three enneads [i.e., weeks consisting of nine days].

Again we find strong formal, syntactic, and semantic correspondences to the Indic and Germanic materials, but no phonetic correspondence in the precise terms, for Old Irish *alt* ("joint") and *féith* ("sinew," "vein," or "nerve") bear no etymological relation to their counterparts in these other sources. The situation is different, however, when we turn to previously unrecognized Greek variants. First, consider the Hippokratic *Aphorism* 7.28: "Any bone or cartilage or sinew in the body that is cut through does not grow." This statement also occurs in Hippokratic *Aphorism* 6.19, where two further anatomical items are added to the list and a second verb is added to give greater precision to the sense:

> When a bone or cartilege or sinew, or the thin part of the jaw or the tip of the foreskin is cut through, it does not grow, nor does it grow back together.

What is most peculiar about these two statements, and what has puzzled all commentators on them from Galen down to the present, is that they fly in the face of all direct observation. Bones, cartilege, and sinew *do* knit back together, even when cleanly broken or cut.[20] This fact could not have escaped the well-cultivated empirical powers of the Hippokratic physicians—and yet the text twice denies the possibility of such healing. Why should this be so?

The answer, I would suggest, emerges when we consider the transformation wrought by Hippokratic medicine on the older healing arts. When considering *Aphorism* 7.87, I noted that all hints of "magic" or "superstition" seemed to have been carefully weeded out. *Apho-*

risms 7.28 and 6.19 assert that certain injuries that in truth are curable cannot be cured. Given that this particular cure—restoration of severed bones, cartilege, and sinew—formed an important part of magical healing among the Celts, Germans, Indians, and others, it seems quite likely that the Hippokratics were here combating the claims of earlier Greek healers, who likewise had sought magically to set "bone to bone, blood to blood, and flesh to flesh." That charms of this precise type were preserved and circulated in Greece is further suggested by the occurrence of such phrases, albeit in a different context, in Plato's *Phaido* 96D. There, while discussing his youthful interest in theories of physiology, especially in the nutritional process, Sokrates states: "When one takes food, flesh to flesh is added, and bones to bones . . ."

If it is correct to conclude on the strength of such evidence that a charm of the type "For Injury to Limbs" was known in Greece, then we may recover yet another phonological correspondence within the various versions of this charm, for Greek *osteon*, "bone," used by Plato and the Hippokratics alike, is cognate to Sanskrit *asthi-* (*AV* 4.12.4– 5), both being derived from PIE *H_1os-$t(H_2)$-.[21] We may thus posit a set of speech acts that regularly accompanied the healing rituals performed among numerous Indo-European peoples for sprains, broken bones, and the like. But these speech-acts must also have been accompanied by gestures that increased their efficacy, and these have never been given serious study.[22]

Most of our texts are mute regarding gestures. Some of the variants from the British Isles make reference to a "wristing (or: wresting) thread," which is tied around the injured limb, apparently as a means of binding together tissues sundered by injury.[23] Others, particularly from Siebenbürg and southern Germany, tell of rubbing grease and salt on the injury.[24] The act of rubbing seems particularly significant, and I will consider it later, but the meaning of the specific ingredients—grease and salt—is opaque to me. The only observations I can make are that they may have served as a disinfecting ointment and that their use together was perhaps suggested by the rhyme of *Salz* and *Schmalz* in German.[25]

Several variants, including the Norwegian charm and *AV* 4.12 cited earlier, state that a leaf or an herb of some sort was placed upon the injury, thus combining two of the three traditional categories of IE medicine—healing by words and healing by herbs.[26] Moreover, in *AV* 5.5.8cd–9, we are told why the specific herb prescribed in *AV* 4.12, the Arundhati, should be effective for broken limbs of horses.

> The horse of Yama, which is brown—you (O Arundhati,) are spat-
> tered with his blood!
> That (herb), having been struck with the horse's blood, flows to the
> trees.
> Having become streaming, winged, come to us, O Arundhati!

Brief, though it is, this little snippet of myth is precious, for it connects
the healing charm to the cosmogonic drama. For Yama, according to
Vedic myth (see esp. *RV* 10.10 and 10.14) was nothing other than the
first man.[27] His horse, then, is presumably the first horse, and the
injury here described is presumably the first injury. Blood flew from
the leg of that horse when injured, we are told, and landed on a
nearby blade of grass, transforming it into a spotted herb with certain
healing properties. Forever after, that blade of grass—now the spec-
kled Arundhati herb—will hold within it that blood, which it can
restore to those who have suffered similar injuries. The shape of the
herb when it is placed upon damaged limbs perhaps suggests the veins
or arteries in which blood flows, while its color suggests the blood
itself.[28]

The relation between (origin) myth and (healing) ritual is noteworthy here, for while *AV* 5.5 recounts the story of how a specific
healing plant came into existence from a (dismembered) portion of
the body of some primordial victim, *AV* 4.12 tells how that plant can
be used to restore the material substance needed to mend injuries to
that same bodily member. The myth of *AV* 5.5 is thus something of
a cosmogonic account (albeit a cosmogony on a reduced scale, describing the origin of only one item within the macrocosm, rather
than of the universe in its entirety), while the ritual of *AV* 4.12 is an
anthropogonic reversal of the events described in the myth. Similar
themes and structural relations are evident within a somewhat longer
and more detailed account than the *Lebor Gabála* version of how Miach
restored Nuada's severed hand: that contained in *Cath Maige Turedh*
33–35:

> Nuada was ill, and Dian Cecht gave him another hand, a silver one,
> which had the motion of every hand within it. This did not seem
> good to (Dian Cecht's) son, Miach. He raised up (Nuada's) hand and
> said, "Joint to joint of it, and sinew to sinew," and he healed it in
> three enneads. The first ennead he put it next to his side, and it
> came to be covered with skin. The second ennead, he put it on his
> chest. The third ennead, he cast the white (ashes?) of black bulrushes
> (onto it), after they had been blackened in the fire.

That cure seemed evil to Dian Cecht. He let loose his sword on the head of his son, cutting his scalp down into the flesh. The youth healed that, through the exercise of his skill. (Dian Cecht) struck again, cutting the flesh to the bone. The youth healed that by the same exercise. He hewed a third cut, to the membrane of the brain. The youth healed that by the same exercise. He hewed a fourth cut, and reached the brain, so that Miach died, and Dian Cecht said that there was not any physician who could heal that blow.

After that, Miach was buried by Dian Cecht, and 365 (healing) herbs grew up through his grave, according to the number of his joints and sinews.

In many ways, this myth is quite similar to the sitiogonic accounts considered in Chapter 3. Among the other sources to which this story corresponds most closely are *Zad Spram* 3.42–51 and *Greater Bundahišn* 13.0–9 (TD MS. 93.8–94.15), which tell in elaborate detail how each different edible plant and healing herb was created from a different bodily part of the primordial ox Ēvagdād after he was slain by Ahriman (see Chapter 3). As a result of these events, the texts continue, one may restore any given bodily member by either eating or applying medicinally the plant that originated from the corresponding—that is to say, alloformic—part of the primordial ox. Similarly, according to *AV* 5.5.8–9, a broken limb may be healed with the plant formed from the blood of Yama's horse's leg.

Whereas the Iranian texts include discussions of both the use of plants as food and their medical applications, this Irish version deals with the latter only. As such, it discusses only healing plants ("herbs," OIr *luib*),[29] and posits their origin from the first healer (Miach) rather than from the first animal. Yet with this difference, the ideas contained in *Cath Maige Turedh* 33–35 are quite similar to those in the Iranian sources. Thus, Miach's body is said to have possessed 365 units ("joints and sinews," *altai ocus fethe*), each of which became a different herb upon his death.[30] In the event of an injury to any given bodily member, a cure might thus be effected by application of that specific herb which is the alloform of the damaged member and can thus restore it to wholeness. This may be done because the same essential matter exists in bodily members and in herbs. At Miach's death, this matter moved from its bodily to its herbal form (from microcosm to macrocosm), and the process may be reversed at any time by one who possesses sufficient skill and knowledge to return needed matter from the macrocosm to the microcosm.[31]

While the application of herbs is one gesture that clearly accompanied use of the charm "For Injury to Limbs" on occasion, there were others as well. A nineteenth-century German charm suggests another method of treating injuries to limbs:

> Now take I the stone
> And lay it on your bone
> And press it on the blood
> So it makes it stand straightaway.
> (Repeat three times. The stone should be put back exactly where it belongs.)[32]

It has been suggested that the association of stone and bone here is an accident, occasioned by the rhyme of *Stein* and *Bein,* but I think we are closer to understanding its efficacy if we recall the origin of stone from bone in the Germanic and Indo-European creation myth— "of his flesh the earth was made, and mountains out of bones" (*Gylf* 8, e.g.). Since stone is the alloform of bone, pressing or rubbing with a stone restores the material substance needed for the bone to heal. In this gesture it is not so much that one presses stone to bone, but rather that one presses *bone to bone,* precisely as the Merseburg Charm states, albeit the first-named "bone" is temporarily hidden in its macrocosmic alloform, stone. The act of magical healing here consists of the knowledgeable manipulation of these homologic alloforms.[33] A sixteenth-century German charm makes the same point:

> Our dear Lord went out to matins; he walked into a marble stone very hard. He walked into a marble stone; it sprained and broke his holy flesh, blood, and bone. Our dear Lord went sadly home to his dear mother; he found her alone. "Oh you, my dear darling son of mine! How can you be so sad?"
> "I have walked into a marble stone; it has sprained and broken my flesh, my blood, my bone."
> "Oh son, dearest son of mine! What will you give me with which to put back together your flesh, your blood, your bone?"
> "Mother, I give you heaven and earth, that you may put back together my flesh and blood and bone; therefore I give you heaven and earth . . ."[34]

From the formula "heaven and earth" we are to understand that Jesus gives Mary the physical universe, to be used in the healing of his broken foot (or leg), and it is through the application of the constituent elements of the universe that she is able to make whole his flesh, blood, and bone. Behind this lies the old system of cosmic homologies. One may even speculate that the healing gestures have a precise structure, earth being applied to restore flesh, since its origin is from flesh; stone being applied to restore bone, since its origin is from bone; and water being applied to restore blood, since its origin is from blood.

"Magic," then, is not idle superstition. Rather, as I suggested earlier, it is a system of non-Aristotelian, homologic causality, whereby items connected to one another in a relation of underlying consubstantiality are considered capable of acting on one another. And what is more, the precise terms of these homologies are drawn from cosmogonic and anthropogonic myth. This perspective, which so transforms our understanding of common IE therapy for injury to limbs, also casts a dramatic light on the other bit of ancient healing lore that Kuhn first recognized.[35] This is a charm that might be called "Against Infestation." One of the best examples is the oldest attested example of German "magic," a ninth-century Old Saxon charm that bears the Latin title "Contra Vermes," classed in the Vienna library as MS. 751 (Theol. 259) B1. 188v:

> Go out worm, with your nine wormlings—out from the marrow to the bone; from the bone to the flesh; out from the flesh to the skin; out from the skin to the hoof!

Virtually identical is the Old High German charm "Pro nessia" (Munich *Codex lat.* 18524, 2, B1. 203v), the sole differences being that veins stand in the position here occupied by bones (between marrow and flesh), and that nearly synonymous but not identical terms are used for "skin" (OHG *velle* "pelt" for OSax *hūd*) and "hoof" (OHG *tulli* for OSax *strāla*). In truth, "hoof" is not a fully accurate translation. More precisely, as Gerhard Eis has demonstrated,[36] *tulli* and *strāla* denote the "frog" of a horse's hoof, the horny but elastic triangular pad at the center of the sole. It is thus the outermost extremity of soft tissue in a horse's body, the last stop before space external to the horse. Eis's demonstration is particularly helpful, for it reveals the structure of the charm, whereby a menacing invader is driven from the body's innermost core to its outermost extremity, and thence—presumably—out of the body entirely. This same structure in reverse is apparent in Dian Cecht's attack on Miach, whom he cuts from skin to flesh to bone to brain, this being the process of assault that leads to death, while the opposite process, as described in the Germanic "worm charms" leads to health. The same healing structure is recovered in *Atharva Veda* 2.33.6, a verse within a longer hymn used for the cure of *yakṣma*, a disease characterized by decay, atrophy, consumption, and the like, as if the body were being eaten away by some internal enemy.[37]

> From your bones, from your marrow, from your sinews, from your
> veins;
> I drive away the *yakṣma* from your hands, from your fingers, from
> your nails!

To be sure, the neat and orderly logic apparent in the Germanic spells is here somewhat garbled, but it is clearly present nonetheless. The verse starts with internal components of a limb—bones, marrow, sinews, veins—and calls the disease out from them to the extremities, progressing from hands to fingers to nails as the final point before the ailment leaves the body entirely, the nails providing a strong formal correspondence to the hoof or "frog" of the Germanic texts,[38] while other terms provide semantic (*bēn/asthi-*, *ādra/dhamani-*) or phonetic (*marga* ~ *marge/majjan-*) correspondences.[39] Also note the anomalous position of this verse within the broader hymn: it breaks the entire structure of *AV* 2.33, which, like the closely related *Ṛg Veda* 10.163 (= *AV* 20.96.17–22) and other Indo-Iranian examples, drives the infection out of the body on a vertical axis, starting at the top and working downward.[40] *AV* 2.33.6 thus has the look of an artificial insertion, a fossilized remnant of an earlier charm, sufficiently similar to the bulk of the hymn to have been added to it, but different in its details and origin nonetheless.

To these materials can also be compared a very late reflex that has previously gone unrecognized, a nineteenth-century Byelorussian charm against sorcery (Byel *uroč"* ~ *suroč"*) collected in Smolensk by Vasily Dobrovolskij.[41] The sorcery, which has produced various physical symptoms, is cast out of the patient's body in the following terms:

> Depart, begone, you sorcery, from this servant of man. Go out of
> his bones, out of his strength (muscles?), out of his veins and arteries,
> out of his joints and sub-joints, from his large head, from his swift
> eyes and his rosy face, from his toiling hands, from his swift feet,
> and from all his human innards. Depart you, from this servant of
> man! Go to the mosses, to the swamps, to the stagnant fens!

Once again indwelling monsters that cause disease are driven from the sufferer's body, starting from the innermost core—here, bones—outward through intermediate tissues (veins and arteries, joints and subjoints) to bodily extremities (head, with subparts eyes and face; hands; feet). Only the mention of "human innards" (*nutrinnasti čila-věčeskij*) as the final item in the series represents a deviation from the pattern of the Germanic and Indic variants. Perhaps this item is added as a summation of all that is internal to the body, or perhaps it is meant to denote the intestines as reservoirs of fluids, these being suggested by association to the swamps and fens to which the illness is ultimately directed. But whatever its meaning and possible motivation, this item would seem to be an anomalous excrescence on a basic structural pattern, the ancient nature of which is familiar to us from other reflexes.

Not only does the Byelorussian charm mention the same basic bodily parts as do the Germanic "worm charms" and *AV* 2.33.6; these also are essentially the same bodily parts as those mentioned in the charms "For Injury to Limbs."

As can be seen from table 10, the bodily parts named fall into four general groupings, organized around two taxonomic systems that are only imperfectly correlated. The first taxonomy is by relative hardness: most solid (bones); next most solid (flesh and marrow); liquid (blood and veins, with sinews as a substitution for veins because of their resemblance in shape and a consequent terminological ambiguity in many languages);[42] and an anomalous fourth category, which ought to be filled by the lightest and least dense items (hair could be thus defined, but not so the other parts here—skin, nails, hooves, limbs, joints). This last group is better defined as extremities, a term that covers all the parts included, and which suggests the basis for the second taxonomy: proximity to or distance from the central core of the body. Thus, under this system the first term is the most central (marrow and bone); then next most central (flesh); then still closer to the surface (blood, veins, and sinews); and finally extremities (limbs, joints, skin, hair, nails, and hooves).[43] As will be seen, the two systems yield identical patterns of organization, with the sole difference that marrow must shift from the first class when defined by centrality to the second when defined by density.

Any number of fascinating details emerge when the data are organized in this fashion. For instance, note the great consistency with which bones are always mentioned in these charms (only *Cath Maige Turedh* and the OHG worm charm lack a reference to bones), in contrast to the tremendous variation permitted with regard to the extremities (all texts mention one or another, but there is no consistency as to which will be specified). Again, in the charm "Against Infestation," which is structured on motion from core to periphery, marrow is regularly specified, while in that "For Injury to Limbs," where such motion is not involved, marrow appears only rarely. But by far the most important point here is that the four items I have posited as fundamental to this system of charms—bone, flesh, blood, and extremities—three figure prominently in the microcosmic-macrocosmic homologies established in IE creation myths, possessing clear macrocosmic alloforms: bone/stone, flesh/earth, and blood/water. With regard to extremities the case is a little more complex, for within this generalized category is expressed something on the order of "that which lies at the very limits of the organism," for which a possible macrocosmic alloform might be "that which lies at the ends of the earth."

It is not just the charm "For Injury to Limbs" that works simultaneously on microcosm and macrocosm, appropriating the latter to restore the former's health. The charm "Against Infestation" also has a macrocosmic dimension, for in driving pests or disease out of a human patient it simultaneously drives evil out of the world, moving it from the core of the earth to the outer extremities, where its threat to life is reduced, and thence into ultimate nonbeing. This emerges clearly in a previously unrecognized reflex of the charm "Against Infestation," which has gone unnoticed precisely because it describes the workings of the charm at the macrocosmic rather than the microcosmic level and because it treats this process as myth rather than as healing ritual. The myth is the account of "the first battle the Evil Spirit waged against the water of the rivers" as told in the *Greater Bundahišn* 6B and *Zad Spram* 3.7–25, both of which are Pahlavi expansions of an idea already present in the Avesta (*Yašt* 8.43): the cleansing of poisons from the earth by the rainwaters brought by the star Tištar (< Av *Tištrya-*, most probably Sirius) at the onset of the rainy season.[44] At that time, "each drop of rain is as large as a bowlful" (*GBd* 6B.5: TD MS. 62.10–11), and the deluge drowns all *xrafstars* (< Av *xrafstra-*) on the earth, these being vermin and noxious creatures, including snakes, frogs, insects, rodents, vicious predators and the like.

According to Zoroastrian doctrine, the xrafstars are created by Ahriman to war against the earth.[45] Once these creatures die, their corpses pose a problem, for as *GBd* 6B.8 (TD MS. 63.3–6) relates,

> The dead xrafstars remained in the earth, and their venom and stench were mixed up in the earth. In order to carry away that venom from the earth, Tištar came down into the sea in the form of a white horse with a long tail.

Table 10. Correspondences of bodily parts in the charms "For Injury to Limbs" and "Against Infestation."

	Central		Inner			Outer		Extremity		
	Hardest	Hard	Hard	Liquid	Liquid			Least Hard	Least Hard	
	Bone	Marrow	Flesh	Blood	Vein	Sinew	Limb, Joint	Skin	Hair, Nails, Hooves	Hand/Foot
"For Injury to Limbs"										
Second Merseberg	ben	—	—	blout	—	—	lid	—	—	—
Norwegian	been	marv	kjöd	—	—	—	—	—	—	—
Devonshire	bone	—	—	—	vein	—	—	—	—	—
Codex Vatican	pain	—	fleisch	pluet	adern	—	gelid	—	—	—
16th-cent. German	bain	—	fleisch	blued	—	—	—	—	—	—
Cath Maige Turedh	—	—	—	—	—	feith	alt	—	—	—
Atharva Veda 4.12	asthi	majjan	carman māṃsa	asṛj	—	—	—	tvac	loman	—
Hippokratic Aphorism 7.28	osteon	—	—	—	—	khondros neuron	—	—	—	—

Table 10 (*continued*)

"Against Infestation"

	Stone	Earth	Water					Outer Limits
Old Saxon	bēn	flēsg	—	—	—	hūd	strāla	—
Old High German	—	fleisk	ādra	—	—	fel	tulli	—
Atharva Veda 2.33.6	asthi	majjan	dhamani	snāvan	pāni aṅgula	—	nakha	—
Byelorussian	kos'c'	—	žyla	—	sustau	—	—	ruka naga
Cosmic Reference	Stone	Earth	Water					Outer Limits

At first Tištar encounters difficulty; he has to defeat the demon Apaoša, "Dearth" or "Nonthriving," the Pahlavi account generally following the lines of *Yašt* 8.20–29.[46] Having despatched his enemy, however, Tištar causes it to rain again "much harder," this time "in drops like a bull's head" (*GBd* 6B.13: TD MS. 64.1–2).

> He made it rain that way for ten days and nights. The venom of the xrafstars was all within the earth, and it mixed into the water, and it made this water most salty. (*GBd* 6B.15: TD MS. 64.7–10)

This salt water—salt being the mark of its pollution, the evil that came to reside in it as the result of Ahriman's assault, while the water itself remains fundamentally good, being a creation of Ohrmazd—is driven off by the wind. Its fate according to *ZS* 3.17 is relatively simple: it enters the three great salt seas, Pūdīg, Kamerōd, and Gēhān-būn, all of which border on the great cosmic ocean, known in Pahlavi as the Frāxkard Sea and in Avestan as the Vouru.kaša.[47] (It must be stressed that these various bodies of water, like those I will presently discuss, are part of a mythic geography, however much Iranians of one age or another sought to identify them with actual physical landmarks.) Of the Kamerōd and Gēhān-būn we are told relatively little, although *GBd* 10.18 (TD MS. 84.6–9) does give a clear picture of the nature of salt seas in general:

> One is not able to go as near as a league to the salt seas because of the stench nearby. A huge amount of that stench and salt will become sweet again through the beating of the wind when the Renovation is established.

One need not wait for the Renovation, the final eschatological drama of Zoroastrian belief, for a certain amount of the salt water to be purified. For a clear process of purification takes place in the Pūdīg Sea, the very name of which (Pahl *pūdīg* < Av *pūitika-*) means "the Purifying."[48] The process is already described in the Avesta (*Vd* 5.18–19), and is spelled out in detail in *GBd* 10.9 (TD MS. 83.2–7):

> Between the Frāxkard Sea (the world ocean) and the side of the Pūdīg ("Purifying") Sea, there is what they call the lake of Sadwēs. Whatever coarseness and salt and impurity wishes to go from the Pūdīg Sea to the Frāxkard Sea, a great wind from the lake of Sadwēs

beats it back. But whatever is bright and pure goes into the Frāxkard
Sea, to the Spring of Ardwīsūr, while the rest flows back to the Pūdīg.

From the Frāxkard Sea the pure water is cycled back to all creation,
the salt remaining in its distant reservoir, where it ceases to be a threat.
In the *Greater Bundahišn* the final result is much the same, although
the polluted water travels a slightly more complex path than it does
in *Zad Spram,* moving first to two lakes, one of which is good and one
of which is hostile to all life;[49] then to two rivers, one of which is good
and one of which infested with serpents and xrafstars;[50] then to the
Frāxkard Sea, whence it is sent via a hundred thousand golden chan-
nels to the top of Mount Hugar (< Av *Hukairya-*) "the mountain of
good ability," where it is purified and returned to the Frāxkard for
redistribution to the entire earth, making its passage to the Frāxkard
via a single special golden channel.[51]

The myth thus tells us how a poison came from the bodies of
xrafstars—these being a macrocosmic version of the worms in the
Germanic worm charms[52]—and how this poison was lodged in the
earth. As the result of the god Tištar's intervention, the poison was
driven from the earth into the water, the water thus becoming salt,
impure, infected. Now itself a threat to life, the salt water was driven
further, to the very ends of the earth, where it was either purified
(according to the *Greater Bundahišn*), or isolated and rendered harm-
less (according to *Zad Spram*). Earth to water to the borders of the
cosmos—flesh to blood to the extremities of the body. Only the first
term of the series is missing: bones, which might have been represented on the macrocosmic scale by stone in order to complete the
series, had the authors of the Pahlavi texts found a way to have poison
penetrate stones.

The two charms are thus hardly to be understood as scattered items
of a petty and casuistic "magic," as they have often been interpreted.
Rather, they are intimately connected to each other and to the system
of homologies and creation mythology discussed in the preceding
chapters. Within this system, the cosmos and the human body are
seen as interchangeable: one thus heals the microcosm by appropriating the elements of the macrocosm, and one heals the macrocosm
by working on its human alloform.[53]

In considering the IE vocabulary for the act of healing I noted that
one term commonly used in this context, *kai-lo-,* signified "wholeness,
integrity." It now becomes apparent just how awesome a task the
production or restoration of such integrity must be, for it is not just

a damaged body that one restores to wholeness and health, but the very universe itself. I also noted that the verb used to denote "healing," *med-*, stressed the knowledge and authority that enabled a healer to create proper order in an ailing patient. The full extent of such knowledge is now revealed in all its grandeur: the healer must understand and be prepared to manipulate nothing less than the full structure of the cosmos.

6

Death and Resurrection, Time and Eternity

If the process of aging is seen as a form of erosion whereby life and the body are gradually worn away,[1] there is an inevitable end to such a process. For even if erosion is slowed and the threats posed by time, illness, and accidents are countered with proper nutrition and healing practices, still the end to human existence may only be postponed a bit, never avoided altogether.

All life ends in death, just as all erosion ends in total collapse or pulverization. And just as the PIE verb *ĝer- straddles the meanings "to age" and "to fall apart,"[2] so also the verb *mer- combines the senses "to die" (thus: Skt marate and mriyate [the latter with a reduced grade vocalism]; Av miryeite; Arm meṙanim [first person singular]; Lt morior; Lith mìrštu, mìrti; OCS mrěti; Hitt me-ir-ta [third person singular pret-erite]) and "to reduce to small pieces" (thus: Skt mṛṇāti "to crush, grind"; Gk marainō "to rub away, grind down"; Lt mortārium "mortar"; ON merja "to strike, pound"; Serb mȑva "crumbs"; ORuss moromradi "to gnaw, erode, crumble"; Hitt marriattari "to be shattered, crushed").[3]

Such semantics have strong implications for the understanding of death common among the Indo-European peoples, which—as we shall see—cast death as the dissolution of a complex entity, which was reduced to its constituent parts after a long process of erosion. One of the most obvious ways this dissolution was envisioned was as the separation of body and soul—a falling apart of sorts—that is the hallmark of death in countless texts;[4] other analyses go further and consider the ways in which the body itself crumbles into smaller pieces after death.[5]

A convenient starting point for consideration of these ideas is one of the earliest Greek inscriptions in which the post mortem fate of the soul is discussed: that placed at the burial spot of the Athenian soldiers who died at the Battle of Potidaea in 432 B.C.[6] It states, simply, of the dead, "Aither received their souls, and earth their bodies."[7] Here it is important that the term used to denote souls, Gk *psykhē*, most literally means "life-breath, being derived from the verb *psykhō*, *psykhein* "to breathe, to blow."[8] The "soul" is thus most fundamentally the air that temporarily resides within a human organism. When it is present, the organism is alive. When it departs once and for all, the organism is dead. And—what is most significant to the present inquiry—when that lifebreath leaves the body, it enters the air, its macrocosmic alloform, from which it first came and to which it returns. Similarly, in many Greek anthropogonic accounts the human body is said to be created from earth,[9] and this inscription informs us that at death the body returns to the earth once more. This point is made explicit in Euripides, *Suppliants,* ll. 531–534:

> Let the corpses now be covered with the earth,
> From which each of them came forth to the light
> Only to go back thither: breath *(pneuma)* to the aither,
> And body to earth.[10]

Something similar is found in two closely related passages from the oldest Russian epic that has come down to us, the *Slovo o P"lku Igorevě* ("The Song of Igor's Campaign"), written shortly after 1185. In both passages the fate of those fallen in battle is metaphorically compared to the treatment of cereal grains. The first, ll. 157–158, reads:

> On the Nemiga (river-banks), sheaves
> Are spread out with heads on them;
> They are threshed with flails of Frankish steel (i.e., enemy swords).
> They lay life down on the threshing floor,
> And winnow soul from body.
> The bloody banks of the Nemiga
> Were unhappily sown—
> Sown with the bones of Russian sons.

Here, as in the two Greek texts cited above, the separation of body and soul is correlated with the return of the body—more specifically, the bones—to the earth. To this is added complex agricultural symbolism. First the corpses are compared to grain that is threshed and winnowed, the souls presumably being associated to grain and the

bodies to chaff that is let fall to earth. In line 158, however, the bones—
the most solid and enduring part of the body—are further compared
to seed, which is sown in the earth in order to produce a rebirth of
the grain. In another passage of the *Slovo* (l. 67), this anticipated
rebirth is made explicit and given a brilliant poetic twist.

> The black earth underneath (the horses') hooves
> Was sown with bones
> And watered with blood:
> These sprouted as grief
> On the Russian soil.

The power of this image derives primarily from the fact that the
reader—or better, the audience, since this work began in an oral
tradition and drew on conventions from even older oral traditions—
is led to expect a very different type of resurrection. Seed that is
planted and watered ordinarily comes to birth as grain of the same
sort that produced the seed in the first place. Grain comes from the
earth and returns to the earth, only to spring forth again in a never-
ending cycle. And if the body is compared to grain, we anticipate a
similar cycle of bodily death and rebirth. Yet in this decidedly somber
description, all that is born is grief.

Another point must be made regarding these lines from the *Slovo*.
Whereas lines 157–58, like the Potidaea inscription and the verses
from the *Suppliants*, propounded a single fate for the body—return
to earth—line 67 describes a differentiated transformation of bodily
matter: the bones enter the earth while the blood becomes water, and
it is the reunion of bones/seeds-in-the-earth and blood/water that pro-
vokes expectations of rebirth. Here, the traditional homology of blood/
water has been faithfully preserved, while those of flesh/earth and
bones/stones seem to have fallen together.

The Greek sources, being less specific—only the undifferentiated
"body" *(sōma)* returns to the earth—avoid this issue entirely, but a
similar conflation of homologies that are more often held separate is
evident in an Iranian text, *Zad Spram* 34.7, which gives a detailed
description of the body's fate. This verse occurs within a broader
discussion in which the Wise Lord, Ohrmazd, answers Zarathuštra's
question (ZS 34.1): "Concerning the corporeal ones who have passed
away into the earth—at the Renovation, do they become corporeal
again, or are they like shadows?"[11] To this Ohrmazd answers immediately (ZS 34.2): "They become corporeal again. They rise up." Con-

cerning the details of their reincorporation, as presented in *ZS* 34.8–
19 and elsewhere, I shall have more to say later. But before Ohrmazd
passes to that topic, he first describes the corporeal effects of death.

> There are five collectors, receptacles of the corporeal substance of
> those who have died. One is the earth, which is the keeper of flesh
> and bone and sinew (or: fat) of men. The second is water, which is
> the keeper of blood. The third is the plants, preservers of bodily
> hair and hair of the head. The fourth is light, recipient of fire. Last
> is the wind, which is the life-breath of my own creatures at the time
> of the Renovation.

Here three traditional and broadly attested homologies are presented quite straightforwardly: blood/water, breath/wind, and hair/
plants. The first two of these we have already encountered in Greek
and Slavic descriptions of the effects of death. To these, a fourth
homology specific to Iran is added: fire/light, the fire in all likelihood
being the internal digestive fire that converts food into bodily warmth.[12]
In all of these instances, death effects the transfer of material substance from microcosm to macrocosm: blood entering into water—its
homologic "collector" or "receptacle"—breath into wind, and so forth.
Yet the final cosmic element—earth—is said to be the receptacle not
only of the body's flesh (the normal alloform of earth, as we repeatedly
have seen) but of its bone and sinew (or fat, if the reading *pīh* is
preferred to *pay*) as well, which is to say that in Iran—as in Greece
and Russia—the earth was treated as the residual category, to which
all bodily matter not assigned other cosmic resting places was allocated.
Presumably, this formulation derives from burial practices, either primary or secondary, in which bodily remains of varied sorts were, quite
literally, consigned to the earth.[13]

Indic sources present much the same analysis of the body's fate as
does *ZS* 34.7, although they go into still greater homologic detail. At
death, the body is seen to break down into numerous constituent parts,
which then become part of ("enter into") those elements which are
their macrocosmic alloforms. One famous treatment of this theme is
Bṛhadāranyaka Upaniṣad 3.2.13, in which the same homologies appear
as in *ZS* 34.7 (breath/wind, flesh/earth, hair/plants, blood/water), along
with certain other traditional alloformic pairs (eye/sun, mind/moon)
and others found only in India, drawn from the *Puruṣasūkta* and
elsewhere (voice/fire, ears/cardinal directions, self/atmosphere, se-
men/water). Like *ZS* 34, this Upaniṣadic passage takes the form of a

dialogue on matters of ultimate concern. Here, the great sage Ārtabhāga interrogates the even greater sage, Yājñavalkya.

> "Yājñavalkya," he said, "when the voice of a dead man enters the fire, his breath the wind, his eye the sun, his mind the moon, his ear the cardinal directions, his flesh the earth, his self (*ātman*) the atmosphere, his bodily hair the herbs, the hair of his head the trees, and his blood and semen are deposited in the waters, what then does this man become?"
>
> "Take my hand, dear Ārtabhāga. Only we two will know of this. It is not (to be spoken of) by us here in the presence of others."

What Ārtabhāga presents here is an ancient, authoritative teaching on the nature of death and the body's fate, which is preserved in many other IE sources and given in slightly different form elsewhere in the same Upaniṣad (*BṛhadUp* 1.3.11–16). Yet, in what follows, Yājñavalkya adds new ideas to this old theme, for we are told that once the two sages had gone off in private, "They spoke: karma was what they spoke about. Then they praised: karma was what they praised." *Karma*—the theory of cyclical rebirths that depend on deeds performed in previous lives—is a new tenet in the early Upaniṣads, absent from earlier sources, that quickly became a dominant concern of Indian religion and philosophy. In *BṛhadUp* 3.2.13 it is presented as a sacred secret, a mystery reserved for the private conversations of the most elevated sages.[14] The ideas it replaced, however—those presented by Ārtabhāga, in which death is treated as a form of sacrifice, as signaled by his consistent use of *puruṣa*, the name of the first sacrificial victim, to denote "man" in general—are much older, and are found in earlier Indic texts, as for instance *SB* 10.3.3.8, which begins by asking what happens to the fire when it is extinguished, and then considers as a parallel process the fate of the body when life is extinguished:

> When the fire goes out, it is dispersed into the wind. Therefore, they say "It is finished," for truly it is dispersed into the wind. When the sun sets, it enters the wind. The moon and the cardinal directions are established in the wind, and they are born again from the wind.
>
> He who knows thus—he goes forth from this world. He enters the fire with his voice, the sun with his eye, the moon with his mind, the cardinal directions with his ear, the wind with his breath. He, having become one who is made thus, having become whichever of the deities he desires—he is at rest.

When the fire is said to be finished, it is not really finished, it has merely entered the wind; similarly, the sun does not die at sunset but also enters the wind. And just as the sun reappears each morning, so too fire can reappear from its temporary residence in the wind, as is seen when the wind blows on hot coals and causes flame to leap up. Similarly, human death is only an apparent end, for the body enters the cosmos, and there is a strong implication that the body will be reborn from the cosmos, like fire and sun from the wind. After his dispersion to the elements, the dead man is said to be resting (Skt *ilayati*), a verb usually used for the state of sleep or temporary quiescence, from which there is inevitably a reawakening.[15]

The earliest attestation of this view of death is found in an extremely important hymn of the *Ṛg Veda* devoted to the funerary fire, dating perhaps as early as 1200 B.C. In *RV* 10.16.3, the attending priest instructs the deceased:

> Your eye must go to the sun, and your self (must go) to the wind.
> You must go to heaven and earth, according to what is right—
> Or you must go the the waters, if that is fated for you; you must
> stand in the plants with your flesh.

This brief text is among the most fascinating we have seen, for it presents two alternative destinations for the corpse. In the first, articulated in *RV* 10.16.3ab, parts of the body disperse to the three vertical strata of the cosmos: the eye goes to the sun in the highest heavens; the self (*ātman*), understood here as the life-breath, passes to the intermediate wind;[16] and the rest of the body goes to the residual category, the earth.[17] This dispersal, like those in *BṛhadUp* 3.2.13 and *SB* 10.3.3.8, is on the cosmogonic model, whereby pieces of the body join their macrocosmic alloforms at death, just as the same bodily pieces of the first human victim established those elements upon the performance of the first, cosmogonic sacrifice. Whereas the other Indo-Iranian texts develop this theme in some detail, however, *RV* 10.16.3ab presents it in rather abbreviated, almost shorthand fashion, as do the Greek and Russian sources I have considered: soul to wind or air, body to earth being the minimal, irreducible form that the idea may take, as in the Potidaea inscription.

In addition to this analysis of death, *RV* 10.16.3cd offers a second possible fate for the body, introducing this alternative with the contrastive particle *vā* "or". According to this hemistich, the body may enter the waters and plants instead of the three cosmic levels; an adaptation of the sitiogonic pattern to the theme of the body's fate.

Should, for some reason, the corpse not replenish the entire cosmos with its material substance, as did the first man at the dawn of time, another possibility exists: it may follow the model of the primordial bovine, and become food in the form of fluids and plants. The same sitiogonic transformation of the corpse is attested in Iran; in *Vīdēvdāt* 5.18–20 the Wise Lord answers two related questions: how does he dispose of corpses, and how do the cosmic seas work:

> I, Ahura Mazdā, carry away the corpse. I, Ahura Mazdā, carry away the afterbirth. I, Ahura Mazdā, cause bones to be sent away. I, Ahura Mazdā, wash off that which is impure. I wash these together to the Pūitika ("Purifying") Sea.
>
> These (contents) stream into the sea. By virtue of their purification (there), the waters run from the Pūitika Sea to the Vouru.kaša Sea (the cosmic ocean), to the tree of the good waters. There all my plants grow, all growing by the hundreds, the thousands, the myriads of myriads.

> I cause all these to rain down together,
> I, who am Ahura Mazdā,
> As food for the Right-possessing man,
> As pasture for the beneficent cow.

> My grain—man shall eat (that); the pasture is for the beneficent cow.

As in *RV* 10.16.3cd, the deceased here enters the waters and the plants, and we are explicitly told that these are to be understood as food, which will be consumed by men and cattle alike and from which their bodies will be rebuilt. To the best of my knowledge, only these Indo-Iranian sources preserve mention of the sitiogonic alternative, and we also lack any discussion whatsoever of the fate of animals at death. Yet perhaps it is not too much to assume that animals at death repeated the fate of the first animal, from whose body food was created. If this is so, then we might speculate further and suggest that just as an animal victim might do service for a human victim in sacrifice, its body becoming the cosmos instead of just food, so too a human corpse might assume the fate ordinarily reserved for animals, becoming food instead of the cosmos.

Whether these last suggestions hold true or not—and they should be considered no more than suggestions in the absence of further data—the contents of *RV* 10.16.3 may no longer be lightly dismissed as a feeble reworking of themes drawn directly from *RV* 10.90, as some authorities have claimed,[18] for nowhere in the latter does the sitiogonic alternative appear.

Having come to the earliest attestation of this set of ideas, I must also consider one of the most recent: the Fourth Meditation of John Donne's *Devotions upon Emergent Occasions.* The *Devotions,* written in 1624, are a set of reflections on the "Variable, and therefore miserable condition of Man" (First Meditation), and purport to have been written during a grave illness, from which Donne expected to die. They follow the course of the illness and its treatment to Donne's final cure, which he compares to a rebirth like that of Lazarus.[19] The Fourth Meditation occurs at the point where Donne recognizes the full seriousness of the disease, along with the strong possibility of death, and accordingly sends for the Physician. While thus contemplating death and disease, he muses:

> It is too little to call *Man* a *little World;* Except *God,* Man is a *diminutive* to nothing. Man consists of more pieces, more parts, then the world; then the world doeth, nay then the world is. And if those pieces were extended, and stretched out in Man, as they are in the world, Man would bee the *Gyant,* and the world the *Dwarfe,* the world but the *Map,* and the Man the *World.* If all the *Veines* in our bodies, were extended to *Rivers,* and all the *Sinewes,* to *vaines of Mines,* and all the *Muscles,* that lye upon one another, to Hilles, and all the *Bones* to *Quarries* of stones, and all the other pieces, to the proportion of those which correspond to them in the *world,* the *aire* would be too little for this *Orbe* of Man to move in, the firmament would bee but enough for this *star;* for, as the whole world hath nothing, to which something in man doth not answere, so hath man many pieces, of which the whol world hath no representation.

To be sure, few of these ideas are original with Donne. The theme of microcosm and macrocosm appears frequently in his writings, and it has been shown that in large measure he took it from the works of Paracelsus, who in turn drew on a variety of Neoplantonic and Hippokratic sources,[20] behind which lay the full Indo-European heritage. In some measure, these ancient ideas still seemed valid and acceptable to a high-ranking Anglican clergyman and prominent intellectual of the seventeenth century.[21] Yet at other points Donne pits himself against the system, as when his powerful humanism requires him to make the self-consciously audacious assertion that the human organism is grander than the universe, having in it parts—one assumes he means the "soul" in a Christian sense—for which there are no macrocosmic alloforms. Donne's Meditation is particularly precious for us no matter how late its date or idiosyncratic its final conclusions, for it reveals the enduring power of the traditional IE view of death to provide some measure of solace to an individual at death's door. The other sources I have examined—funerary inscriptions, tragic choruses, epic laments, and ritual or theological texts—view death from the standpoint of an observer, an outsider. Yet countless human beings—and Donne was not the last of them—have drawn comfort from the expectation that when dead they would not disappear but would merge with the cosmos.

Donne's Meditation is a relatively recent variant on a traditional theme—the nature of death—on which the Greek, Slavic, Indic, and Iranian materials offer us more ancient testimony. Within this tradition, death was understood to be a process whereby matter was transmuted from a bodily to a cosmic form, along the lines of well-established homologies. At a bare minimum, the lifebreath became or "entered into" the wind, while the body "entered" or became the earth. Beyond this, other homologies might be added: blood/water appears fairly frequently, as do bones/stones (or some variant thereof) and hair/plants.[22]

Further, this material translation from microcosm to macrocosm was seen as a form of sacrifice, indeed, as the last sacrifice that all human beings perform, in which their very bodies are offered up to ensure the continued existence of the universe. In *Atharva Veda* 12.3, a hymn in which cremation is treated as a form of sacrifice, the priest repeatedly addresses the deceased in terms such as these: "I cause you, who are earth, to dwell in the earth; this body of yours, which was whole, is (now) cut apart" (*AV* 12.3.22ab); "I unite you, who are earth, with the earth" (*AV* 12.3.23b). In the most grandiose statement of all, the corpse about to be consumed by flames is told that it will sustain the world: "Preserver, preserve yourself in the preservation of the earth; the deities must cause you to move on, you who have not yet moved on" (*AV* 12.3.35ab).

Like all sacrifice, death is a repetitive, ritual act. Each death repeats every other death and every other sacrifice: above all the first death, which was also the first sacrifice and, most important, effected the creation of the universe. For while death is the fate of all human beings, death is also a cosmogonic act. Whenever people die, their bodies replenish, sustain, or even re-create the universe at large.

As always, there is more. For by now it should be apparent that within the common IE system of cosmological speculation there is no movement without a counter-movement, no cosmogony without an answering anthropogony, no shift of matter that is not balanced by a shift in the opposite direction.[23] It is thus no surprise that there are numerous texts that describe the body's resurrection at the end of time—or, to put it more precisely, at the end of each cosmic cycle.[24]

Iranian sources provide several detailed descriptions of the resurrection of the dead (Pahl *ristāxez*), which is already mentioned in earlier Avestan passages.[25] Consistently, the resurrection is presented as a culminating act in the Renovation or "Making-Wonderful" (Pahl *frašagird*) of the cosmos, which takes place at the end of the twelve thousand years Zoroastrian theology assigns to the history of the material world.[26] A fairly straightforward account is given in the *Pahlavi Rivayat accompanying the Dādestān i Dēnīg* 48.54–55:

> He who is the chief—Sošyans [the eschatological hero], the accomplisher of the Renovation—and those who are his assistants, set out on the resurrection of the body. And Ohrmazd summons bone from the earth, blood from the water, hair from the plants, and life-breath from the wind. He mixes one with the other, and he keeps creating the form proper to each.

The process described here is the reverse of death's effects as described in *ZS* 34.7, for the "receptacles" into which bodily parts fall at death now return them in response to the Wise Lord's call. From this bodily matter, each individual human being is restored. *ZS* 34.8–19, the passage immediately following the discussion of death, presents this same picture of the resurrection, with the added—almost comic—motif that when Ohrmazd issues his summons, the "receptacles" balk at first, saying that they have received the bones or blood or whatever of so many dead bodies that they cannot possibly tell them all apart. It is thus left to the omniscience (*wisp dānišnīh*) of the Wise Lord to distinguish them all and to reassemble each individual as she or he was in life. The process begins with Gayōmard, the first man, from whose body the cosmos was created. The eschaton thus reverses the cosmogony, as the man from whom the cosmos was made is now made from the cosmos. Nor is the point valid for Gayōmard alone: it applies with equal force to each individual. When their bodies are de-created at death, they create the cosmos, and when the cosmos is de-created at the Renovation, their bodies are recreated from it.[27]

Ideas of resurrection are also preserved in numerous Russian folk songs and formal laments, although these are not placed within any grander world-eschatological scheme. Also, just as the Russian discussions of the body's dispersal at death that I considered earlier made use of a very limited set of homologies, so also these texts in which resurrection is suggested make use of only the same few items. Given the late date of these lamentations (eighteenth and nineteenth centuries A.D.), this may be due to gradual attrition of an originally fuller ideology. Two examples may be cited: the first a lament for the Czar, collected at Simbirsk; the second a north Russian lament for one's mother.

> Flow, flow, threatening cloud,
> Pour out, strong dense rain,
> Soak up, damp mother earth!
> Open yourself, damp mother earth
> In all four directions!
> Open, you coffin boards,
> Fling yourself open, thin white shroud,
> Get up, get up, you righteous Czar!

> Roll from the mountains, springtime streams:
> Soak the yellow sands.
> Lift up the coffin lid,
> Open the shrouds.
> Grant to me—I who am stooped with sorrow—to glance once more
> At my parent, my little mother![28]

In both examples the call is made to the same elements: water, in the form of either rain or rivulets, and earth, in the form of soil or sand. These are to flow to the grave of the deceased, where they will unite and restore life to him or her; recall that in the *Slovo*, l. 67, the bones of the dead entered the earth and their blood became water, which—when poured on the earth—called forth hopes of a resurrection. Yet in the lament for the Czar there is still a hint that the full cosmos must combine to effect his resurrection, for the water is to flow from all four cardinal directions, which is to say, from the totality of space.

It is doubtful that the speakers in these laments truly expected such a resurrection to take place. Rather, such phrases seem to have been part of the standard expressions of grief: the proper things to say at the death of a loved one. The very similarity of these laments with each other and with others like them shows their stereotyped nature. Yet behind them stands a long tradition, only part of which we can trace. A similar lament is found in the twelfth-century Russian *Slovo*, ll. 168–183, where the princess Jaroslavna, believing her husband, Igor, to be dead, calls on the wind, the river Dnepr, and the sun (which Roman Jakobson has shown to represent the cosmic realms of heaven, sky, and earth)[29] to return him to her. The request is granted, for immediately after her lament—and so it is explicitly called—Igor returns, having miraculously escaped from captivity.[30] Already in the *Slovo* this theme has been rationalized, and limited to an exceptional individual case, but the idea that the elements of the macrocosm may restore the life and substance of the dead is apparent nonetheless.[31]

Certain texts hint at a belief in resurrection among some of the Thracian peoples[32] and also the Celts,[33] but the evidence is too scant to afford certainty. That both Thracians and Celts had elaborate views of an existence beyond physical death is quite certain,[34] but whether this was an immortality of the soul, a metempsychosis, a resurrection, or some other mode of continuity is not clear from the vaguely worded testimonies that have come down to us.[35] Most suggestive, perhaps, is Lucan, who addresses the Druids directly in *Pharsalia* 1.454–458:

> According to you as authorities, the shades
> Do not travel to the silent abodes of Erebus and the pallid dominions
> Of Dis in the deep. The same spirit rules over bodily members (*artus*)
> In the other world: death is the midpoint of a long life,
> If you sing things which are rightly known.

In contrast to the usual bland assertion that the Druids taught the immortality of the soul,[36] Lucan here ignores the soul and discusses the fate of the body. Moreover, he strongly implies that the material components of the body—*artus* "limbs" is a very striking term in such a context—are reconstituted after death, death being only a moment of transition between different loci of existence. In some ways, this is most similar to the ideas I have been considering, and it is maddening not to know more.

Germanic sources are a bit fuller, but once again there is less than one might like. For while we have several lengthy accounts of Germanic eschatology, as well as some pieces of iconographic evidence, the bulk of it deals with the world catastrophe of the *Ragnarǫk* ("Fate of the gods"), with only brief hints of the resurrection that followed the destruction of the cosmos.[37]

Most scholars now accept that the Old Norse Ragnarǫk mythology represents an independent variant of broader and more ancient eschatological traditions, although earlier researchers who noted the striking similarities to certain Indo-Iranian data were more inclined to argue that motifs or even full scenarios diffused from east to west.[38] Similarly, the portions of the myth that tell of the world's restoration after its near-total destruction are now usually considered to be part of the pagan Germanic system, and not (as some had argued) the result of Christian influence.[39] The most authoritative source for these is *Vǫluspá* 59–63, in which the sibyl (ON *vǫlva*) prophesies to Oðinn. The passage follows immediately upon the description of the collapse of the earth and the heavens, and the death of gods and monsters alike.

> I see it come up   another time—
> The earth from the sea,   green again.
> Waterfalls flow,   an eagle flies over,
> Who hunts for fish   on the fells.
>
> The Aesir meet   at Iðavǫllr
> And talk of the mighty   earth-encircler (i.e., the Midgard Serpent),
> And there recall   the mighty dooms
> And Fimbultyr's (Oðinn's?)   ancient mysteries.
>
> Then afterward   they will find
> The wondrous gold gaming-pieces   in the grass,
> Which in olden days   they had possessed.
>
> Unsown fields   will grow,
> All misfortune will heal.   Baldr will come;
> Hǫðr and Baldr dwell there   in Hropt's (i.e., Oðinn's) battlefield,
> The temple of the gods of the slain.   Would you know more, or what?
>
> Then Hœnir is able   to work the sacrificial wands,
> And the sons of the brothers   of Tveggi dwell
> In wide Wind-home.   Would you know more, or what?

This passage systematically presents the period immediately after the cataclysm as a repetition of the paradisal age following cosmogony, and also as a reversal of the eschaton. Thus, the earth rises up from the sea, into which it has sunk as a culminating act of the world's end (*Vsp* 57).[40] The gods meet at Iðavǫllr ("Shining Meadow"), where first they gathered (*Vsp* 7), and there recover the gaming pieces with which they amused themselves before any strife broke into the world (*Vsp* 8). In fact, world history seems to be nothing more than the working out of the gods' game, one round of which was concluded with the Ragnarǫk, and now the game begins again.[41]

Of greatest interest to us, however, is the resurrection of Baldr and Hǫðr, the two slain sons of Oðinn. That this is a literal resurrection of the dead there can be no doubt: Snorri, in his version of the same events (*Gylf* 53), states "they came from Hel," the subterranean realm of the dead, from which Baldr could not be released until after the cosmos was destroyed. Regrettably, we are told nothing of the precise way their resurrection is accomplished, nor whether others will be resurrected after them.

Other features of the *Vǫluspá* account are of considerable interest for the ways in which the end of the world recalls its beginnings. Thus, sacrifice resumes once more with Hoenir's working of the "sacrificial wands" (*hlautvið*),[42] and the mysterious Tveggi appears (*Vsp* 63), a figure who is barely known elsewhere, but whose name means nothing other than "Twin," being derived from the genitive form (*tveggja*) of the numeral "two" (ON *tveir*). Tveggi, who appears at the end of time, thus recalls those primordial figures whose names also mean "Twin": Tuisco and Ymir.[43]

In many ways, the Germanic eschatological tradition shares important features with Iranian accounts of the Renovation. In both, a resurrection is one of the culminating acts of cosmic restoration after the cataclysm, and new men appear—or, perhaps better yet, new versions of the first men reappear—immediately after the world has been destroyed. This same coalescence of themes is evident in at least three different Greek traditions.

To begin, there is the myth of Deukalion and Pyrrha. Mentioned earliest in Hesiod and Pindar,[44] it is given most fully in Apollodoros, *Bibliotheka* 1.7.2, and Ovid, *Metamorphoses* 1.245–415. Throughout Greco-Roman lore, Deukalion and Pyrrha are honored as the sole survivors of the flood with which Zeus put an end to the Race of Bronze, and they are thus the first humans of our own age. Moreover, they are the first man and woman in another fashion, for they are the first mortal children born of immortal titans—Deukalion being the son of Prometheus and Pyrrha the daughter of Epimetheus by Pandora—whereas all other humans of their age were created by Prometheus out of water and earth.[45]

With the flood, one world age ends, and with the emergence of Deukalion and Pyrrha from their ark, another age begins. The two survivors face a problem: how to repopulate the earth. Piously, they seek an oracle from the goddess Themis to guide them in this endeavor. Ovid (*Met* 1.381–413) tells what happened:[46]

> The goddess was moved and gave an oracle: "Depart from the temple,
> Cover your head, unbind your girded garments,
> And throw the bones of your dear mother behind you."
>   For a long time they stood amazed, and Pyrrha first broke
> The silence with her voice. She refused to obey the goddess's
>   commands.

Trembling, she asked forgiveness for herself, (for) she feared
To offend her mother's shade by tossing her bones about.
Meanwhile, they repeated in their dark hiding places the obscure
Words of the oracle given, each considering them separately.
Then Prometheus's son soothed Epimetheus's daughter
With tranquil words. "Either our ingenuity is deceitful," he said,
"Or nothing is pious and the oracles advise a sinful deed.
Our dear mother is the earth; I believe the stones in the earth's body
Are what we called bones. We are ordered to throw *them* behind us!"
Although (Pyrrha) was moved by her husband's interpretation,
Still her hope was in doubt. What is more, both of them distrusted
The heavenly prophecies. But what could it hurt to try?
They separated, covered their heads, ungirded their tunics,
And threw the stones behind their own footsteps.
The rocks—who would believe this, if antiquity did not testify to
    it?—
Began to give up their hardness and their rigidity,
And gradually to attain a softer, more pliable form.
Soon, when they had been born, a milder nature was reached
By them, and it seemed like a human form:
Not plainly, but more like a statue as it is in the beginning.
Of these rocks, that part which was damp with moisture somewhere
And earthy—that turned into the flesh of the body.
That which was solid and unable to bend changed to bone,
And that which was the veins remained under the same name.
And in brief time, according to the will of the gods, the rocks
Thrown by the man's hands assumed the figure of men,
And from (each) female throw, a woman was remade.

Here is the very same scenario encountered in Scandinavia and Iran: the resurrection of humanity, starting with figures of the first-man type, immediately after the destruction of the world. The only difference is that the cataclysm is somewhat more limited in this myth, affecting only the surface of the earth, not the entire cosmos. Moreover, the myth of Deukalion and Pyrrha goes beyond the Germanic accounts in its detailed description of how humanity was re-created, in this resembling the Iranian and Slavic materials. For the new people who are brought into being by Deukalion and Pyrrha are constructed out of the material remnants of the macrocosm, particularly the elements earth and water, and are built up on the basis of homologic alloforms. Thus, their flesh is made out of the soft earth, their bones out of the hard stones, and their blood vessels from rock striations, this last homology resulting from the fact that one word, Latin *vena*, denotes both, as does its English cognate, vein. These are essentially

the same homologies that inform the Russian laments; they also resemble closely the earliest homologies explicitly attested in any Greek
source, those in the fragment from Khoirlos considered briefly in
Chapter 1: "Stones are the bones of the earth; rivers are earth's veins."

What Deukalion and Pyrrha ask of the goddess after the flood is
essentially the same question posed by Zarathuštra to Ohrmazd in *GBd*
34.4 (TD MS. 221.12–14): "Whence is the body remade, which the
wind leads off and the water carries away, and how does the resurrection come to be?" What they seek is nothing less than a reversal of the
world's end and a reversal of death, or, to put it differently, a re-creation
of humanity and a repetition of the anthropogony. In *Metamorphoses*
1.413, which reads *Et de femineo reparata est femina jactu* "And from
(each) female throw, a woman was remade," the verb used is *re-parō* "to
make or prepare again." With some metrical adjustment, such verbs
as *creō, faciō,* or *formō* could easily have been used, as could *parō* without
the *re-* prefix. Yet Ovid chose a verb that would emphasize the repetitive
nature of this anthropogony. It is not just that men and women were
created thus by Deukalion and Pyrrha. He makes a stronger point:
they were created thus *before*. Recall *Metamorphoses* 1.363–364, where
Deukalion wishes he could create people out of earth as did his father,
Prometheus.[47] When we consider how it is that human bodies can be
built out of these elements, we must also bear in mind the Greek and
other IE sources, in which at death the body passes into the earth and
the blood into water, from which they can be recalled when the cosmos
is de-created at the end of a world age.

Similar ideas are found in the great myth of Plato's *Politikos* 269C–
274E, the most elaborate of Plato's discussions on the topics of death
and rebirth and cosmic cyclicity.[48] Here, Plato describes the cosmos
as a sphere, the motion of which alternates between two phases. In
the first of these, the sphere is guided by God's hand, which spins it
in one rotational direction (presumably clockwise). The motion is steady
and secure, and the world partakes of both moral and physical well-
being, this being the paradisal Age of Kronos when animals and humans lived peacefully, the earth produced abundant fruit of itself,
and the climate was so mild as to make clothing and shelter unnec-
essary. But at a certain moment, God releases his hand from the
cosmos, and it begins to spin in the opposite direction. The following
period is the Age of Zeus, our own age, in which moral and physical
conditions gradually deteriorate as the world spins ever more disas-
trously out of control, ultimately threatening to destroy all. In the
face of this threat, God intervenes once more and starts the world
rotating again in the same direction it had during the Age of Kronos.

The moments of transition from one rotational direction to another—or from one world age to another—are moments of catastrophe, when "beginning and end rush in opposite directions" (273A). The change of cosmic spin is said to be "the greatest and most complete change" that ever takes place (270B), altering all things. When God lets go of the universe, setting it into the Age of Zeus, earthquakes destroy almost all living creatures (273A), and when he takes control once more there is again a tremendous jolt and great loss of life (270D). Only a very few humans survive, and those survivors experience a total reversal of their lives. Consistent with the reversal of cosmic rotation, the course of life turns backward, and

> all mortal beings stopped coming to seem older; changing back, as it were, they grew younger and softer of skin. The white hairs of the older people turned black, and the cheeks of those with beards became smooth again, restoring the bygone prime of youth to each one. And the bodies of those made young became smoother and smaller every day and night, returning to the state of a newborn child, being made like (such a child) in soul and in body. Thereafter, they faded away altogether and wholly disappeared. (270D–E)

In the Age of Kronos, human beings do not age, but rather grow younger, until they pass beyond infancy and disappear. The mechanism whereby this disappearance is accomplished is spelled out later in the dialogue (272E), where we are told that people in the Age of Kronos "fall into the earth as seeds." It comes as no surprise, then, when we are told that the process of birth is also reversed in the Age of Kronos, people being born at a full old age, from which they grow younger thereafter. Moreover, they come to birth from the soil itself. The Eleatic Stranger, who recounts the *Politikos* myth, explains how this is accomplished:

> When the transition of the old people to the nature of a child is completed, it follows that those lying (dead) in the earth are put back together there and brought back to life, the process of birth being reversed with the reversal of the world's rotation (271B).

What is described is nothing other than a resurrection of the dead: a reversal of the process of death, whereby bodies are "put back together" *(palin . . . xunistamenous)* and spring forth alive from the ground, into which ordinarily bodies are buried or "enter" when dead. Further, this takes place immediately following an eschatological upheaval, the end of a world age, and marks the beginning of a new cycle.

So similar is this mythic scenario to Iranian descriptions of the Renovation that some scholars have argued for direct diffusion of the *Politikos* myth from Iran, specifying Eudoxos of Kyzikos as a possible intermediary, who entered the Academy around 367 B.C. and could have acquainted Plato with Iranian ideas.[49] But while the similarities are undeniable, the Greek sources Plato himself specifies or implies are fully sufficient to have permitted him to construct his myth,[50] and given the evidence of the Deukalion myth and the texts from Empedokles and Anaxagoras I will consider shortly, there is no reason to assume foreign origin for a myth involving resurrection of the dead and cosmic cycles.[51] Rather, Plato—like the Iranian accounts, the Slavic laments, and the *Vǫluspá*—seems here to be drawing on traditional ideas that had come down to him, in which the end of the world is seen to produce the re-creation of mankind from the material substance of the de-created macrocosm. The same theme is apparent in Plato's great predecessor Empedokles.

As we have seen, Empedokles—following Parmenides in this—rejected any idea of absolute cosmic creation or destruction, holding that the universe is eternal in its fundamental nature. Attempting to restore a sense of dynamism to the static cosmos that Parmenides envisioned, however, Empedokles argued that the universe was not totally without change but was best described as being "motionless in its cycle" *(akinētoi kata kyklon;* fragment B17.14), which is to say, ever changing, but always in the same repetitive (and thus changeless) pattern. This cosmic cycle he described as involving an alternation between two opposite states: a unified sphere, in which the four cosmic elements—which together comprise all the material substance of the universe—are unified; and a fragmented state, in which the elements stand separate from one another. Two forces produce the oscillation between these two states: Love, which draws all matter together, and Strife, which tears it apart (see Chapter 1).

The history of the cosmos is thus an infinite repetition of this cycle: from unity to separation to unity again. And what is more, individual lives follow the same pattern, for each living organism is nothing more than a mixture in which the four elements are temporarily combined,[52] and these elements separate out at death, only to be recombined again when the soul enters a new body.[53] Four existing fragments spell out Empedokles' views on this topic:

> I will tell you another thing. There is no "origin" of all
> Mortals, nor is there any end in accursed death.

But there is only mixture and interchange of the things mixed,
And this is called "origin" with reference to humans. (B8)

And when (the elements) are mixed into man—
Or into the race of wild animals, or into bushes,
Or into birds—then people call that "birth."
And when they separate out, that is "the evil-spirited destiny" (i.e.,
    death).
That which is correct, they do not call by name, and customarily I
    myself speak in similar fashion. (B9)[54]

Infants! For their thoughts are not far-reaching.
Truly, they suppose that that which did not exist formerly has been
    born,
Or that anything dies out and is annihilated everywhere. (B11)

For it is impossible that things are born from that which never existed,
And (it is) unheard of and incapable of fulfillment that that which
    is perished utterly.
For things will always be, eternally, wherever anyone pushes them.
    (B12)

Empedokles' contemporary Anaxagoras shares this view, perhaps
having been influenced by Empedokles, or perhaps having drawn on
a common tradition. One of the few surviving fragments of Anaxagoras's own writings (B17) lays out his opinions:

> The Greeks do not believe rightly concerning birth and annihilation.
> For nothing is born and nothing is annihilated, but (everything) is
> mixed together out of existing things, and separates (back into those
> things). Thus, they rightly ought to call birth "mixture," and anni-
> hilation "separation."

The picture could not be clearer. At death, a body dissolves into its
constituent elements, which rejoin the cosmic totality, and at birth
those elements are drawn out of the cosmos and recombined into a
human (or animal or plant) organism. Never is there any birth for
the first time: every birth is a rebirth, or better yet, a reconstitution
of organic shape, a shifting of matter from the macrocosm to the
microcosm, and a resurrection. Death, conversely, is never final. It is
merely the temporary separation of elements, a shifting of matter
from the microcosm to the macrocosm. In this analysis, as in so many
others, Empedokles and Anaxagoras are heirs to an extremely ancient
tradition, which they adapt in fascinating and novel ways, but which
they also preserve with great fidelity.

The outlines of that system are fairly clear by now, although not all details are preserved with equal clarity in every text. Still, it is apparent that traditional IE thought on the topic of death and resurrection rests upon the same premise that informed creation mythology, healing practices, sacrificial ritual, and nutritional theories: the conviction that the material cosmos and the human body are complementary opposites, intimately interrelated and infinitely interchangeable along homological lines. When the world is created, it is created out of man— whether in cosmogony, sacrifice, or death. And when mankind is created—whether in anthropogony, nutrition, healing, or resurrection—it is created from the cosmos. The creation of one always implies the destruction or de-creation of the other. Alternatively, one might also say that the same matter always has existed and always will exist, forever alternating between human and cosmic forms. The processes we "infants" (as Empedokles put it) are accustomed to call "birth" and "death" are nothing other than moments of transition between temporary macrocosmic and microcosmic incarnations of matter. "Cosmogony" and "eschatology" are also such moments of transition, albeit on a larger scale.

What we see is that death and resurrection are reciprocal processes, in which matter passes from microcosm to macrocosm and back again. Death, moreover, is a form of sacrifice, a repetition of the cosmogony—which was simultaneously the first sacrifice, the first death, and the creation of the universe. And just as cosmogony and sacrifice are reversals of anthropogony and nutrition, so also death reverses the last two processes. Similarly it may be said that resurrection repeats the anthropogony and the action of nutrition, while reversing the effects of death, sacrifice, and cosmogony.

I have now reached the point where I can pick up a thread left hanging since the end of Chapter 3. There, after analyzing theories of nutrition, I offered figure 12 as a summary of cosmic processes, including cosmogony, anthropogony, sitiogony, sacrifice, and nutrition. Since then, I have shown that healing, like nutrition, is a form of anthropogony, whereby the body is rebuilt out of matter appropriated from the cosmos, and also that death and resurrection are varieties of cosmogony and anthropogony respectively, matter flowing from microcosm to macrocosm at death, and the flow being reversed with resurrection. Finally, I have shown that eschatology—the destruction of the cosmos at the end of a world age—is not only a destruction but also a creation, for human beings are (re)-created from the matter that is supplied when the cosmos is de-created. These processes can now be added to those described in figure 12 (see p. 86), and the result is a broader, more complex, more inclusive, and also more neatly symmetrical account of cosmic processes, as can be seen in figure 14.

Figure 14 represents the various ways matter flows between people, animals, and the universe, with food—a complex and highly important component of the universe—also figuring prominently. In this diagram there is no starting point and no termination. Matter is always in flux, although a dynamic equilibrium prevails: perhaps Empedokles' description is best and all things are "motionless in the cycle." If we arbitrarily start with the matter incarnated in cattle, however, we can follow a turn of the cycle conveniently. Thus, when matter leaves its animal form, either through animal sacrifice or through the natural death of an animal, it becomes food, following the pattern established in the sitiogonic myth. From food, matter passes back into animals when animals eat and drink, or into human form when humans do the same. Matter moves from man to the cosmos, via human sacrifice or natural death, repeating the model established in the cosmogonic portion of creation myth. From the cosmos, matter may shift back to a human locus in healing—as portions of earth, for instance, are appropriated to restore damaged flesh—and also through the resurrection that takes place at the end of a (not *the*) world. Such shifts

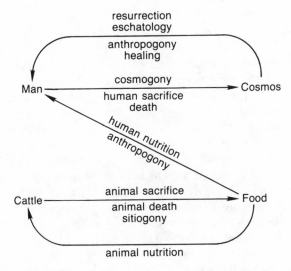

Figure 14. Cosmic processes: cosmogony, sitiogony, anthropogony, sacrifice, nutrition, healing, death, resurrection, and eschatology.

from the cosmos to man follow the pattern of the anthropogony. Finally, this constant and varied motion of matter from one entity to another may easily occur, for at the most fundamental level people, animals, and the universe are all the same, their apparent differences being ony superficial distinctions of form. Each one is merely an alloform—an alternative shape—of all the others.

The circle is now complete. The myths of cosmic creation lead inevitably to those of cosmic destruction, creation and destruction being perfectly, symmetrically balanced processes. In truth, there appears to be no such thing as "creation" or "destruction" *tout court.* Rather, every act of creation entails a destruction, and every destruction a creation—for whenever something is created, its alloform must be de-created.

The myths I have discussed are concerned primarily with the nature of man and the cosmos, not with gods and the "supernatural." The analysis of material existence set out in these myths is enormously rich and complex, as we have seen, incorporating scores, if not hundreds or thousands, of homologic details and welding them into a coherent, cohesive system. The fundamental premises of this system might be summarized in four points:

1. Man and the cosmos are alloforms of each other.
2. Matter is eternal in its existence, but subject to infinite recombination.
3. Time is infinite.
4. Change is constant, but the same processes cyclically recur.

One who fully understands such points—who comprehends the nature of matter, the various forms it takes, and the interrelations of those forms—can manipulate all things in the universe. Cosmological knowledge is not theoretical only, but emphatically, even radically, instrumental, as seen from the fact that the "requests" in the Vedic hymns are set in the imperative mood, not the subjunctive. They are not requests at all, but commands, commands whereby a fully knowledgeable priest bends the cosmos to his will. Vedic priests, like their Druidic counterparts, regularly claimed that they possessed the ability to create and de-create the universe through the performance of sacrifice,[55] and Empedokles claimed that he could teach how to bring rain, heal disease, and raise the dead (fragment B111). Such confident and audacious claims follow logically from the myths, in which were coded ideas considered nothing less than the secrets of the universe.

7

Reflections on Myth and Society

In the common Indo-European mythic system, as we have seen, the human body was understood to be the homologic alloform of the cosmos and vice versa. Thus, speculation on the nature of bodily parts yielded an understanding of the parts of the cosmos, and the reverse was equally true, mythic physiology and mythic cosmology being opposite sides of the same coin.

Analysis of human existence was not limited to consideration of the individual (physical) body, however, for a major section of this mythic system—what I have called the sociogony—dealt with the origin and nature of the social body. In the preceding chapters, for the most part, I have paid little attention to the social side of things. The time has now come to redress this imbalance, and to explore the subtle interconnections between cosmic and social concerns. I wish to address three simple, but fundamental questions: What have these myths to say about the nature of society? Who propagated such myths? Who benefited from their propagation? These are questions that ought be asked with reference to any myth, and in the case at hand, the answers are most revealing.

Recall from Chapters 1 and 2 that in numerous sociogonic accounts, social classes were formed from the dismembered body of the first man, who was often also the first king, and each class derived its nature and status from the bodily member from which it had emerged. Thus, in those variants where the well-known "tripartite" structure characteristic of many IE societies is evident,[1] the priestly class came from the head, priests being characterized by their superior powers of thought, perception, and speech.[2] The warrior class came from his upper torso, warriors being characterized by the superior force of their arms, their courage ("heart"), and the abundant energy that manifests itself as bodily heat—what we would now probably call adrenalin.[3] Finally, the commoner class came from the lower torso of the primordial victim, an area including both the belly and the genitals, commoners being characterized by superior abilities of food production (most often through herding and agriculture) and reproduction (through abundant sexuality), and also by powerful appetites.[4] These points are summarized graphically in figure 15.

Beyond these straightforward characterizations of the supposedly inherent gifts of each class and the activities proper to them, other conclusions were drawn from this type of sociogonic myth. Most important were those regarding social hierarchy and relations among the three classes. But rather than discuss these in the absence of solid data, it is preferable to begin with a classic sociogonic account, *Mānava Dharmaśāstra* ("Laws of Manu") 1.87-93.

> For the sake of the protection of all that had been created, the most radiant one
> Appointed separate occupations for those who had been born from his mouth, arms, thighs, and feet.
> He appointed teaching, study, sacrifice on their own behalf, and sacrifice on behalf of others,
> Generosity, and the acceptance of gifts for the priests.
> He prescribed protection of the people, generosity, the patronage of sacrifice, and study,
> And noninvolvement in (other) spheres of activity for the warrior.
> The protection of cattle, generosity, patronage of sacrifice and study,
> The merchant's path, usury, and agriculture for the commoner.
> But the lord presented only one mode of action for the servant:
> Obedience to the (other) classes.
> Puruṣa ("Man") is reputed to be more fit for sacrifice above (than below) his navel.
> Therefore, the Self-existent (lord) declared his mouth to be the most fit for sacrifice (i.e., most sacred, pure).
> The priest came into being from the highest part of the body: he is the most powerful and he preserves the sacred ritual formulas (*brahmaṇas . . . dhāraṇāt*).
> According to what is right, he is lord of all that has been created.

To the three classes characteristic of IE societies, a fourth was added in India: the *śūdra* class, consisting of servants, who remained always outside and beneath the proper borders of Indic society. In this passage, their lower status is emphatically marked by their origin from

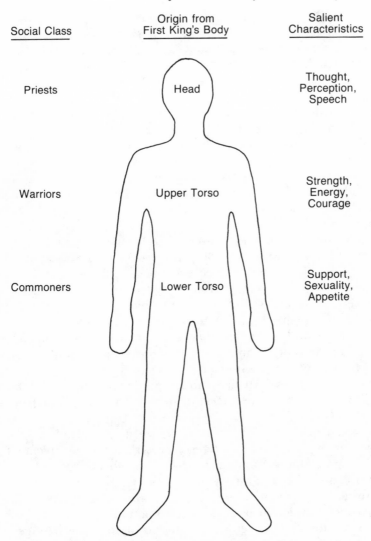

Social Class	Origin from First King's Body	Salient Characteristics
Priests	Head	Thought, Perception, Speech
Warriors	Upper Torso	Strength, Energy, Courage
Commoners	Lower Torso	Support, Sexuality, Appetite

Figure 15. Sociogony and social organization.

Puruṣa's feet and by the stress on their radical subordination: their sole calling in life is to obey their class superiors. Furthermore, whereas all three of the upper classes are explicitly given the right to take part in sacrifice, such a statement is lacking for the śūdras, and in practice they were not admitted to the grounds where sacrifice was performed.[5]

For just as the priests, given their origin from Puruṣa's mouth, were "most fit for sacrifice," so the śūdras, given their origin from his feet, were "least fit for sacrifice"—and, as Louis Dumont has elegantly demonstrated, ritual purity, "fitness for sacrifice," forms the basis of the traditional Indian social hierarchy, which has persisted in large measure until the present day.[6] Sacrifice and the myth of the first sacrifice defined social borders and established who was at the top and who at the bottom of the pecking order.

Certain specific activities, moreover, were charged to members of the three upper classes, these activities being presented as the logical extensions of that bodily part from which each class had its origin: the bodily alloform of the class, as it were. Thus, one activity is presented as the exclusive prerogative of the warriors as the "arms" of society: "protection of the people" (*prajānāṃ rakṣanaṃ*), which must be contrasted with one exclusive activity proper to members of the commoner class, "protection of cattle" (*paśūnāṃ rakṣanaṃ*). Whereas no other activities were assigned exclusively to the warriors—in fact, they were explicitly barred from involvement in most other areas reserved for members of other classes, which were either too high or too lowly for them—commoners, as the thighs or support of society, were charged with a large variety of concerns, almost all of them being related to the production of food (via agriculture and herding) and wealth (via trade and moneylending). A strong note of condescension is evident, however, particularly with regard to the last-named activity, for the neuter Skt noun *kusīdam* "usury" is derived directly from the adjective *kusīda-* "lazy."[7]

The activities reserved for members of the priestly class, society's "voice," form a particularly interesting set, since they complement the set formed by those activities charged to members of all three of the upper classes. The exclusively priestly prerogatives are teaching, the performance of sacrifice, and the acceptance of gifts; the duties or obligations charged to all classes in common being study, the patronage of sacrifice, and generosity. On the strength of this passage from *Manu*, one may thus perceive a system of exchanges between priests and others, operating in three areas (teaching/study, sacrifice/sacrificial patronage, acceptance of gifts/generosity), in which priests give nonmaterial service and benefits to others in return for material payments,[8] as is graphed in table 11.

A much less elaborate variant on this same sociogonic pattern, lacking any explicit discussion of class duties and relations, is found in the Old Russian "Poem on the Dove King" (*Stič o golubinoj knig"*), a text discussed in Chapter 1.

Czars and czarinas come into being
From the head of honest Adam.
Princes and heroes come into being
From the bones of honest Adam.
The orthodox peasants come into being
From the knee of holy Adam.

Here the same vertical hierarchy of social classes—which have their origin from the first man's body—is evident as in India, with a few variations of detail. First, only three classes are specified, and in this, the Russian reflex is more conservative than even the most ancient Indic version (*RV* 10.90.11–12), where a fourth class, that of the śūdras, already appears. Political sovereigns—czars and czarinas—replace priests in the paramount position, and their origin is from the head, not the mouth. On this detail the Russian version is again more conservative than the Indic, where fascination with the creative powers of sacred speech (*brahman-*, neut) led to the view that the speech organ alone was the alloform of the priestly class (*brāhmaṇa-*, masc).[9]

Again, the bodily locus of the warrior class—"princes and heroes" (*knjaz'ja so bojarami*) being characterized by nothing so much as their prowess in battle—is given in rather general terms, being only the "bones," but their intermediate position in the order of presentation sets them between head and knee. Finally, the knee, from which sprang the lowest—but most productive—of classes, the peasants, may well be a euphemism for the genitals, as the terms for "knee" in many IE languages often served thus.[10] Beyond the details, however, the over-arching structure corresponds quite closely to that of *Manu* 1.87–93; the vertical hierarchy of social classes being correlated to the parts of the first man's body, from which all classes are said to have emerged.

Table 11. Exchange relations among the three upper classes according to *Mānava Dharmaśāstra* 1.87–93.

Class	Instruction		Sacrifice		Generosity	
	Teach (for pay)	Study (and pay)	Practice (for pay)	Patronize (and pay)	Accept gifts	Give gifts
Priests	X	X	X	X	X	X
Warriors		X		X		X
Commoners		X		X		X

Iranian sources preserve several different sociogonic accounts, among them that of *Škend Gumānīg Wizār* 1.20–24, which is quite similar to the Indic and Slavic materials already considered, although unlike them it simply posits homologies between bodily parts and social classes, without describing the origins of the latter from the former: "And in the microcosm which is man is revealed a likeness (*hōmānāgīh*) to the four social classes of the world. The head is like the priesthood, the hands like the warriorhood, the belly (or womb) like the commoners, and the feet like the artisanry."[11] Again, there is the myth of how the royal glory-nimbus (*x^varənah-*) of the first king, Yima ("Twin"), was divided into three portions and distributed to representatives of the sovereign, warrior, and commoner classes (*Yt* 19.30–39).[12]

Other myths also present Yima as first king and founder of the social hierarchy.[13] Another Iranian account has Frēdōn (< AV *Thraētaona-*), Yima's rightful successor as king, for its hero.[14] The story—which is found in *Ayādgār i Jāmāspīg* 4.39–41, and which resembles certain Greek and Germanic myths[15]—tells how both space and society were divided among three sons of a primordial king.

> Three sons were born of Frēdōn. They were named Salm and Tōz and Ēric. He called each of the three before him, and he said to each of them: "I will apportion the world among you all, as seems proper to each of you. I will give to each of you that which each desires."
>
> Salm desired much material wealth. Tōz desired strength. And Ēric—since the royal glory (*xwarrah i Kayān*) was over him—desired the law and the religion. Frēdōn said: "As you desired, so may it come to be."
>
> He gave the land of Hrōm (i.e., the Byzantine empire) unto the shore of the sea to Salm, and he gave Turkestan and the desert unto the shore of the sea to Tōz, and Iran and India unto the shore of the sea came to Ēric.

The unified realm over which Frēdōn ruled was thus carved into three empires, each of which took its name from one of his sons: Hrōm in the west from Salm, Turan or Turkestan in the east from Tōz, and Iran plus India—the best of all realms, located at the center of the world—from Ēric. Moreover, the chief attributes of the three social classes were distributed among the three sons: the law and religion (*dād ud dēn*) proper to priests being given to Ēric, who was already a king by virtue of possessing the royal glory (Pahl *xwarrah* < Av *x^varənah-*); physical might (*tagīgīh*), the mark of the warrior, to Tōz;

and great wealth (*was xīrīh*), the mark of the successful commoner, to Salm.

For all that this account differs markedly from the sociogonies cited above, such differences are only superficial. For here, in place of physical and sacrificial dismemberment, we find dynastic inheritance, whereby the division of a primordial king's realm into three parts replaces the tripartite division of his body. In both instances, each of the three pieces is homologized to one of the social classes. In those variants of the sacrificial type, the *king's body* is divided into three socially coded and hierarchically differentiated portions, while in those of the dynastic type, it is the *kingdom* that is so divided.

As for the ranking, duties, and relations of the classes, Iranian accounts tally closely with Indic. A good example is *Mēnōg i Xrad* 31, which is also noteworthy in that its discussion is confined to the three IE classes, ignoring the fourth, Iran-specific class of artisans.[16]

> The wise one asked the Spirit of Wisdom: "What is the proper function created for priests, warriors, and commoners (*wāstaryōšān*),[17] each individually?"
>
> The Spirit of Wisdom answered: "The proper function of priests is to preserve the good religion; sacrifice; invocation of the good gods; to make observations regarding the law and justice and custom and social bonds as revealed in the pure Mazdā-worshipping religion; to make men know the goodness of virtue; and to point out the path to heaven, the fearfulness of hell, and the defense against hell.
>
> The proper function of warriors is to smite the enemy and to keep their own land and country peaceful and without fear.
>
> And the proper function of commoners is to do the work of cultivation and —to the extent of their ability—to make the world flourish and to keep it cultivated.

Obviously, the priests again had many more responsibilities than did the other classes, sacrifice figuring prominently among these. Beyond what we would see as their specifically religious functions, priests also had certain legal and political responsibilities, although these were hardly regarded as secular. Thus, the text states straightforwardly that it was the task of priests "to make observations regarding the law and justice and custom and social bonds, *as revealed in the pure Mazdā-worshipping religion.*" While the law may have regulated society, society was considered no less sacred than the cosmos, and regulation of society through law was no less sacred an activity than regulation of the cosmos through sacrifice. The law rested on sacred principles and was administered by priests. Perhaps it is because law came under the control of "secular" authority that "czars and czarinas" replace priests in the higher position in the Old Russian variant of the sociogony.[18]

An interesting ambiguity shows up in the brief account of warriors' duties in *MX* 31. Two different tasks are mentioned: "to smite the enemy" and "to keep their own land and country peaceful and without fear." The question is, were these two synonymous or not? As for the first, it is clear that the "enemy" (*dušmen* lit "the evil-minded one[s]") was meant to be seen as a foreign enemy, who had to be repulsed or conquered. But was the elimination of foreign threats sufficient to secure domestic tranquillity, or were internal police functions also necessary for the warrior class "to keep their own land and country peaceful and without fear"? If the latter, against whom was the warriors' might to be directed? The text provides no answers, but it is perhaps worth noting that the priests were directed only "to make observations regarding the law," not to enforce their judgments in any way. Given this, I think it is possible that the force of the warrior class—or at least, the threat of that force—served to back up priestly authority on legal and sociopolitical matters.

Productive labor was prescribed for the commoners, who engaged in herding as well as agriculture. As in India, there is a certain condescension evident toward them in this text, which was composed by priests. Thus, while it is the commoners' duty "to make the world flourish" by increased production of crops and herds, they may make the world flourish only "to the extent of their ability," the broad implication being that the ability of commoners to sustain creation is, at best, rather limited.

A still more detailed discussion of the duties of the three social classes is found in Caesar's account of Gaulish society, *De Bello Gallico* 6.13–15, which closely resembles those given in *Manu* and the *Mēnōg i Xrad*. The passage is long, but it merits close attention, particularly for its detailed description of a functioning priesthood.

> In all of Gaul, there are two classes of men who are in any rank and honor at all, for the masses (*plebes*) are held almost in the place of servants; they dare nothing by themselves, and are not admitted into public deliberations. The majority, pressed down by debt, by the size of tributes, or by injuries inflicted by those more powerful, give themselves up in servitude to the nobles, who exercise over them the same rights as lords over servants. But of these two (noble) classes, one is the Druids and the other the Knights (*equitum*). (The Druids) take part in all things divine, manage the public and private sacrifices, and interpret the holy things (*religiones*). A large number of youths

flock to them for instruction, and they are in great honor among them. They decide almost all controversies, public and private, and if a crime is committed, if a murder is performed or there is a dispute over an inheritance or over boundaries, they judge that and fix the awards and penalties. And if someone—an individual or a whole people (*populus*)—does not abide by their decision, they proscribe him or them from the sacrifices. This, according to them, is the heaviest penalty of all. Those who have been thus proscribed are placed in the number of the ungodly and polluted. Everyone shrinks from their approach or mention, not wishing to obtain trouble from contact with them. Justice is not granted to them should they seek it, nor is any honor shared with them . . .

The Druids habitually are absent from war, do not pay tributes along with the rest, and have freedom from military service and immunity in all things. Excited by such great advantages, many enter instruction, sent by their parents and relatives, or of their own free will. There, they are said to learn a great number of verses by heart, and some spend twenty years in instruction. They do not consider it right to commit these (verses) to writing, but with almost all other things, public and private, they make use of Greek letters. They seem to me to have established this (practice) for two reasons: they do not wish their knowledge (*disciplinam*) to be disseminated to the masses (*vulgum*), nor (do they wish) that those who have come to rely on letters should devote themselves less to the art of memory. It usually happens that with the aid of letters, people relax their diligence in learning things thoroughly and also (relax) in the art of memory. Above all, they wish to convince people that souls do not perish (lit "become lost"), but after death pass from certain bodies to others, and this they believe to excite courage most greatly, the fear of death being neglected. Beyond this, they dispute concerning the stars and their motion, the size of the universe and the earth, the nature of things, and the immortal gods and their power, and this they teach to their youths.

The other class is that of the Knights. When there is need, and a war breaks out—which before the arrival of Caesar was wont to happen almost yearly, since they either inflicted injuries themselves or would redress those (injuries) perpetrated (against them)—all the Knights take part in the war, and whoever among them is greatest by birth and by riches, that one has the most retainers and clients around himself. This is the only (form of) service (*gratiam*) and authority they have invented.

By now, the picture is largely familiar. The priests occupied the highest rung of the social ladder, not only as an elite intelligentsia—although they were that—but also through their control of ritual and legal processes. The two, in fact, were closely connected, for the most severe punishment (*poena . . . gravissima*) meted out was exclusion from sacrifice, which was—as the text makes clear—equivalent to total ostracism, participation in the sacrifice being what established one as a member of the social body.[19]

Sacrifice, law, study and teaching—all these are familiar to us from Indic and Iranian accounts of priestly duties, and the Druidic rejection of writing in favor of strenuous training in the art of memory also finds Indo-Iranian parallels.[20] Further, the topics to which the Druids devoted their attention were very much those I have explored in the preceding chapters: the nature of matter (*de rerum natura*), the relations of microcosm and macrocosm (*de mundi ac terrarum magnitudine*), and the redistribution of the human entity at death.

Careful attention should also be paid to the financial dealings of the Druids, as to those of the other classes. Two details within Caesar's account are most instructive. First, we are told that the Druids "do not pay tributes along with the rest" and that this "advantage" (*praemium*, lit "premium, primacy") was so great that coupled with exemption from warfare and "immunity in all things," it induced youths to flock to the Druids for training, and they were willing to endure up to twenty years of instruction in order to join their ranks. Second, we are told that a disproportionate share of tribute was expected of the commoner class, so much so that "the majority, pressed down by debt, or the size of tributes, or the injuries inflicted by those more powerful, give themselves up in servitude to the nobles (*nobilibus*), who exercise over them the same rights as lords over servants." The text goes on to specify that the two noble classes were the Druids and the Knights (*equites*).[21] It thus follows that the Druids received tribute but did not themselves pay any; the Knights both paid and received tribute; and the commoners (*plebes*) received no tribute but paid to the extent that most of them (*pleri*) fell into a state of serfdom as the result of the debts they incurred, priests and warriors alike benefiting from their misfortune.

Most of what we are told regarding the commoners is how they furnished wealth and labor to their class superiors. While the plight of debtors seems most acute, all the plebes—even those who had not been forced to surrender their freedom as the result of debt—were "held almost in the place of servants" (*plebes paene servorum habetur loco*). In such a situation, they had little recourse. Law was controlled by the Druids, as we have seen, and the plebes were excluded from all political power: they were "not admitted into public deliberations" (*nullo adhibetur consilio*). In the face of this, they "dared nothing by themselves."

In general, Caesar seems quite sympathetic to the commoners' plight, although—like Posidonios, his chief source for Celtic ethnography[22]—he could afford sympathy, being an outside observer. Had we an indigenous Gaulish account, the attitudes displayed toward the plebes might be considerably more condescending or even contemptuous, as is the case in indigenous accounts from India, Iran, and Greece.[23]

One phrase in which Caesar reveals his sympathy is of particular interest, for he speaks of "the injustices inflicted by those more powerful" (*injuria potentiorum*) on the commoners. Such injuries are classed with the burdens of debt and tribute as the means whereby commoners were reduced to serfdom. Obviously such "injuries" had a powerful effect, but we are given no clue as to what they were, nor are we told who "those more powerful" were. Coercive force threatened or perpetrated by members of the warrior class is not outside the realm of possibility.

Of the warriors we are told rather little, their tasks being quite clearly defined and narrowly delimited. War and raiding were their regular profession, and Caesar tells us—taking credit for putting a stop to this state of affairs—that each year the Gaulish *equites* went forth to battle, whether provoked or unprovoked. In battle, honor and riches were to be won, and high-ranking warriors assembled large followings around themselves, using distribution of booty to ensure the allegiance of their followers.[24] A leader thus had considerable need for wealth. A skilled leader was able to compound his wealth, for by attracting a large number of followers he could make further success in battle much more likely. Success in battle brought more wealth in the form of booty, and this wealth could be translated into a larger following, although some of it was needed for tribute, most probably paid to the Druids.

The picture of Celtic society that Caesar offers corresponds closely to the picture of Iranian society given in the *Mēnōg i Xrad*. Yet neither of these connects its description of social relations and processes to a sociogonic myth, nor does the Old Russian "Poem on the Dove King" connect its sociogony to a description of social reality. Of the sources I have discussed thus far, myth and experience are explicitly correlated only in the *Mānava Dharmaśāstra* 1.87–93. Yet the same correlation is found in two of Plato's most important dialogues, the *Timaios* and the *Republic*.

Several important studies of the *Republic*, particularly those by Georges Dumézil and more recently Bernard Sergent, have established that Plato's ideal city possessed a system of social classes on the general IE pattern.[25] The sole major variation, predictably, is that for Plato, philosopher-kings replaced priests as the sovereign class, although like priests before them, they ruled by virtue of superior intellectual powers. But Plato did not merely outline a tripartite utopia: his goal was much more ambitious, and together with the description of proper social structure contained in Books 3 and 4 of the *Republic*, he offered an analysis of the nature of the human soul. These two projects were unified at *Republic* 440E–441A, where the question of whether the soul has two or three parts is resolved:

> "So then, is (the spirited faculty) separate from the rational, or is it some form of the rational, and thus there are not three, but two forms in the soul: the rational and the appetitive? Or, just as in the city there are three classes (*genē*) that comprise it—the commercial, defensive, and deliberative—so also in the soul is there a third (part): the spirited, which is by nature defender to the rational, if it is not corrupted by an evil rearing?"
> "Of necessity," he said, "there is a third (part)."

Although his terminology fluctuates somewhat through the *Republic*, Plato here names the three social classes "commercial" (*khrēmatistikon*), "defensive" (*epikourētikon*), and "deliberative" (*bouleutikon*), these being the commoners (who produce the bulk of wealth, engaging in trade as well as pastoral and agricultural activities), warriors, and philosopher-kings respectively.[26] The parts of the soul—and again, there is some fluctuation in usage throughout the Platonic corpus— are here named the "appetitive" (*epithymētikon*), "spirited" (*thymoeides*), and "rational" (*logistikon*). But what is most important is the homology established between these two sets. For Plato states that the "spirited" part "is by nature defender (*epikouron*) to the rational (part), if it is not corrupted by an evil rearing," using the nominal form (*epikouros*) of the same term that as an adjective (*epikourētikon*) denotes the warrior class. Thus, the "spirited" portion of the soul was seen as defender of the individual, just as the warrior class was defender of the city. Moreover, the spirited part of the soul properly served at the bidding of the rational part ("if it is not corrupted by an evil rearing"), just as the warrior class properly served at the bidding of the philosopher-kings (see, e.g., *Tim* 70A, *Rep* 439D–441A, 442B). Finally, it is implied here and stated explicitly in other passages I will consider, that these defenders were to guard against threats internal as well as external, for it was the excessive demands ("appetites") of the lower portions of city and soul alike that posed the greatest dangers to stability (*Rep* 442A–E). Worst of all situations was that in which the defenders—

Table 12. Homology of soul and society in Plato's *Republic*.

Portion of soul	Characteristics of social class	Social class
Rational	Deliberative	Philosopher-Kings
Spirited	Defensive	Warriors
Appetitive	Commercial	Commoners

either the spirited portion of the soul or the warrior class—themselves came under the sway of base desires (that is, those characteristic of the lower portion of the soul and the lower social strata), and rebelled against their proper superiors.[27]

Starting from the homology between the spirited faculty and the warrior class, a full correlation follows between the portions of the soul and the social classes, as shown in table 12. In the *Timaios*, written some years after the *Republic*, Plato went further, homologizing the three portions of the soul to parts of the human body, once again preserving traditional IE themes and images.

In the *Timaios*, Plato also refined his analysis of the soul, and—while still preserving the schema of three parts characterized by reason, spirit, and appetite—he now argued that the first of these constituted the immortal and divine portion of the soul, while the other two parts were mortal only. With this as a starting point, *Timaios* 69D–70A described how the creator gods set each part of the soul in a different bodily locus. The pattern is virtually identical to that found in the Indic, Iranian, and Old Russian sociogonic myths.

> Fearing to defile the divine (portion of the soul) unless it was entirely necessary, the demiurges settled the mortal (portion of the soul) apart from it—in another residence within the body—constructing an isthmus and a border for the head and breast, setting the throat between them so that they will be separated. And they pressed the mortal type of soul into the breast and into what is called the thorax. And since one of these (portions of the mortal soul) is better and the other worse, they built a separation once more, in the hollow of the thorax, setting the midriff and diaphragm between these, and separating the residence of men and women. That part of the soul which participates in manliness and spirit (*andrias kai thymou*), which is victory-loving, they settled closer to the head, between the midriff and the throat, so that—attentive to reason and in common with reason—

it would hold down by force that type (of mortal soul) characterized by appetites, when that one is totally unwilling to be persuaded by the command and reason from the lofty citadel.

Reason—the divine part of the soul—was thus situated in the head, elsewhere called the most perfect part of the body (*Tim* 73C–D). In its "lofty citadel" (*akropolis*), reason was set apart from the lesser forms of the soul, to which it issued commands. Ordinarily these were obeyed, for although the head is the smallest part of the body, Plato saw it as the most divine and best suited to rule over all bodily parts (*Tim* 44D).[28] Problems might arise, however, when the appetitive part of the soul—set in the largest but lowliest section of the body—resisted the commands of reason. In such an eventuality, it was the task of the spirited part of the soul (mention of *thymos* here corresponds to the designation *thymoeides* used in the *Republic*)—which was most martial ("victory-loving," "manly") and was located in the chest, between reason (head) and appetite (lower torso)—to suppress by coercive force the appetitive soul's rebellion (*biāi to tōn epithymiōn katekhoi genos*). Combining the homology between body and soul developed in this passage from the *Timaios* with that between soul and society developed in *Republic* 440E–441A yields the broader set of relations graphed in table 13.

Proper hierarchy—within society and within the individual as well—is vertical and pyramidic. The smallest section of the total entity is placed at the top; it is assisted by the next smallest, placed in the middle; and the largest section is placed at the bottom. Ideally, the top section should control the lower two, prevailing over them by virtue of its superior mental powers. Should the lowest section balk, the physical force of the intermediate section is brought to bear in support of the highest sections's rule. The greatest disaster of all

Table 13. Homology of body, soul, and society in Plato's *Republic* and *Timaios*.

Bodily part	Portion of soul	Characteristics of social class	Social class
Head	Rational	Deliberative	Philosopher-Kings
Upper torso	Spirited	Defensive	Warriors
Lower torso	Appetitive	Commercial	Commoners

occurs when the two lower sections combine and resist or even overthrow the command of the highest section, which, being smallest, is unable to prevail over their combined force. We have already seen these schematic relations worked out with regard to the soul in *Timaios* 69D–70A. *Republic* 431A-D repeats this analysis and extends it to include, by homology, the social order, taking as its starting point the meaning of the expression "self-mastery."

"It seems to me that such an expression professes to say that with regard to the soul, inside the same man there is a better (part) and a worse, and whenever by nature the better is master of the worse, this is called "self-mastery." One applauds it, at any rate. And whenever the better part, being smaller, is mastered by the worse part, which is larger, owing to evil rearing or company, this is censured and one so disposed is called "yielding to himself" or "undisciplined."

"It looks like that."

"Now, consider our new city, and you will find therein one or the other of these (conditions). For you will say that (the city) is justly called self-mastered if the better rules the worse and it is reputed to be moderate and master of itself."

"I do consider it, and you have spoken truly."

"And again you will find a host of motley appetites, pleasures, and pains, above all among children, women, household slaves, and among the masses and common people (*en tois pollois te kai phaulois*) who are called free."

"Just so."

"But you will find simple and moderate (appetites) which are managed by reason along with intellect and right belief, in only a few (*en oligois*), and these are the best by nature and best by education."

"True."

"And do you not see within your city, that the appetites within the masses and the common people are mastered by the appetites and the prudent judgment within those who are fewer in number and most reasonable?"

"I do."

"If then, there is need to call any city master of its pleasures and appetites, and master of itself by itself, then this (city which we have just described) is to be called thus."

"Absolutely."

To Plato self-mastery was thus a situation in which a small upper portion, characterized by moderation and lofty intellect, ruled over a large lower portion, characterized by base appetites. In the individual, we might refer to such a state as ego control; in society, as class domination.[29]

Like *Manu*, Plato thus combined a detailed description of the workings and organization of social classes with a myth in which bodily parts and social classes were set in homologic relation to one another. These two accounts find strong, although partial, correspondences in the Slavic, Iranian, and Celtic sources I have discussed. One difference, however, must be noted between the myth in *Manu* and that in Plato: whereas the former recounts how the constituent classes of society were created *from* the body of the first man, the latter tells how the essential characteristics of those classes were placed *into* the body of the first man.[30] Elsewhere Plato argued that any just (*dikaios*) man—which is to say, any man fit to rule—would combine within himself these three separate parts, each in its proper place (*Rep* 434DE, 435B, E, 441DE, inter alia). The just man, like the first man, is thus a social microcosm, combining all three social orders within himself and resolving their differences. From such an individual—and only from such an individual—a proper society could emerge, for in such a one all the necessary constituents were conjoined. It is no accident that in many IE creation accounts, this first-man figure (to whom Plato's "just man" corresponds) was specified as the first king.[31]

Kings were thus viewed as the alloform of society in its normal hierarchical differentiation. A corollary of this is the fact that there was no specialized royal class evident among the Indo-Europeans: kings were not themselves a part of the stratified social system, but somehow stood apart from it.[32] Yet sociogonic myths regularly recount how from division of the first king's body (or realm) the three social classes were formed, and how in each king's body (or realm) those classes were fused, the king himself being a social microcosm. Recently, in two probing studies of rituals of royal investiture in ancient India and Ireland, Daniel Dubuisson has shown that the transformation of a member of the warrior class into a king was accomplished by priests, who bestowed upon him a set of carefully chosen symbolic items, each of which represented one of the three social classes.[33] Upon receipt of this set of gifts, he left his warrior identity behind, and was regarded as a person who transcended all class distinctions and allegiances. Moreover, there is a classic mythic treatment of such royal investiture: Herodotos 4.5–6, which preserves the Skythian creation account.

> The Skyths say that they themselves are the youngest of all peoples, and this is how it came to be so. A first man was born in that earth, which had been desolate. His name was Targitaos. The parents of

this Targitaos, they say—I don't trust it—were Zeus and the daughter of the river Borysthenes (the Dnepr). This was the lineage from which Targitaos was born, and of him were born three sons: Lipoxais, Arpoxais, and Kolaxais, the youngest. In the time of beginnings, certain gold objects fell from the sky to Skythia: a plow and a yoke, a Skythian sword, and a libation cup.[34] Seeing these first, the oldest went nearer, planning to take them, but the gold burst into flame as he—wishing to remove it—approached. Then the second (son) approached, and it happened again. When they had departed from the flaming gold, the fire died out just as the third, the youngest, came near, and he carried it off to his own home. The older brothers then agreed to give over the kingship to the youngest.

And from Lipoxais are descended those Skyths who are called the Aukhatai class (*genos*); and from the middle (brother), those who are called Katiaroi and also Traspies; and from the youngest himself, from the king, those who are called Paralatai. And the name of all together is the Skolotoi, an eponym from the king. The Greeks named them Skyths.

It must be stressed that there are two different sections to this myth that, while closely interrelated, are still separate in their structure. The second of these (Hdt 4.6) is rather like the story of Frēdōn's sons: a sociogony on the dynastic pattern in which the three social classes are divided among three brothers, as is clear from the most convincing interpretation yet offered of the name given to the four *genē* founded by the sons of Targitaos—himself the first man, son of heaven and earth.[35] Thus, as almost all authorities have recognized, the Greek form *Paralatai* renders Iranian *Paraδāta* "foremost" or "first created," with a lambda (Λ) replacing a delta (Δ) through a simple graphic error. In the Younger Avesta and later Iranian texts, *Paraδāta-* is a royal title, particularly associated with a first-king figure renowned for his victories over sorcerers and demons, Haošyaɳha Paraδāta.[36] Yet—like Indo-Iranian *Kavi-*, a priestly title that came to denote a type of sacred ruler in Iran—*Paraδāta* originally denoted a priestly sovereign, as is indicated by the cognate Sanskrit term *purohita-*, the title given to the priest who serves as a king's chamberlain, advising the king on all things and providing sacred direction to his reign.[37]

If the Paralatai thus represented the priestly or sovereign class, the Aukhatai were warriors, their name being derived from Iranian *augah-* "(physical) force" (GAv *aogah-*, YAv *aojah-*; Skt *ojas-*), to which a Skythian plural in *-tai* has been added: they were thus "the forces," or perhaps "the strong."[38] Finally there were the two groups descended from Arpoxais, the Traspies and the Katiaroi, whose names are somewhat more opaque. All that can be said with any confidence is that they seem to have been connected with herding of livestock, for the element -*aspa*- "horse" (Av *aspa*-, Skt *aśva*-) is certainly present in the name *Traspies*,[39] and *-čahr-* "pasture" perhaps yielded the element -*tiaro* in *Katiaroi*.[40] If this is so, Traspies and Katiaroi alike represented the commoner class. The full passage (4.6) thus describes how the social classes were distributed among and derived from the three sons of the first man.

The first section of the myth (Hdt 4.5) is quite different, however: instead of the creation of the three social classes from a primordial unity embodied in the first man (Targitaos), we are told how the first king (Kolaxais) was created from the diversity of the three social classes. For the fiery golden objects that descend from the sky as gifts of the gods are unmistakably emblems of the three classes: the yoke and plow represent the commoners, suggesting their production of food and wealth through herding and agriculture; the sword, the warriors and their force of arms; the cup, which is used for the pouring of libations, as the independent testimony of Curtius Rufus makes clear, the priestly class.[41] But what must be stressed is that Kolaxais became king—and also eponymous ancestor of the Skyths[42]—when he received *all* of the golden objects, for at that moment the three social classes merged in him. Having become a total, all-encompassing social microcosm, he was fit to rule.[43]

The myth of Kolaxais and the gold objects is thus the reverse of the account of how Targitaos's sons founded the social classes. And if the latter is rightly considered as a sociogony, a new term is needed for the Kolaxais story. At the risk of unduly multiplying neologisms, I suggest calling it a "regiogony"—a myth of the origin of kingship, regiogony and sociogony being understood as symmetric counterparts like cosmogony and anthropogony, sacrifice and nutrition, disposal of hair and cures for baldness. Insofar as the king and the social hierarchy are alloforms of one another, when the one is created, it can only be created from the other: the unity within the king divides into the social classes, and the diversity of the classes merges into the king.

An important Irish legend, the story of Lugaid Red Stripes; displays the same alternation of sociogony and regiogony evident in the Skythian myth. Although parts of this pseudohistory are preserved in numerous sources, nowhere is it given in full, and we must piece it together from various overlapping versions.[44] The first act of the drama does not involve Lugaid himself, but tells of a rebellion against his grandfather, Eochaid Feidleich, high king of Tara. This rebellion culminated in the battle of Druim Criaich, and it is within a discussion of this place name that the *Rennes Dindsenchas* (140) tells us the following:

> Whence is Druim Criaich named?
> That's not difficult. At first, its name was Druim n-Airthir ("Eastern Ridge"), until the three Find-eamna gave battle to their father there: to Eochaid Feidleich, the king of Ireland. Bres and Nár and Lóthar were their names, because they were reared at Emain Macha—or, because *eamain* ("twins, triplets") means all things that are bound together, and they were born all at one birth . . .

I will consider the individual names of these rebellious brothers later, but for now note their collective title: *Find-eamna*, for which the passage offers two possible etymologies.[45] Of these, the first—which relates the brothers' name to the putative site of their birth, Emain Macha (itself named for twins born to Macha)—has little to recommend it. The second, however, is of considerable interest. For OIr *e(a)main* (also *emuin*) does mean "twins" and is also attested elsewhere to mean "triplets." Moreover, it is derived from PIE **yemo-no-*, an extension built upon the same root from which we have the names of numerous mythic figures of the first-man/first-king type: Skt *Yama*, Av *Yima*, Lt *Remus* (with a deformation of the initial consonant), and ON *Ymir*.[46] The three sons of Eochaid Feidleich, then, seem to have been known as the White (OIr *find*) Triplets or the White Twins.

The *Dindsenchas* account goes on to tell how the brothers marched across Ireland with their army, and also describes certain scandalous carryings-on with their sister, Clothru (of which more later). Eochaid, meanwhile, raised an army against his sons, and attempted to win a month's truce from them before giving battle. When they refused, "Eochaid cursed them then, and said: 'May they be like their names' " (*beidid mar tad a n-anmann*). Battle was joined, and the Find-eamna defeated. Their army shattered, the brothers fled, only to be tracked down, killed, and beheaded. Then, the *Dindsenchas* tells us, "They took the three heads to Druim Criaich toward night, and then Eochaid issued a proclamation that no son would take the sovereignty of Tara from that time onward without someone coming between (him and his father)."

As always, the *Dindsenchas* is interested above all in the origin of place names, and here it offers the dreadful folk etymology of Druim Criaich from *ria n-aidchi*, because the severed heads of the defeated Find-eamna were carried to their father "toward night" (*ria n-aidchi*).

But if this piece of wordplay is of little interest to us, other etymological lore is crucial to any understanding of the story's import. This is signaled by Eochaid's curse: *"May they be like their names."* What do these names—Bres, Nár, and Lóthar—mean?

Among the first to struggle with this problem was Whitley Stokes, whose translation of the *Rennes Dindsenchas* remains standard. In parentheses inserted into his translation, Stokes rendered these names "Noise and Shame and Trough," systematically employing the most pejorative sense that could be borne by each of the common Irish nouns *bres, nár,* and *lóthar,* that is, the sense he considered most appropriate for a curse. In so doing he seriously misrepresented the normal denotation of these words, and led others to misunderstand the structure and significance of the story.[47] Let us thus consider these words once again.

To begin, *bres* has the primary meaning "fight, battle, combat," as in the common phrases *bri co mbreis* "cause of combat" and *bai bresse* "advantage in combat." Derived from the PIE verb **bhr(e)i-*, "to cut, break, wound," it is closely related to Breton *brezel* "war" and Welsh *brwydr* "battle," the latter coming from a form **bhrei-trā-*. Only as a secondary development does *bres* carry the sense of "noise, uproar, din," particularly to denote the tumult of battle.[48]

Still more misleading is Stokely's treatment of OIr *nár,* which has as its primary denotation "noble, magnanimous, honorable, modest," as is made clear in the indigenous glosses. Thus, O'Clery's Glossary defines *nár* as "good, noble" (*maith*), while O'Davoren's Glossary gives two definitions. The first of these is "high, noble" (*uasal*), while the second is more elaborate: "*nár* means generous (*fial*) or full (*lán*) or holy (*noeb*) or true (*idan*)." Used of people and things, *nár* occurs often as an adjective of kings and of heaven, and is derived from PIE **ner-* "man, male," from which are also derived Welsh *ner* "hero," Bret *nerz* "force, might" (= OIr *nert*, Welsh and Cornish *nerth* "manliness" < PIE **ner-to-*), and Skt *nara-*, Av *nar-*, Gk *anēr*, all of which mean "man, male." Occasionally, *nár* occurs with the secondary sense of "diffident, abashed"—although the Royal Irish Academy's *Dictionary of the Irish Language* marks this definition with a question mark, adding that as a tertiary development the term came at times to denote that which causes diffidence or shame, whence Stokely's tendentious translation.[49]

Only for *lóthar* (earlier *loathar*) did Stokely preserve the usual sense of the term, which is glossed variously by Lt *pelvis* "basin," *alveus* "trough," and *canalis* "channel, canal," and also by OIr *coire* "kettle, tub." The word thus apparently denotes low-lying vessels for water, a sense thoroughly consistent with its derivation from PIE **lou-* "to

wash." Other nouns formed from this verb with the same agent suffix
-tro- display similar meanings: Bret *lovazr* "trough"; Gall *lautro* "bath";
Gk *loutron* "bath"; ON *lauðr*, OE *lēaþor* "soap, lather."[50]

In place of Stokely's "Noise and Shame and Trough," then, we
would do better to translate these names as "Combat, Noble, and
Washing Vessel." But what can be the sense of this? Consideration of
texts describing the second act of the story of Lugaid Red Stripes will
help to resolve this problem.

As numerous sources relate, the night before the battle of Druim
Criaich, the three Find-eamna were approached by their sister, Clothru,
who cried out to them in lamentation for her childless state and persuaded them all to have sexual relations with her.[51] As a result of this
incestuous union, she conceived a son, who came to be known as
Lugaid Raib nDearg or Lugaid Reo nDerg, "Lugaid Red Stripes," as
the result of an anatomical peculiarity. A text devoted to explicating
the "Fitness of Names" (*Coir Anman* 105) describes this as follows:

> *Lugaid Reo nDerg:* this means "Red (*derg*) Stripe (*sriab*)." Two red
> stripes were around him: a belt around his neck and a belt around
> his waist. His head looked like Nár ["Noble"], his breast like Bres
> ["Combat"], and from the belt downward, he looked like Lóthar
> ["Washing Vessel"].

Lugaid's triple paternity thus resulted in a triple resemblance, the
nature of his three fathers—the White Triplets—fusing in his very
body. Moreover, a specific bodily locus was assigned to each one: the
head to the noble Nár, the upper torso to the martial Bres, and the
lower torso to the lowly Lóthar, who—to judge from his name—may
be associated with dirt, impurity, and service. This system of correlating social classes to vertical bodily strata is precisely that found in
other variants on the sociogonic and regiogonic pattern: Plato, the
Puruṣasūkta, SGW 1.20–24, the "Poem on the Dove King," and others.[52]

It now becomes clear that the first act of the Irish drama—that
centering on the Find-eamna—is sociogonic. It tells of the creation of
the three separate classes from the king, and concludes that the Find-
eamna were unsuited for kingship precisely because they represent
the divisive, rebellious tendency of the classes in separation. The second act, however—that centering on Lugaid Red Stripes—is regiogonic, describing the reunion of all three classes within a single
individual, who by merging all classes within himself transcends class
antagonisms and is thus ideally suited to be king. And indeed, other
texts still relate how Lugaid ascended to the high kingship of Tara,

having been tutored by Cu Chulainn himself, elected within a ritual Bull Festival (*Tarbfess*), and acclaimed by the hosts of Ireland. Succeeding the great Conaire Mór (who followed Eochaid), Lugaid reigned wisely and well for twenty-six years.[53] And although it is less than certain, there may be another sociogonic episode in the final act of his story, for Lugaid was killed by a group of three men who had slain other great kings, Conaire and Conall Cernach, before him. Moreover, the names of these three, who are known collectively as the Three Redheads (*na trí Ruadcind*), have some suggestion of class identify: White Man (*Fer Gel*), Choice Man (*Fer Roguin*), and Lomna the Fool or Lomna the Lewd (*Lomna Druth*).[54] The cycle thus passes from kingship and unity (Eochaid) to class division and strife (the three Find-eamna) to kingship and unity (Lugaid Red Stripes) to division and strife once more (the Three Redheads): sociogony and regiogony ever alternating, "motionless in the cycle."

It may be helpful now to step back from the details of specific texts and to seek some generalizations. At the start of this chapter, I posed three questions: What have the myths to say about the nature of society? Who propagated such myths? Who benefited from their propagation? I am ready to answer the first of these, and the process of so doing should make the answers to the other two become clear.

Two interrelated themes recur in the myths considered in this chapter, dealing explicitly with social issues. These I have called the sociogony and the regiogony—stories of the creation of the social hierarchy and of kingship. Of these, the first was told in two different fashions. First, the sacrificial pattern (as in *RV* 10.90.11–12, *Manu* 1.87–93, the "Poem on the Dove King," *SGW* 1.20–24, and *Yašt* 19.30–39) tells how the first man—who is often also the first king[55]—was dismembered, and from the pieces of his body the three distinctive social classes came into being: priests from his head, warriors from his chest and arms, commoners from his abdomen, genitals, and legs. The second pattern is the dynastic pattern (as in *Ayādgār i Jāmāspīg* 4.39– 41, *Germania* 2, Herodotos 4.6, and the story of the Find-eamna), which presents similar ideas while making use of genealogic and/or topographic rather than sacrificial imagery. Here, instead of the first king himself being divided, it is his realm and/or progeny that are divided into three portions, each of which is associated with one of the social classes—one marked by ritual and intellectual capabilities, one by physical and martial abilities, and one by service to the other units and the production of wealth through herding and agriculture.

In both of these patterns of sociogonic myth, the king and the social hierarchy are presented as alloforms of each other. The king was equivalent to a social microcosm, and creation flowed from him. The dispersed population, divided into classes of priests, warriors, and commoners, was but the king writ large, for the king incarnated and represented the total social unit. Society was dependent upon the king for its very existence, and when he took action he acted not just *on behalf of* society as a whole, but *as the very embodiment* of the social totality.

Beyond this sweeping homology king/society, precise homologies were posited for each of the three social classes, these being priests/ head, warriors/upper torso, commoners/lower torso. A vertical hierarchy was thus established in which the group smallest in numbers, the priests, occupied the position of highest authority and prestige, followed by the warriors, and the largest group, the commoners, came last. As alloforms of the head, priests pursued intellectual matters; warriors, as alloforms of the arms and chest, fought and showed courage; commoners, as alloforms of the legs, quite literally supported the other two classes. Associated also with the belly and the genitals, commoners were expected to be concerned with the production of food and the reproduction of population, and to possess near-insatiable appetites.

In contrast, regiogonic accounts such as *Timaios* 69D-70A, Herodotos 4.5, the story of Lugaid Red Stripes, and the investiture rituals studied by Dubuisson,[56] reversed the process of the sociogony. Kings— following the model of the first king—were created when the essential characteristics of the three social classes were placed within or upon their bodies. The exercise of kingship thus demanded priestly intellect, warrior might, *and* the powers of production and reproduction characteristic of commoners, while proper kings were expected to ensure the well-being of *all* their people. Being presented thus as an individual whose identity and allegiance were to the total society and not to any specific class, the king was expected to rise above or even reconcile any potential class conflicts. Such reconciliation, however, might realistically be expected to take the form of support for the established hierarchy in which priests outrank commoners as the head outranks the body. Indeed, even in a king the head should outrank the body, and an evil king—of which there were, no doubt, all too many—was one in whom the belly ruled.

What I have presented thus far, however, is only the social ideology encoded in IE creation myths. As such, it presents more a picture of how things ought to be than how things were, describing the social order in the best light.[57] But an ideology—any ideology—is not just an ideal against which social reality is measured or an end toward the fulfillment of which groups and individuals aspire. It is also, and this is much more important, a screen that strategically veils, mystifies, or distorts important aspects of real social processes. Like any other ideology, myth largely serves to create false consciousness in many members of society, persuading them of the *rightness* of their lot in life, whatever that may be, and of the total social order.

It is thus important to examine the descriptions of social organization and relations contained in such texts as *Mēnōg i Xrad* 31, Caesar's *Bello Gallico* 6.13–15, Plato's *Republic* 431A-D (and more broadly, Books 3 and 4 as a whole), and the *Mānava Dharmaśāstra* 1.87–93. When these are read with a critical, dialectically analytic eye, IE social structures and processes appear somewhat different from their mythic (that is, ideological) representation.

Thus, I would argue that we may accurately view the priestly class as an elite intelligentsia, devoted not only to speculation on the nature of man and the cosmos, together with the performance of rituals attendant to such speculation, but also to the propagation of a social ideology encoded in sociogonic and regiogonic myths. Although the smallest class numerically, priests were the highest hierarchically, and they possessed disproportionately large quantities of wealth, power, and prestige. While the claim was made—and sincerely believed—that the entire order of the cosmos depended on priests' fully knowledgeable performance of sacrifice, at a more mundane level it is apparent that the activities of priests were not directly productive in a material sense. Priests were, in fact, wholly dependent on the labor of other classes for their material support. No sacrifice ever produced food *de novo*, and other people had to work in order for priests to eat. The priestly class, in large measure, was a leisure class, permitted the luxury of lengthy training—Caesar mentions twenty years (*BG* 6.14), and Indic sources up to thirty-six (*Manu* 3.1)—followed by a lifetime free from manual labor. In this they were supported by a steady flow of institutionalized generosity—gifts, tribute, stipends, and the like—in exchange for which they provided such nonmaterial services as recitation of prayers, performance of rituals, and working of magical cures.

The class of priests was effectively the ideological apparatus of society. As such, the priests propagated myths—the mode of ideology most characteristic of the preindustrial world—that encoded the dominant, normative view of reality, cosmic as well as social. We must be careful not to denigrate unduly the ideological activity of these priests, or to impugn their sincerity and integrity. It is important not to adopt a facile anticlericalism in our attitude toward them.[58] Priests viewed themselves as discovering, articulating, and transmitting the most sacred and profound of all truths, in which were revealed nothing less than the fundamental structures of reality—cosmic as well as social. Their self-image must not be mistaken for objective reality, however, nor can we take their truth-claims at face value. However much these priests felt themselves to be concerned with sacred and eternal truths, their actual concern was a set of ideas and norms peculiar to a certain society and period of history, which enabled that society—among other things—to organize and replicate itself along hierarchic and exploitative lines. And the norms and ideas they propagated granted the priests a position of great power and privilege. Here was a classic symbiosis of ideological and sociomaterial factors, in which the privileged position of priests permitted them to formulate and disseminate a brilliantly persuasive ideology, while that ideology—among its other effects—chartered and legitimated the privileged position of priests.

Warriors also benefited from the myths propagated by priests, for although subordinate to priests, they were consistently classed as a "noble" class.[59] If the priestly class may be considered as the ideological apparatus of society, the warrior class must be seen as its coercive apparatus, for the warriors possessed an effective monopoly on the legitimate use of force. Such force might be used purely defensively, to repel enemy attacks, or it might be applied aggressively in raiding and warfare, in which livestock, booty, and pasture lands were won. Unlike those of the priests, warriors' activities were materially productive, as victory in battle yielded not only increased wealth but also an increased food supply.[60]

Aggressive and defensive actions alike directed warriors' violence toward external enemies, which is to say, non-Indo-Europeans. Yet there was another utilization of warriors' might: repression of the commoner class. For among the Indo-European peoples, as in any stratified society, the lower social orders ever posed a potential threat to the privileged classes: the threat that they might seek to disrupt the status quo and redress its inequities. This threat being potential only, in most instances the repressive use of warriors' violence remained also potential. The threat of repressive force was itself sufficient to act as a powerful check on unrest.

Moreover, the sociogonic myth chartered and legitimated repression in two important ways, as Plato recognized.[61] First, warriors were placed above commoners, pressing down upon them just as the upper torso presses down on the lower torso. Second, the commoners were believed to have excessive, uncontrollable appetites, for sex as well as for food, because they were formed from bodily alloforms that included the belly and the genitals. Such appetites—which might, for example, take the form of demands for a larger share of the food that the commoners themselves produced—were to be held in check by the superior rational control of the priests and the superior force of the warriors.

Another danger, which Plato also recognized, was perhaps even more threatening to the social order than potential unrest among the commoners: loss of control over the warrior class.[62] For if the warriors once began to pursue their own self-interest instead of overall stability, there was little that could effectively stop them.[63] Against such an eventuality, however, numerous checks existed. First, the warriors were supplied with a large share of the available wealth, power, and prestige, to avoid their possible discontent. Second, desires for more of these valued commodities were condemned as greedy or appetitive behavior more appropriate to the commoner class than to the upper classes.[64] Third, warriors and priests were grouped together and defined as "noble" classes, so that warriors felt themselves closely allied to priests and separated from commoners by a wide gulf. Fourth, warriors felt that they held a large share of political power by virtue of the fact that kings always came from the warrior class. Finally, most important of all, the subordination of warriors to priests was firmly established as rightful or natural, being chartered by the sociogonic myth.

Mythic ideology also provided the key for control of the commoner class. For while the commoners were potentially the most powerful class in IE societies, being largest numerically and effectively controlling the internal means of production (herding, agriculture, and artisanry, as well as trade), they remained ever at the bottom of the hierarchy, supporting their class superiors and accepting as rightful their lowly station. Much less than the coercive force of warriors— although that was there if needed—it was the ideological hegemony of priests that kept commoners in their place.[65] Successful propagation of the sociogonic and regiogonic myths among the commoner class resulted in false consciousness for the commoners, and this false consciousness made it nearly impossible for them to dispute their lot in life. For the myth established it as a given—that is to say, as something right, normative, and eternally true—that the commoners should support the upper classes just as (or even, within the logic of the myth, *because*) the lower torso supports the upper body. Further, the myth established that the commoners should be lower hierarchically than the "noble" classes, just as (or again, *because*) the lower torso sits beneath the rest of the body. And finally, if the lower classes suffered repression, this too was established as rightful, for the weight of the upper body does, quite literally, press down upon its lower members.

The material consequence of such a view was that the commoners turned over a large share of the wealth they produced to members of the "noble" classes. "Gifts," tribute, stipends of various sorts were expected, and these enabled the upper classes to devote their time and energies to pursuits other than productive labor. In return for the "gifts" they proffered, commoners received ritual and ideological services from the priests, and "protection" from the warriors.[66] While Indo-European populations—commoners as well as nobles—viewed this as an exchange that was beneficial to the commoners, an outside observer may be permitted some doubts.

There is one further aspect to the ideological subjugation of the commoner class, a time-honored strategy of ruling elites everywhere: blaming the victim. Mythically homologized to the lower portion of the body—the ignoble region "below the navel," as *Manu* 1.91 put it— commoners were associated with the belly, the genitals, the anus, and the feet. At best regarded by their class superiors with condescension, often with contempt, commoners were thus characterized as greedy, appetitive, lascivious, and dirty. Insofar as these characterizations were accepted as part of the commoners' own (false) consciousness, they engendered feelings of self-worthlessness and supported the conclusion that the myths were right in their depiction of the commoners' origin and proper place.

In times of greatest hardship, commoners always felt that they could turn to the king, and there was a sound ideological foundation for this sentiment. As established in the regiogony, the king transcended class divisions and thus had the commoners' interests at heart as much as those of the upper classes. The king was expected to be just and truthful (supposedly attributes of the priestly class) brave and protective (like the warriors), but he was also expected to be generous (like the commoners), and could be turned to in time of need.[67] Yet again, one must stress the difference between ideology and actual practice. However much a king was *supposed* (in the sense of "ought" and that of "believed") to transcend class boundaries and antagonisms, kings in reality rarely, if ever, did so. Born to the warrior class, tutored and advised by priests, the interests of kings remained firmly with the upper classes.

In contrast to the official ideology of the king as himself a social microcosm stands the damning popular appellation of king as "eater of the masses." Consider, for example, Akhilles' denunciation of Agamemnon in *Iliad* 1.223–232:

> And Akhilles answered Agamemnon
> With baleful words, and did not lay down his anger at all:
> "Wine-sodden one, you with the eyes of a dog and heart of a deer—
> You have never dared in your breast to arm yourself for battle
> Along with the host, nor to go into ambush
> With the best of the Akhaians: that seems to you to be death itself.
> Truly, it's better for you to carry off the gifts
> Of anyone throughout the broad army of the Akhaians who speaks against you.
> You king, devourer of the masses (*dēmoboros basileus*), you rule over worthless men—
> For otherwise, son of Atreus, you would now commit outrages for the last time."

Akhilles here draws on a well-established set of images appropriate to satire and the poetry of blame.[68] Of particular interest to us are the comparison of the king to a timid deer (when a king more properly ought act like a lion, bull, or other proud, powerful beast), and the accusation that he is one who feeds on the members of the lower social class (the *dēmos*), instead of seeing to it that they are fed. These images recur in an Indic text, *Śatapatha Brāhmaṇa* 13.2.9.8, in which an explication is offered for the ritual formula "When the deer eats the grain":

> "When the deer eats the grain"—truly, the grain is the common people (*viś*) and the deer is the kingship, for (the king) makes the common people into something to be eaten for the good of the kingship. Therefore, the kingship eats the common people (*rāṣṭro viśam atti*).

No phonological correspondences exist between the Gk *dēmoboros basileus* and the Skt *rāṣṭro viśam atti*. Rather than reflecting a precise poetic phrasing that existed at some point in linguistic prehistory, they seem to indicate a more general language of invective that was commonly used—in either anger, satire, or dispassionate description (as is the case in the *SB* passage)—to discuss a side of kingship well known to the people but conveniently omitted from the official ideology. Although the phrase "eater of the masses" does not occur, the same perceptions and attitudes encoded in this phrase are evident in an Irish myth of the origin of satiric verse. The story, recounted in *Cath Maige Turedh* 36–40, has it that the primordial king Bres exacted undue services from his people and failed to show generosity to them: in particular, he did not give them adequate food or drink. Finally, when Bres gave the poet Corpre extremely meager fare (three dry cakes), Corpre composed a satire against the king—the first of its kind. So powerful was this satire that Bres was deprived of the kingship as a result. Later, when asked by his father what had lost him his rule, Bres responded: "Nothing save my own untruth and arrogance. I defrauded them of their wealth and their treasures and their own food." Quite distant from the official, dominant, or hegemonic ideology of kingship as presented in sociogonic and regiogonic myths, where the king appears as a perfect individual and reconciler of class divisions, is the picture presented in this popular, unofficial, or counter-hegemonic (but equally traditional) ideology, in which the exploitative and oppressive side of kingship leaps into prominent relief.

The evidence and the kinds of issues considered in this chapter may seem rather different from those in Chapters 1–6. There, I concentrated primarily on myths and their correlated rituals that had a cosmic focus: that struggled to make sense of heaven and earth, life and death, time and eternity, as well as such mundane affairs as broken bones, digestion, and baldness. All these and more were integrated within the same mythic schema, bound together in a rich synthetic understanding of the nature of the universe. In contrast, the myths and correlated rituals treated in this chapter have a social focus: indeed, they provided the ideological legitimation for an exploitative and oppressive—and exceedingly stable—social hierarchy. For the sake of analytic clarity I have treated the cosmic and social sides of this Indo-European tradition as if they were separate, but in fact they are inextricably intertwined. Like the dismembered pieces of the first victim's body, they can and must be put back together again. Having analyzed the tradition's various contents—that is to say, having broken it down into constituent parts in ways reminiscent of sacrificial dismemberment—I must now resynthesize those contents and restore the sundered unity.

The general lines of the creation myths common among the Indo-European peoples are, *au fond,* relatively simple, telling how a primordial victim (or victims) was (were) cut into pieces and put back together. The subtleties and complexities derive not from this core narrative but from the alloformic homologies with which the core was elaborated. Among these were the homologies man/cosmos, with separate homologies for the various bodily parts (eyes/sun, flesh/earth, and so on); king/society, with separate homologies for each of the social classes (priests/head, and so on); and lastly, cattle/food.

Using these basic homologic building blocks, priests—the intellectual and ideological specialists among the Indo-European peoples—told and retold variants of the myth, explicating them and applying their specific contents and general structure to ever more areas of human experience and activity, which were explicitly or implicitly synthesized to one another. Thus, for instance, sacrifice was shown to be a process homologous to cosmogony. It being also demonstrated that death was a process homologous to cosmogony, the conclusion logically followed that death and sacrifice were homologous as well. To this set could also be added the division of society into stratified classes, for all of these processes (and others as well) were but variations on a common pattern in which a microcosmic unity was broken into pieces, pieces that were then transmuted into macrocosmic alloforms. Conversely, all instances where scattered macrocosmic entities were transmuted into microcosmic alloforms and then (re)united were also homologous: nutrition, healing, royal investiture, and the like.

The fantastic persuasive power—the real genius—of such a system is its potential for synthesis. One feels that there was absolutely nothing that might not be satisfactorily subsumed within the pattern of homologic thought, which sought to integrate all existence within one encompassing structure.[69] When members of the priestly class successfully propagated at least a superficial understanding of this powerful system of religious ideology through all social strata, two major results followed. First, people of all classes felt the cosmos to be an intelligible and reassuring entity, a place in which death was but temporary and every destruction was followed by a restoration. Second, people of all classes felt society to be legitimate, and also reassuring: stable, eternal, well-founded, and rightful. What is more, this sentiment contributed dramatically to the *actual* stability of society.

The ability of this myth to synthesize all manner of phenomena was crucial to its persuasive power, for the greater the number and variety of entities and processes it could integrate, the greater the credence it commanded. Thus, for instance, if people accepted the interpretations of nutrition that were offered on the basis of this myth, their acceptance of that application made it easier for them to accept the myth's application to healing or to cures for baldness. Further, acceptance of this whole set of applications (nutrition-healing-baldness) facilitated and simultaneously was facilitated by acceptance of other such sets (such as sacrifice-death-disposal of hair). Every strand within the whole fabric of thought was thus reinforced by every other strand. A highly significant specific instance of this mutual reinforcement and interweaving was the way the system's cosmic contents supported its social counterpart.[70]

Employing a different terminology from mine—using "world view" instead of "cosmic contents" and "ethos" instead of "social contents"—Clifford Geertz has offered some penetrating remarks on the interrelation of cosmic and social concerns: "Religion, by fusing ethos and world view, gives to a set of social values what they perhaps most need to be coercive: an appearance of objectivity. In sacred rituals and myths values are portrayed not as subjective human preferences but as the imposed conditions for life implicit in a world with a particular structure."[71]

While the structure of the cosmos may be eternal, the structure of society certainly is not. Yet within the materials considered in this book—and the same could be said of countless others as well—the two were placed on the same plane. Sociohistoric contingencies and natural "laws" were treated within the same mythico-ritual discourse, and were endowed with the same status of utter facticity and eternal truth. To challenge any part of the system was to challenge all, and a challenge to any part could be refuted with overpowering arguments. One could not, for instance, suggest that commoners ought be the equals of priests without, as an inevitable corollary, suggesting that sacrifice did not re-create the cosmos each time it was performed, sacrifice being a process parallel to sociogony. To challenge sacrifice, moreover, forced one to argue that at death the body was not dispersed to its cosmic alloforms, death being parallel to sacrifice and sociogony alike. And if one rejected such an interpretation of death, belief in bodily resurrection had also to be rejected. In order to preserve a belief in resurrection—that most reassuring of beliefs—*out of logical necessity* one was forced to accept the subordination of commoners to priests.

Starting with a social concern, one was thus led inevitably to a cosmic concern, and vice versa. Wondrous revelations yielded to insidious ideology, which yielded in turn to wondrous revelation again. For—so it seems—among the Indo-Europeans, discourse on society and discourse on the cosmos, insidiousness and wonder, ideology and revelation, all of these were alloforms of one another.

Notes

1. Cosmogony, Anthropogony, Homology

1. See, for instance, Adolf Jensen, *Die getötete Gottheit* (Stuttgart: Syndikat Verlag, 1968); G. Hatt, "The Corn Mother in America and Indonesia," *Anthropos* 46 (1951): 853–914; and the challenging recent studies of Cristiano Grottanelli, "Cosmogonia e Sacrificio, I. Problemi delle cosmogonie 'rituali' nel R̥g Veda e nel Vicino Oriente Antico," *Studi Storico-Religiosi* 4 (1980): 207–235; idem, "Cosmogonia e Sacrificio, II. The Lord of the Dead," *Studi Storico-Religiosi* 5 (1981): 173–196.

2. In general, I have tried to avoid in this book formulations that involve positing a hypothetical "Proto-Indo-European" community, ethnic group, homeland, body of myth and religion, or social system. Rather, I prefer now to speak in terms of a shared tradition: a body of myths, ritual practices, thought about the nature of the universe and of society, that is preserved in the literatures and oral traditions of the various peoples whose languages fall within the Indo-European grouping. Multiple explanations are possible for the commonalities that can be observed: common genetic origin (the so-called *Stammbaum* theory), diffusion, overlapping circles of influence and connectedness, and so on. The whole question remains highly controversial. For some of the more recent arguments against an overhasty and uncritical acceptance of the *Stammbaum* theory, see Ulf Drobin, "Indogermanische Religion und Kultur? Eine Analyse des Begriffes Indogermanisch," *Temenos* 16 (1980): 26–38; Bernard Sergent, "Penser—et mal penser—les indo-européens," *Annales: E.S.C.* 37 (1982):669–681; Franco Crevatin, *Ricerche sull' antichità indoeuropea* (Trieste: Edizioni LINT, 1979): Cristiano Grottanelli, "Temi Dumeziliani fuori dal mondo indoeuropeo," *Opus* 2 (1983): 365–389; Paolo Ramat, "Linguistic Reconstruction and Typology," *Journal of Indo-European Studies* 4 (1976):189–206; B. Schlerath, "Ist eiu Raum/Zeit Modell für eine rekonstruierte Sprache möglich?" *Zeitschrift für vergleichende Sprachwissenschaft* 95 (1981):175–202.

3. Names meaning "Man" include Skt *Manu-*, Av **Manuš* (preserved in the name of another primordial man, *Manuš.ciθra* "Son of *Manuš), and Gmc *Mannus* (all of which are cognate, from a base form **Manu-*). Other names with the same meaning include Skt *Puruṣa* (on which see J. Otrębski, "Aind. puruṣah, pūman und Verwandtes," *Zeitschrift für vergleichende Sprachforschung* 82 [1968]: 251–258) and Lt. **Vir-inos* (in Romulus's divine name, *Quirinus* [< **Co-vir-inos*]; see Jaan Puhvel, "Remus et Frater," *History of Religions* 15 [1975]: 146–157). Gk *Minos* presents serious phonological problems, but the mythic materials remain suggestive.

Names meaning "Twin" include multiple formations from a form **yem-* "geminate." Thus, with full vowel grade, the proper names Skt *Yama-* and Lt *Remus* (the latter with deformation of the initial consonant); with full vowel grade and a suffix *-ono-*, the common nouns OIr *emuin* (which occurs in numerous creation accounts) and Lt *geminus* (used of Romulus and Remus); with zero vowel grade, the proper names ON *Ymir* and Av *Yima-*, as well as the common noun Av *yə̄ma-* (which appears in the cosmogonic myth *Y* 30.3–4). Other terms with similar meaning are Gmc *Tuisco~Tuisto* (from a form **dwis-* "double") and OPruss *Bruteno* "Brother," the first priest, who dies a sacrificial death alongside his brother the first king, in an important but as yet unstudied set of legends recorded in Simon Grunau's *Preussische Chronik* (see esp. 2.2.2–3, 2.4.1, and 2.5.3).

4. On this text see Stanislas Schayer, "A Note on the Old Russian Variant of the Purushasūkta," *Archiv Orientalnì* 7 (1935): 319–323; and V. N. Toporov, "O Strukture Nekotorykh Arkhaiceskikh Tekstov, Sootrosimykh s Koncepciej 'Mirovogo Dereva,' " *Trudy po Znakovym Sistemam* 5 (1971): esp. 43–46. The latter is extremely rich in its presentation of data and its methods; I am grateful to Jaan Puhvel for calling it to my attention. The text I have translated is found in Schayer, p. 320.

5. On the interrelation of social and cosmic levels of discourse, see my discussion in "The Tyranny of Taxonomies," Inaugural Lecture of the University of Minnesota Center for Humanistic Studies (Minneapolis: Occasional Papers of the Center for Humanistic Studies, University of Minnesota, 1985). More broadly, on the sociopolitical dimensions of myth, see my articles "Die politische Gehalt des Mythos" (with special reference to creation myths), in Hans-Peter Duerr, ed., *Alcheringa: oder die beginnende Zeit* (Frankfurt: Qumran Verlag, 1983), pp. 9–25, and "Mito, Storia, Sentimento, e Società: Osservazioni preliminari su un grande tema" (which supplants aspects of the analysis offered in the article just cited), forthcoming in *Thélema* (Cagliari).

6. See, e.g., Willibald Kirfel, *Die Kosmographie der Inder* (Bonn and Leipzig: Kurt Schroeder, 1920), pp. 3–5.

7. Julius Pokorny, *Indogermanisches etymologisches Wörterbuch*, (Bern: Francke Verlag, 1959), p.1061; Alois Walde and Julius Hofmann, *Lateinisches etymologisches Wörterbuch*, 4th ed. (Heidelberg: Carl Winter, 1972), II, 655.

8. One of the few places where it is attested is *Greater Bundahišn* 28.

9. See Manfred Mayrhofer, *Kurzgefasstes etymologisches Wörterbuch des Altindischen* (Heidelberg: Carl Winter, 1956–1976), II, 573f., 631f.; Pokorny,

Indogermanisches etym. Wb, pp. 726–728, 731–732; Carl Darling Buck, *A Dictionary of Selected Synonyms in the Principal Indo-European Languages* (Chicago: University of Chicago Press, 1949), pp. 54–55, 1198–1199.

10. I have studied this myth in two earlier works: "The Indo-European Myth of Creation," *History of Religions* 15 (1975):121–145; and *Priests, Warriors, and Cattle: A Study in the Ecology of Religions* (Berkeley: University of California Press, 1981), pp. 69–95.

The earliest significant treatments of this myth in its various versions are Wilhelm Wackernagel, "Die Anthropogonie der Germanen," *Zeitschrift für deutsches Altertum* 6 (1848):15–20, and Rudolf von Roth, "Die Sage von Dschemschid," *Zeitschrift der deutschen morgenlandischen Gesellschaft* 4 (1850):427–433. More important—indeed, fundamental—are Max Förster, "Adams Erschaffung und Namengebung," *Archiv für Religionswissenschaft* 11 (1908:477–529; Albrecht Götze, "Persische Weisheit in griechischem Gewande," *Zeitschrift für Indologie und Iranistik* 2 (1923):60–98, 167–177; and above all, Hermann Güntert, *Der arische Weltkönig und Heiland* (Halle: Max Niemeyer, 1923), pp. 315–395. Franz Rolf Schröder's attempt, in "Germanische Schopfungsmythen: Eine vergleichende religionsgeschichtliche Studie," *Germanisch-romanische Monatsschrift* 19 (1931):1–26, 81–99, to extend Güntert's arguments only served to weaken them, leading to the attack of Franz Börtzler, "Ymir: Ein Beitrag zu den eddischen Weltschöpfungsvorstellungen," *Archiv für Religionswissenschaft* 33 (1936):230–245.

More recently, see Aram M. Frenkian, "Puruṣa—Gayōmard—Anthropos," *Revue des études indo-européennes* 3 (1943): 118–131; A. W. Macdonald, "A propos de Prajāpati," *Journal asiatique* 240 (1953):323–328; G. Bonfante, "Microcosmo e macrocosmo nel mito indoeuropeo," *Die Sprache* 5 (1959):1–8; Walter Burkert, "Caesar und Romulus-Quirinus," *Historia* 11 (1962):356–376; Hoang-son Hoang-sy-Quy, "Le mythe indien de l'homme cosmique dans son contexte culturel et dans son évolution," *Revue de l'histoire des religions* 175 (1969):133–154; Giorgio Locchi, "Le mythe cosmogonique indoeuropéen: réconstruction et réalité," *Nouvelle école* 19 (1972):87–95; Jaan Puhvel, "Remus et Frater"; and Geo Widengren, "Macrocosmos—Microcosmos," *Archivio di Filosofia* (1980):297–312.

Two as yet unpublished treatments of considerable importance and value are William Sayers, "Fergus and the Cosmogonic Sword," *History of Religions* (forthcoming), and Richard Dieterle, "The Hidden Warrior: The Social Code of the Vǫlundarkviða." I am most grateful to both authors for generously sharing the results of their research with me.

Finally, on the precosmogonic state of things as imagined by the Indo-Europeans, for which we have the evidence of RV 10.129, *Manu* 1.5, *Vsp* 3, the Wessobrunner Prayer, and other related materials, see Edgar Polomé, "Vedic Speculations on the Ultimate," in Polomé, ed., *Man and the Ultimate* (Austin: Symposium of the Southwest Branch of the American Oriental Society, 1980), pp. 39–52.

11. A similar account is found in a Zoroastrian (or perhaps Zervanite) creation narrative, *PRDD* 26, a full translation of which is available in R. C.

Zaehner, *Zurvan: A Zoroastrian Dilemma* (Oxford: Oxford University Press, 1955), pp. 360–367. Here, the world is again made from a primordial being, who contains within his body particles of light. He is said to fashion creation "piece by piece" out of himself: the sky from his head, the earth from his feet, the water from his tears, plants from his hair, the primordial bull from his right hand, and fire from his mind. Of these, the homologies sky/head, water/tears, and plants/hair are well attested elsewhere: the others are rather idiosyncratic.

12. The name *Kūnī*, which has usually been thought to derive from Av *Kundī*, a demon of whom virtually nothing specific is told and who is mentioned only in *Vd* 11.9 and 11.12, is—in my opinion—more likely to have been a feminine formation from Pahl *kūn* ("anus"). Note, for instance, *GBd* 28.4: "The anus (*kūn*) is like hell underneath earth, (for) the anus is the lowest seat of the body." Text in TD Ms. 190.12–13.

13. On the theme of the imprisoned light and on the general Manichaean devaluation of the material world, see Geo Widengren, *Mani and Manichaeism* (New York: Holt, Rinehart, and Winston, 1965), pp. 45–50, 54–56.

14. Note also *Odyssey* 1.53, where Atlas is said to be guardian of the pillars of heaven, and *Theog* 517, where he holds up the sky.

15. See above all Förster, "Adams Erschaffung," pp. 487–489, 500–502, 511–521. Note also Götze, "Persische Weisheit," pp. 171–174; Güntert, *Arische Weltkönig*, pp. 328–330; and J. M. Evans, "Microcosmic Adam," *Medium Aevun* 35 (1966):38–42.

16. Thus two OE texts, the *Rituale Ecclesiae Dunelmensis* and the *Dialogue of Solomon and Saturn*.

17. One might attempt to reconstruct an IE theory of the senses and of perception working from such evidence as this text, *Manu* 1.16–20, Empedokles fragment B109, and the Welsh "Song of the Great World," (*Kanu y Byt Mawr*) from the *Book of Taliesin*. Such a project, however, is considerably beyond the scope of this book.

18. The most comprehensive study remains the masterful treatment of Max Förster, "Adams Erschaffung," in which most of the relevant primary sources are cited. See also, more recently, Evans, "Microcosmic Adam"; H. L. C. Tristram, "Der 'homo octipartitus' in der irischen und altenglischen Literatur," *Zeitschrift für celtische Philologie* 34 (1975):119–153; and Alex Wayman, "The Human Body as a Microcosm in India, Greek Cosmology, and Sixteenth-Century Europe," *History of Religions* 22 (1982):172–190.

19. Reference is made to an Enoch or Book of Enoch in the 6th-to-7th-century *List of the Sixty Books;* in the *Stichometry of Nicephorus,* written prior to the 9th century; and in Mechithat of Airivank's *List of the Secret Books of the Jews,* written around 1280; but there is no assurance that this is II Enoch and not the totally unrelated I Enoch (also referred to as the Ethiopic Enoch). Moreover, there is no assurance that the crucial passage (II Enoch 30.8–9) was found in a Gk or Lt antecedent. The plain fact is that we have no direct evidence for the existence of II Enoch prior to the 16th century, or for its circulation anywhere outside of Slavic areas. All the arguments for derivation

of the anthropogonic myth from II Enoch are inferential and circular: it does *not* follow that where one finds a story of the Eight-Part Adam, II Enoch must have circulated earlier. While this may have occurred, there is no way of proving it given the present state of the evidence.

20. Text in Wilhelm Heusler, *Altfriesisches Lesebuch* (Heidelberg: Carl Winter, 1903), pp. 87f. Similar Germanic texts include the OE *Rituale Ecclesiæ Dunelmensis* and *Dialogue of Solomon and Saturn*, as well as the MHG "Poem on the Four Gospels," quoted in Jacob Grimm, *Teutonic Mythology* (London: George Bell, 1883), II, 566.

21. Text first published in Whitley Stokes, *Three Irish Glossaries* (London: Williams and Nordgate, 1862), pp. xl–xli; also in Tristram, "Der 'Homo Octipartitus'," p. 120. For further Irish materials, see David Greene and Fergus Kelly, eds., *The Irish Adam and Eve Story from Saltair na Rann* (Dublin: Dublin Institute for Advanced Studies, 1976), esp. canto 152, sts. 41–43.

22. Discussed in Förster, "Adams Erschaffung," pp. 477–478, 483–484. The fullest discussion of this text in a western language is R. Nachtigall, "Ein Beitrag zu den Forschungen über die sogenannte 'Bes"da Trex" Svjatitelej' (Gespräch dreier Heiligen)," *Archiv für slavische Philologie* 23 (1901):1–95; 24 (1902):321–408. While most authorities have seen the "Poem on the Dove King" as derived from the "Discourse of the Three Saints" (thus Schayer, "Old Russian Variant," pp. 322f., although he questions this conclusion at points), a theory of such simple textual dependency is quite impossible. Schayer (p. 323) stresses that the sociogony (which I have labeled part B) of the "Dove King" finds no antecedent either in the "Discourse of the Three Saints" or in any other Slavic text, and the same is true of the anthropogonic section (part C).

23. Text in Vatroslav Jagič, "Slavische Beiträge zu den biblischen Apocryphen. I. Die altkirchenslavischen Texte des Adambuches," *Denkschriften der Kaiserlichen Akademie der Wissenschaften* (Vienna), *Philosophisch-Historische Classe* 24 (1893):60.

24. Text in Förster, "Adams Erschaffung," pp. 527f.

25. The convincing arguments for grouping Russ *kost'*, Hitt *ḥaštai*, and Lt *costa* within this reconstruction were advanced primarily by André Martinet, for a summary of whose views see Edgar Polomé, "The Laryngeal Theory So Far," in Werner Winter, ed., *Evidence for Laryngeals* (The Hague: Mouton, 1965), p. 38. See also Max Vasmer, *Russisches etymologisches Wörterbuch*, 3 vols. (Heidelberg: Carl Winter, 1953–1958), I, 643, with a summary of the earlier literature, prior to the development of laryngeal theory, in which a $*k$- prefix was regularly suggested.

26. Examples of such detailed analyses are found in the *Greater Bundahišn* 28 and the Pseudo-Hippokratic *Peri Hebdomadōn*, ch. 6, both of which will be treated later in this chapter. An interesting set of Irish myths that depends on the homology urine/swamp has been studied by William Sayers, "The Mythology of Loch Meagh," *Mankind Quarterly* (forthcoming).

27. It is worth quoting one of these two texts here, for they exhibit wide and interesting variation from the forms in which these homologies are more usually given. Many of their novel features are also shared with a 9th-century

text in Latin, filed as Vatican Codex Reg. 846, folio 106b, the text of which is given in Förster, "Adams Erschaffung," p. 495. The following is the text of the *Rituale Ecclesiae Dunelmensis,* which in content (although not in style) is virtually identical to the *Dialogue of Solomon and Saturn.*

Concerning the eight pounds from which Adam is made.
From eight pounds of these Adam is made:
A pound of loam, from that flesh is made.
A pound of fire, from that the blood is red and hot.
A pount of salt, from that are salt tears.
A pound of dew, from that sweat is made.
A pound of blossoms, from that is the coloration of the eyes.
A pound of clouds, from that is the unsteadiness and instability of thought.
A pound of wind, from that is the cold breath.
A pound of grace, from that is man's thought.

28. See de Vries, *Altnordisches etym Wb,* p. 567; Pokorny, *Indogermanisches etym Wb,* p. 1043. That Snorri Sturlason understood *sveiti* in this passage to denote "blood" is suggested by his presentation of the homology as one of blood *(blóð)* and sea or water in *Gylf* 8, a passage in which he made clear use of the *Grímnismál* text.

29. Tears/sea appears in Vatican Codex Reg. 846; blood/dew in II Enoch 30.9; sweat/libation in *TB* 2.1.2.1; semen/water in *Ait Up* 1.4 and 2.4; urine/rain in *BṛhadUp* 1.1; and sweat/dew in *Rituale Ecclesiæ Dunelmensis.*

30. For instance, Arm *aregakn* "sun," originally a compound meaning "eye (akn) of the sun (*arew*)," on which see Antoine Meillet, *Esquisse d'une grammaire comparée de l'armenien classique,* 2nd ed. (Vienna: Imprimerie des Pères Mekhitharistes, 1936), p. 50. One of the very few surviving pieces of old Armenian poetry preserves the homology of eyes and sun, along with a less common homology of the red beard of the hero Vahagn (whose birth is being described) and fire. The text is found in Moses Xorenaci 1.31: "Truly, he had flames as his beard/And his little eyes were like suns."

31. This is the traditional explanation of the etymology, accepted by Joseph Vendryes, *Lexique étymologique de l'irlandais ancien* (Dublin: Dublin Institute for Advanced Studies, 1959–1978), pp. S–201f. The objections made on semantic grounds by O. Szemerenyi, "Principles of Etymological Research in the Indo-European Languages," in R. Schmitt, ed., *Etymologie* (Darmstadt: Wissenschaftliche Buchgesellschaft, 1977), pp. 313–314, should be answered by my discussion of the homologic relation between sun and eye. The formal objections raised by Szemerenyi have now been convincingly answered by Alfred Bammesberger, "Le mot irlandais designant l'oeil," *Etudes celtiques* 19 (1982):155–157; Bammesberger has also recognized in the -*i*- stem of **sūli* an old dual form, marking the eyes as "the two suns."

32. On IE theories of vision, and also on the mythology of creatures possessing ocular deformities (a theme that draws heavily on the homology

of eyes and sun), see several rich, interrelated studies by Françoise Bader: "Autour de Polyphème le Cyclope: diathèse et vision," *Die Sprache* 30 (1984):109–137; "Problèmes d'onomastique mythique: 2. Cyclopes," in M. A. Jazayery, ed., *Festschrift for Edgar Polomé* (Austin: University of Texas Press, 1985); and "Introduction à l'étude des mythes i.e. de la vision: les Cyclopes," in a forthcoming volume edited by Enrico Campanile.

33. Pokorny, *Indogermanisches etym Wb*, pp. 881 and 775–777, respectively.

34. Duchesne-Guillemin, "Persische Weisheit in griechischem Gewande?" *Harvard Theological Review* 49 (1956):115–122. The text for this portion of the *Peri Hebdomadōn* has been lost, and what survives is a Lt translation. Behind the Lt phrase *locus sensus apparuit judicium,* Duchesne-Guillemin argues, there originally stood Greek *phrenes,* which permitted no simple translation. On *phrenes* see Hjalmar Frisk, *Griechisches etymologisches Wörterbuch* (Heidelberg: Carl Winter, 1973), II, 1041–1043.

35. Pokorny, *Indogermanisches etym Wb*, p. 82.

36. Grimm, *Teutonic Mythology,* II, 568f.

37. Güntert, *Arische Weltkönig,* pp. 328–330.

38. For the difficulties in assuming II Enoch as the source for the European Eight-Part Adam tradition, see note 19 to this chapter. Beyond this, while an origin for II Enoch in Hellenistic Alexandria seems possible, it is by no means certain; still less is it certain that there was any Iranian influence on the text.

39. Duchesne-Guillemin, "Persische Weisheit," written in opposition to Götze's theses of Iranian influence on Greek microcosmic-speculation, a thesis warmly embraced by members of the *Religionsgeschichtliche Schule,* esp. Richard Reitzenstein and H. H. Schaeder, *Studien zum antiken Synkretismus aus Iran und Griechenland* (Leipzig: B. G. Teubner, 1926). Most recently on this question, see J. Mansfield, *The Pseudo-Hippocratic Tract Peri Hebdomadōn Ch. 1–11 and Greek Philosophy* (Assen: Van Gorcum, 1971), pp. 21–24; and M. L. West, "The Cosmology of 'Hippocrates' De Hebdomadibus," *Classical Quarterly* 21 (1971):385–388.

Although still not fully acceptable, Götze's case could have been strengthened significantly had he taken *ZS* 30.4–11 as the starting point for his comparison. Not only does this passage preserve some of the specific details that are found in *PeriHeb* 6.1–2 and nowhere else outside of Iran (especially the homology of skin and heaven), but it also arranges both microcosm and macrocosm as a system of seven concentric circles, the same model found in the Hippokratic text. The Pahlavi passage reads as follows:

"The material body is complete in seven layers. The innermost is the marrow. Around the marrow is the bone, around the bone is the flesh, around the flesh is the fat, around the fat are the veins, around the veins is the skin, around the skin is the hair.

"And the marrow corresponds (?) to the Moon . . . And above the Moon is the planet Mercury, and its habitation is over the bone. And above Mercury is the planet Venus, and its habitation is above the flesh. And above Venus is the Sun, and its habitation is above the fat. And above the Sun is the planet Mars, and its habitation is above the veins that convey blood. And above Mars is the planet Jupiter, and its habitation is above the skin, the beautifier of the body. And above Jupiter is the planet Saturn, and its habitation is above the hair."

40. The text exists in four different manuscripts, one Gk, two Lt, and an Arabic translation. The first three, and a German translation of the fourth, are assembled in Wilhelm Roscher, *Die hippokratische Schrift von der Siebenzahl* (Paderborn: Ferdinand Schöningh, 1913). The Gk text lacks ch. 6, however, and we are left with only the Lt and Arabic translations. I follow the version of the Codex Lat. Ambrosianus G 108.

41. See Kranz, "Kosmos und Mensch," pp. 125–130; Duchesne-Guillemin, "Persische Weisheit," p. 118. The homology of heaven and skin is one detail that continues to suggest direct borrowing in one direction or another between Greece and Iran, occurring, as it does, in *GBd* 28.4, *SGW* 16.10, *PeriHeb* 6.1, and nowhere else.

42. Text in G. Kinkel, ed., *Epicorum Græcorum Fragmenta*, I (Leipzig: B. G. Teubner, 1877), 271, fragment 11. See further Ingrid Waern, "Gēs ostea: The Kenning in Pre-Christian Greek Poetry" (Ph.D. diss., University of Uppsala, 1951), esp. pp. 95–96 and 111.

43. Kranz, "Kosmos und Mensch," pp. 125, 143; Duschesne-Guillemin, "Persische Weisheit," p. 118.

44. "The text is as follows: "The center of the earth, which is stable and unmoving, (being) of stone, is an imitation of bones, which are impassable and unmoving in nature. Moreover, that which is around that is man's dissolvable flesh. Moreover, that which is moist and warm in the earth is man's marrow, brain, and semen. Moreover, water in rivers is an imitation of veins and the blood that is in the veins. Moreover, the swamps are the bladder and intestines. Truly, the seas are the humors (i.e., organic fluids) of men inside their organs. Truly, air is the breath that is in man. The place of the moon is where sense prepares judgment.

"Man's heat exists in the world as if in two places. Part is gathered together on earth from the radiance of the sun: that which is warm in man's viscera and veins. Moreover, that which is in the upper parts of the world—stars and sun—is that which is under the skin. And man's heat that is around the flesh, which—being radiant—changes colors quickly, you find that to be just like the planet Jupiter."

45. Text in C. A. Patrides, ed., *Sir Walter Raleigh, The History of the World* (London: Macmillan, 1971), pp. 126f. On the persistence of the theme of microcosm and macrocosm into the early modern period, see Leonard Barkan, *Nature's Work of Art: The Human Body as Image of the World* (New Haven: Yale University Press, 1975).

46. We have almost no direct fragments from Anaximander, although B1 is suggestive. Among the summaries of his doctrines that have survived, note particularly those listed as A9, A10, and A11 in Hermann Diels, *Die Fragmente der Vorsokratiker*, 5th ed., ed. Walther Kranz (Berlin: Weidman, 1934). A rather unsophisticated attempt to treat Anaximander within an IE context was made

by Adolf Dyroff, "Zur griechischen und germanischen Kosmogonie," *Archiv für Religionswissenschaft* 31 (1934):105–123.

47. The classic interpretation of Empedokles' thought may be found, inter alia, in W. K. C. Guthrie, *History of Greek Philosophy,* 6 vols. (Cambridge: University Press, 1981), II, 122–243; G. S. Kirk and J. E. Raven, *The Pre-Socratic Philosophers* (Cambridge University Press, 1964), pp. 320–361; D. O'Brien, *Empedocles' Cosmic Cycle* (Cambridge: Cambridge University Press, 1969); and M. R. Wright, *Empedocles: The Extant Fragments* (New Haven: Yale University Press, 1981), esp. pp. 22–56. This view has come under attack in U. Hölscher, "Weltzeiten und Lebenzyklus," *Hermes* 93 (1965):7–33; J. Bollack, *Empedocle,* 3 vols. (Paris: Minuit, 1965–1969); and Friedrich Solmsen, "Love and Strife in Empedocles' Cosmology," *Phronesis* 10 (1965:109–148; idem, "Eternal and Temporary Beings in Empedocles' Physical Poem," *Archiv für Geschichte der Philosophie* 57 (1975):123–145. Without entering into the details of the debate, which properly belongs to specialists in the study of pre-Socratic philosophy, I would suggest that consideration of the Indo-European background to Empedokles' work strengthens the traditional lines of interpretration.

48. This phrase occurs at B27 and again at B28.

49. The phrase *moniēi periēgei gaiōn,* "Rejoicing, it revolved in solitude," occurs at B27.4 and B28.2.

50. In describing the state of perfection as a sphere, Empedokles is obviously following Parmenides, by whom he was strongly influenced. It is perhaps worth noting that Gayōmart, the primordial man of Zoroastrian myth, in certain texts is also described as having been perfectly spherical in shape. On this theme see Karl Hoffmann, "Gayōmart und Martāṇḍa," *Münchener Studien zur Sprachwissenschaft* 11 (1957):85–103, esp. 98f. On the theme of the sphere in pre-Socratic philosophy more broadly, see O. J. Brendel, *Symbolism of the Sphere* (Leiden: E. J. Brill, 1977).

51. Note particularly its use at *Theog* 458. One might compare *BṛhadUp* 1.3, and *GBd* 4.10 (TD Ms. 42.4–6): "On New Year's day, (Ahriman) assaulted at noon, and the sky was afraid, as sheep are afraid of wolves."

52. The most important fragment in which cosmogonic dismemberment and reunification are described is B20. 1–5:

> This (alternation of Love and Strife) is apparent in the mass of mortal bodies.
> At one time the limbs, which have found a body at the highest point of blooming life,
> Are coming together in a single whole, through (the power of) Love.
> At another time, again cut apart by evil discords,
> Each one wanders separately around the brink of life.

53. See Friedrich Solmsen, "Tissues and the Soul: Philosophical Contributions to Physiology," *Philosophical Review* 59 (1950):436–441.

54. According to fragment B105, thought (*noēma*) is lodged in the blood surrounding the heart, presumably because this fluid is best able to perceive all things with equal clarity, being itself composed of a perfectly balanced mix of the fundamental elements.

55. This is preserved in Simplicius's *Physical Opinions*, quoted in Philip Wheelwright, ed., *The Presocratics* (Indianapolis: Bobbs-Merrill, 1960), p. 153.

56. Text in Hermann Diels, *Doxographi Graeci* (Berlin: G. Reimer, 1879, p. 389. Note, however, that Plutarch, *De Exilio* 17 (*Moralia* 607D) attributes a different view of the soul to Empedokles.

57. The association of humans with fire is less obvious here than are the other associations of species with elements (birds/air, fish/water, plants/earth). The same system recurs in the famous account of Empedokles' series of reincarnations (B117), where he claims to have been reborn in all of the elemental realms (as a plant in the earth, a fish in the water, a bird in the air, and a human in fire). Perhaps one is to understand that the human soul is nearest to divinity, the fiery aither being the heavenly realm beyond the atmosphere. By way of comparison, note the homology of fire with characteristically human attributes: speech in *AitUp* 1–2 and mind (*wárom*) in *PRDD* 26.28.

58. Wright, *Empedocles: The Extant Fragments*, pp. 228f.

59. Note also Gk *ostakos* "crab," < **ost-n̥-ko-* "the bony one" (on which see Pierre Chantraine, *Dictionnaire étymologique de la langue grec* [Paris: Editions Klincksieck, 1968–1977], p. 832), to which one might compare Pāli *aṭṭhitaco* (< Skt **asthi-tracas-*) "the one whose skin is bone."

2. Sacrifice

1. See the discussions in Otto Schrader, *Reallexikon der indogermanischen Altertumskunde* (Strassburg: 1917–1929), 2nd ed. rev. by Alfons Nehring, 2:133–140; and Emile Benveniste, *Le vocabulaire des institutions indo-européennes*, 2 vols. (Paris: Editions de Minuit, 1969), II, 209–231. Also of great interest and value are Joseph Vendryes, "Les correspondances de vocabulaire entre l'indo-iranien et l'italo-celtique," *Mémoires de la société de linguistique de Paris* 20 (1918):265–295; Wilhelm Koppers, "Pferdeopfer und Pferdekult der Indogermanen," *Wiener Beiträge zur Kulturgeschichte und Linguistik* 4 (1936):279–411; and E. Mayrhofer-Passler, "Haustieropfer bei dem Indoiraniern und den anderen indo-germanischen Volkern," *Archiv Orientalnì* 21 (1953):82–205. Several recent volumes contain valuable essays on the sacrificial practices of some of the Indo-European peoples; note esp. Marcel Detienne and Jean-Pierre Vernant, eds., *La cuisine du sacrifice en pays grec* (Paris: Gallimard, 1979); *Le sacrifice dans l'antiquité* (Geneva: Fondation Hardt, 1981); and C. Grottanelli, N. Parise, and P. G. Solinas, eds., "Sacrificio, organizzazione del cosmo, dinamica sociale," *Studi Storici* 25 (1984):829–956.

2. Human victims are attested with certainty among the Celts, Germans, Greeks, Skyths, and Old Prussians. The evidence for the practice among other IE groups is less convincing. On this question see, inter alia, Schrader-Nehr-

ing, *Reallexikon*, 2:56–60; E. Mogk, *Die Menschenopfer bei den Germanen*, *Abhandlungen der philosophisch-historisch Klasse der Sächsischen Gesellschaft der Wissenschaften* 27 (1909):603–643; Friedrich Schwenn, *Die Menschenopfer bei den Griechen und Römern* (Giessen: Alfred Töpelmann, 1915); J. Maringer, "Menschenopfer im Bestattungbrauch Alteuropas," *Anthropos* 37–40 (1942–1945):1–112; Albrecht Weber, "Ueber Menschenopfer bei den Indern der vedischen Zeit," *Zeitschrift der deutschen morgendlandischen Gesellschaft* 18 (1864):262–287; Georges Dumézil, *Flamen-Brahman* (Paris: Musée Guimet, 1935); Renate Rolle, *Die Totenkult bei den Skythen* (Berlin: Walter de Gruyter, 1979); Marija Gimbutas, "Proto-Indo-European Culture: The Kurgan Culture during the Fifth, Fourth, and Third Millennia B.C.," in George Cardona, Henry Hoenigswald, and George Senn, eds., *Indo-European and Indo-Europeans* (Philadelphia: University of Pennsylvania Press, 1970), p. 170; and Albert Henrichs, "Human Sacrifice in Greek Religion: Three Case Studies," in *Le sacrifice dans l'antiquité*, pp. 195–242.

3. This conclusion emerges from the fact that the two examples of horse sacrifice that correspond most closely, the Indic *aśvamedha* and the Irish horse sacrifice reported by Giraldus Cambrensis, *Topographica Hibernica*, ch. 25, are both royal coronations, while the oldest attestations of the rite are in the names of two kings, the Vedic Aśvamedha and the Gallic Iipomiidvos, which are phonetically identical and share the meaning "He whose sacrifice is a horse," this being a royal title. See Franz Rolf Schröder, "Ein altirischer Kronungsritus und das indogermanischer Rossopfer," *Zeitschrift für celtische Philologie* 16 (1927):310–312, and Jaan Puhvel, "Vedic Aśvamedha- and Gaulish Iipomiidvos," *Language* 31 (1955):353–354. The closely related Roman sacrifice of the Equus October is also a royal sacrifice, closely connected with the *regia*. Many treatments of the horse sacrifice—e.g., Koppers, "Pferdeopfer und Pferdekult"; Jaan Puhvel, "Aspects of Equine Functionality," in Puhvel, ed., *Myth and Law among the Indo-Europeans* (Berkeley: University of California Press, 1970), pp. 159–172; Wendy Doniger O'Flaherty, "Sacred Cows and Profane Mares in Indian Mythology," *History of Religions* 19 (1979):1–26—have tended to overstate the importance of horse sacrifice among the Indo-Europeans.

4. See esp. Mayrhofer-Passler, "Haustieropfer." Jaan Puhvel has attempted to argue, in "Victimal Hierarchies in Indo-European Animal Sacrifice," *American Journal of Philology* 99 (1978):354–362, that different species represented the different Dumézilian "functions," but the argument is not persuasive. The standard listing of the "five sacrificial beasts" in Indic sources—man, horse, ox, sheep, goat (*SB* 1.2.3.6; *AB* 2.8 et al.)—is organized strictly on the order of decreasing value, man being the most expensive ("dearest") victim, next horse, next ox, next sheep, with goat being least expensive, and thus in actual practice the most frequent victim. In practice humans were probably never offered in India, the *puruṣamedha* ("sacrifice of a man") remaining only a priest's fantasy of the sacrifice to end all sacrifices (*pace* Weber and the unconvincing arguments of Willibald Kirfel, "Der Aśvamedha und der Puruṣamedha," in *Festschrift für Walther Schubring* [Hamburg: Walter de

Gruyter, 1951], pp. 39–50). Also, as I stated in note 3, the horse was reserved for royal sacrifices. This meant that in normal practice cattle were the preferred offering, being the most expensive and thus most "noble," with sheep and goats being cheaper, fully acceptable, and thus quite frequent substitutes. An interesting instance of such substitution in Germanic sacrifice is found in *Ynglingasaga* 15, where in a time of famine an ox is offered, and that proving ineffective to halt the crisis, a man, and finally a king. For similar substitutions among the Romans, see Gérard Capdeville, "Substitution de victimes dans les sacrifices d'animaux à Rome," *Mélanges d'archéologie et d'histoire de l'école française de Rome* 83 (1971):283–323.

5. See Benveniste, *Vocabulaire*, II, 209–221; and Bernfried Schlerath, "Opfergaben," in *Festgabe für Herman Lommel* (*Paideuma* 7 [1960]), pp. 129–134.

6. For some of the more influential theories of sacrifice, see W. Robertson Smith, *Lectures on the Religion of the Semites*, 3rd ed. (New York: Ktav, 1969); Alfred Loisy, *Essai historique sur le sacrifice* (Paris: Emile Nourry, 1920); Marcel Mauss and Henri Hubert, *Sacrifice: Its Nature and Function* (Chicago: University of Chicago Press, 1964); Walter Burkert, *Homo Necans: Interpretationen altgriechischer Opferriten und Mythen* (Berlin: Walter de Gruyter, 1972); and Victor W. Turner, "Sacrifice as Quintessential Process: Prophylaxis or Abandonment?" *History of Religions* 16 (1977):189–215. Of considerable importance also is Pier Giorgio Solinas, "Caccia, spartizione, società," *Studi Storici* 25 (1984):897–912.

7. Adolf E. Jensen, *Myth and Cult among Primitive Peoples* (Chicago: University of Chicago Press, 1963), esp. pp. 162–190; Eliade, *The Myth of the Eternal Return* (Princeton: Princeton University Press, 1954), esp. pp. 21–27; Christiano Grottanelli, "Cosmogonia e Sacrificio, I," *Studi Storico-Religiosi* 4 (1980):207–235; idem, "Cosmogonia e Sacrificio, II" *Studi Storico-Religiosi* 5 (1981):173–196.

8. Burkert, "Caesar und Romulus-Quirinus," esp. pp. 365–368; Puhvel, "Remus et Frater," p. 155. John Scheid has also recognized sacrificial themes behind the stereotyped accounts of the deaths of certain Roman emperors (Caligula, Nero, Vitellius, and Galerius) in "Le mort du tyran. Chronique de quelques morts programmées," in Yan Thomas, ed., *Le châtiment dans la cité antique* (Rome: Ecole française de Rome, 1984). See also my *Priests, Warriors, and Cattle*, pp. 85–87.

9. The apotheosis legend is given in Ennius, *Annals*, 112–116; Livy 1.16; Dionysius of Halicarnassus 2.56; Plutarch, *Life of Romulus* 27; Ovid, *Fasti* 2.475ff., and elsewhere.

10. The two versions of Romulus's death became embroiled in the political struggles that arose toward the end of the Republic as figures such as Sulla and Caesar sought to identify themselves with Romulus. Thus, the story of Romulus's dismemberment could be told as pro-Sulla or pro-Caesar propaganda, casting the senate as ingrates (Valerius Maximus presents it as the lead item in his treatment of ingratitude [5.3.1, *De Ingratis*]) or as pro-senate propaganda, presenting the senators' actions as the just punishment for a tyrant's

harsh nature (e.g. Florus 1.1.17, *Discerptum aliqui a senatu putant ob asperius ingenium*).

11. Burkert, "Caesar und Romulus-Quirinus," esp. pp. 367f.

12. One might well compare the funerary rituals of the Issedones (a Skythian people) described in Herodotos 4.26: "The Issedones are said to live according to these customs. When a man's father dies, all those who are connected to him in some way bring forth animals, which they sacrifice and cut into pieces. And they cut up the deceased father of him who entertains them, and mixing all the meat together, they set forth a sacrificial banquet (*daita*)." This extraordinary ritual deserves fuller treatment than is possible here, but one must begin by noting that the deceased Issedone father, like Romulus, was the focal representative of a broader social grouping. The corporate identity of the group, which had been concentrated in this individual—indeed, within his very body—was thus returned to the group upon his death, via the mechanism of sacrificial dismemberment, distribution, and (at least in the Issedone case) consumption.

13. On the Feriæ Latinæ see H. H. Scullard, *Festivals and Ceremonies of the Roman Republic* (Ithaca, N.Y.: Cornell Univesity Press, 1981), pp. 111–115; Pierangelo Catalano, *Linee del Sistema Sovrannozionale Romano* (Turin: G. Giappichelli, 1965), pp. 168–173; Jean Bayet, *Histoire politique et psychologique de la religion romaine* (Paris: Payot, 1957), pp. 20f.; W. Warde Fowler, *Roman Festivals of the Period of the Republic* (London: Macmillan, 1908), pp. 96ff.; andF. Münzer, "Feriæ Latinæ," in Pauly-Wissowa, *Realenzyklopaedie der klassisches Altertumswissenschaft*, vol. 6/2, pp. 2213–2216. More broadly on the importance of dismemberment within Roman sacrifices, and with specific reference to the Feriæ Latinæ, see John Scheid, "La spartizione a Roma," *Studi Storici* 25 (1984): 945–956.

14. There are several errors in this presentation. First, the ritual predates Roman hegemony; second, most authors date Roman predominance to the (mythical?) reign of Tullus Hostilius than that of Tarquinius Superbus; third, although the construction of a temple is mentioned, archaeological excavations on the Alban Mount have failed to reveal any such structure. This last detail is worth comparing to the fact that the Celtic, Germanic, Indic, and Iranian sacrifices I will consider are all said to have been performed out of doors, perhaps indicating that the Feriæ Latinæ preserved a general IE pattern of ritual, which Dionysius sought to recast in a more properly Roman mold. Among the other archaic features is the use of a milk libation rather than one of wine (Cicero, *De Divinatione* 1.11.18).

15. The Scholium to Cicero, *Pro Plancio* 23, states: "The adjacent (small) states receive small portions (*portiunculas*) of meat from the victim on the Alban Mount, following the ancient belief. But truly, there are too few men in these cities to receive the meat (which they previously) demanded in solemn fashion." That portions were hierarchically ranked also emerges from the use of the verb *tassō* in Dionysius of Halicarnassus 4.49, a term that has as its primary sense the setting up of an army in military formation, thus "to rank," "to order." Here it is applied to the specific provisions each city was expected

to bring to the Feriæ Latinæ (*taxas ha dei parekhein hekastēn eis ta hiera*) and to the specific portion each city received (*meros hekastē to tetagmenon lambanei*). See the discussion of *tassō* in Pierre Chantraine, *Dictionnaire étymologique de la langue grecque* (Paris: Klincksieck, 1968), pp. 1095f. It is particularly worth noting in the present context that the infinitive form, *taxai*, yielded the Latin *taxāre*, "to tax, assess (differentially)."

16. See Livy 37.3.4, 32.1.9, and 41.16.1–2 for instances of these ritual failings. The last of these passages is particularly interesting, for there it is specified that the offending party must pay the expenses for the repetition of the ritual. It thus appears possible that this was a punishment of those who had failed to pray for the Roman *Quirites*, and one may suspect that the Romans thought such an omission to be an intentional defiance of their authority and an attempt to subvert Latin allegiance to Rome. In its last performance (A.D. 394), the ritual did assume a revolutionary coloration: Virius Nicomachus Flavianus used it to rally the Latin peoples around their old customs and beliefs in opposition to the Christianity of Theodosius, who conclusively defeated Flavianus later that year.

17. Human sacrifice is alleged to have occurred within the Feriæ Latinæ by a great many late authors, amony them Porphyry, *De Abstinentia* 2.56 (the sole non-Christian testimony); Lactantius, *Divinae Institutiones* 1.21.3; *Oratio ad Graecos* 29; Tertullian, *Apologia* 9.5; Minucius Felix, *Octavius* 23.6, 30.4; and Firmicus Maternus, *De Errore Profanarum Religionum* 26.2. These are not trustworthy sources, however, and only spread scandalous rumors of their enemy's rituals, concerning which they knew very little. See Schwenn, *Die Menschenopfer*, pp. 180–181.

18. On this passage, see Alois Closs, "Die Religion des Semnonenstammes," *Wiener Beiträge zur Kulturgeschichte und Linguistik* 4 (1936):549–674; Otto Höfler, "Das Opfer in Semnonenhain und die Edda," in Hermann Schneider, ed., *Edda, Skalden, Saga: Festschrift Felix Genzmer* (Heidelberg: Carl Winter, 1952), pp. 1–67; and above all, L. L. Hammerich, "Horrenda Primordia: Zur 'Germania' c. 39." *Germanisch-Romanische Monatsschrift* 33 (1952):228–233; as well as the valuable commentary of Rudolf Much, *Die Germania des Tacitus*, 3rd ed. rev. Herbert Jankuhn (Heidelberg: Carl Winter, 1967), pp. 432–440.

19. See Much, *Die Germania des Tacitus*, p. 443. The visit of Masyos and Ganna to Rome is mentioned in Dio Cassius 67.5.3.

20. Other Germanic sacrifices are related in *Germania* 9 and 40, Tacitus's *Annals* 1.61, *Eyrbyggja Saga* 4, *Saga of Hakon the Good* 14, *Gautrekssaga* 7, Prokopios *De Bello Gothico* 2.14–15, and Adam of Bremen 4.27. None of these, with the exception of the Nerthus-cult described in *Germania* 40, can compare to the account of *Germania* 39 for its early date, reliability of source, and wealth of detail.

21. Hammerich, "Horrenda Primordia." The most important issue Hammerich addressed was the interpretation of the phrase *celebrant barbari ritus horrenda primordia*. He convincingly argued, first, that *ritus* is a plural nominative (not a singular genitive) and thus is the subject of the veb *celebrant;* second, that *primordia* does not refer merely to the introductory phases of

the ritual, but rather to the beginnings of the Suebian people, as in its occurrence in phrases such as *primordia mundi* (Ovid), *primordia gentis* (Lucretius), *primordia populi Romani* (Tacitus, *Annals* 6.50.19), and the common phrase *in primordiis.*

Hammerich's arguments have been accepted, and enhanced, most prominently by Karl Hauck, "Lebensnormen und Kultmythen in germanischen Stammes- und Herrschergenealogien," *Saeculum* 6 (1955):186—223, esp. 193—195; idem, "Carmina Antiqua," *Zeitschrift für bayerische Landesgeschichte* 27 (1964):1—33, esp. 17—20; and Alfred Ebenbauer, "Ursprungsglaube, Herrschergott und Menschenopfer. Beobachtungen zum Semnonenkult (Germania c. 39)," in M. Mayrhofer et al., eds., *Antiquitates Indogermanicae: Gedenkschrift für Hermann Güntert* (Innsbruck: Innsbrucker Beiträge zur Sprachwissenschaft, 1974), pp. 233—249. All of these are important contributions in their own right.

I have followed the lead of these specialists in viewing the Semnones' ritual as primarily concerned with repetition of their origins and the origins of the world, and have interpreted the phrase *omnis superstitio respicit* in consonance with this view, restoring the proper active sense to the verb *re-spicio* ("to look back," "to respect"), instead of artificially translating it in the passive, as is often done ("the superstition of all is respected," or some such).

22. "Now the Suebi are to be discussed, of whom there is not one (united) people, like the Chatti or Tencteri, for they occupy the greater part of Germany and they are divided into separate tribes and names, although in common they call themselves 'Suebi.'" In this context, note the etymology of the names *Suebi* (Gmc *Swēboz* "those who are under their own law") and *Semnones* (Gmc *Sebnanez* "tribal companions"); see Much, *Die Germania des Tacitus*, pp. 58, 426, 433.

23. On the interpretation of these names see Much, *Die Germania des Tacitus*, pp. 53—55; Güntert, *Arische Weltkönig*, pp. 91—94; Jan de Vries, "Sur certains glissements fonctionnels de divinités dans la religion germanique," in *Hommages à Georges Dumézil* (Brussels: Collection Latomus, 1960), pp. 89—95; Felix Genzmer, "Ein germanisches Gedicht aus der Hallstattzeit," *Germanische-Romanische Monatsschrift* 24 (1936):14—21; and Richard Hünnerkopf, "Die Söhne des Mannus," *Gymnasium* 61 (1954):542—554.

24. Genzmer, "Ein germanisches Gedicht." See also the highly suggestive discussion of Karl Hauck, "Carmina antiqua," pp. 1—33.

25. Güntert, *Arische Weltkönig*, p. 324; Lincoln, *Priests, Warriors, and Cattle*, p. 84. *Tuisto* seems the preferable reading, although *Tuisco* is also well attested in the manuscript tradition. Both are extensions of PIE *dwis-* "two," attested in other Gmc terms such as OSax *twisc*, OHG *zwisc* "twin, double," OE *twist* "twisted thread," ON *tvistr* "deuce (in cards)." See also note 3 to Chapter 1.

26. See *Gylfaginning* 6—8, *Grímnismál* 40—41, and *Vafthrudnismál* 21, plus Chapter 1 above and *Priests, Warriors, and Cattle*, pp. 75—76, 80—142.

27. The question centers on the excavations at Lossow, where some sixty shafts, out of a total of perhaps five hundred containing sacrificial remains, have been systematically studied. The site is near Frankfurt on the Oder, and

attests to the long practice of sacrificial ritual by Germanic peoples in this area. Most striking is the fact that while the skeletal remains of equine and bovine victims are more or less intact, those of human victims are regularly dismembered. Arguing in favor of identification of the Lossow site with the cult place of the Semnones have been W. Unverzagt, "Der Burgwall von Lossow bei Frankfurt/Oder," in Gerhart Rodenwaldt, ed., *Neue deutsche Ausgrabungen* (Münster: Aschendorff, 1930), pp. 159ff.; Kurt Tackenberg, "Die Germania des Tacitus und das Fach der Vorgeschichte," in Dieter Ahrens, ed., *Festschrift Max Wegner* (Münster: Aschendorff, 1962), pp. 61f.; and Hauck, "Carmina Antiqua," p. 17 and n. 55; while skepticism has been voiced by Herbert Jankuhn in Much, *Die Germania des Tacitus,* pp. 173, 435.

28. Thus Hammerich, "Horrenda Primordia," pp. 230–232; Ebenbauer, "Ursprungsglaube," pp. 235–240, 249; Hauck, "Lebensnormen und Kultmythen," pp. 194f. Höfler, "Das Opfer in Semnonenhain," has also located much of this sacrificial pattern in the Helgi-lays of the Elder Edda.

29. Certain variants on the basic mythic pattern contained both cosmogonic and sociogonic sections: for example, *RV* 10.90.11–14 or the Russ "Poem on the Dove King" (see Chapter 1). Among the Germanic peoples, however, a certain division seems evident, whereby the cosmogonic theme was better preserved in Scandinavia (as in *Gylf* 6–8) while the sociogonic theme was prevalent on the continent (as in *Germania* 2). Anthropogonic accounts were preserved in both areas, as in the theme of the Eight-Part Adam and such accounts as the origin of Tuisto from earth (*Germania* 2), Ymir from ice (*Gylf* 6), Askr and Embla from trees (*Gylf* 9), Aschanes (the mythic ancestor of the Saxons, identified with the biblical Ashkenaz), from rocks (*Froschmeuseler Rollenhagens* 1.2: "da Aschanes mit seinen Sachsen aus den Hartzfelsen ist gewachsen"), and the Saxon women from trees (19th-century folksong: "darauf so bin ich gegangen nach Sachsen, wo die schönen Mägdlein aus den Bäumen wachsen"). On this, see the early article of Wilhelm Wackernagel, "Die Anthropogonie der Germanen," *Zeitschrift für deutsches Altertum* 6 (1848):15–20; Franz Specht, "Zur indogermanische Sprache and Kultur II," *Zeitschrift für vergleichende Sprachforschung* 68 (1944):191–200; Gregory Nagy, "Perkŭnas and Perun"," in Mayrhofer, ed., *Antiquitates Indogermanicae,* pp. 124–126; and Edgar Polomé, "Some Comments on Vǫluspá, Stanzas 17–18," in Polomé, ed., *From Old Norse Literature and Mythology* (Austin: University of Texas Press, 1969), pp. 265–290. Recently, Polomé has called attention to the internal complexities of the Germanic cosmogonic tradition and called for reevaluation of all the evidence: "The Background of Germanic Cosmogonic Myths," in Bela Brogyanyi, ed., *Klingenheben Festschrift* (Amsterdam: Benjamins, forthcoming).

30. The entire last sentence is extremely suggestive, for if *iis* is taken as a proper dative rather than an instrumental usage of the dative (as is possible although a bit strained) then it appears that the other Suebi inhabit one hundred cantons as a service *for the Semnones* (*iis*), and thus form the "great body" (*magnoque corpore*) of which the Semnones are the head (*Sueborum caput*) with possible reference to division of the victim's body. Caesar, *BG* 1.37, 4.1,

in fact, does attribute the possession of one hundred cantons to the Suebi rather than to the Semnones.

31. The Feriæ Latinæ are celebrated annually, but this is not certain for the Semnones' cult. Rather, Tacitus merely states that they assemble "at a fixed time" (*stato tempore*). This is usually taken to mean at regular intervals (thus Much, *Die Germania des Tacitus*, p. 434), most probably either every year—which would be in keeping with the well-known ON sacrifice "for the year" (*til ars*, on the cosmic significance of which see Ake Ström, *Germanische und Baltische Religion* [Stuttgart: W. Kohlhammer, 1975], pp. 233f.), or on a nine-year cycle, as at the pagan temple at Uppsala as described by Adam of Bremen 4.27.

32. K. Rönnow, "Zagreus och Dionysos," *Religion och Bibel* 2 (1943): 14–48. See also Olerud, *L'Idée du macrocosmos*, pp. 99–128, 191–208. Rönnow's important researches have not always received the attention they merit, in some measure because of his insistence on linking a broad variety of mythic, ritual, and philosophical materials to an original practice of human sacrifice. That these materials are rooted in sacrifice, be it human or animal, is un-questionable, however, and such a formulation avoids many of the difficulties his theories encountered. See now the treatment of these materials by Marcel Detienne, *Dionysos Slain* (Baltimore: Johns Hopkins University Press, 1979), pp. 68–94; and M. Daraki, "Aspects du sacrifice dionysiaque," *Revue de l'histoire des religions* 197 (1980):131–157.

33. See in particular the hypercritical yet carefully reasoned and influential work of Ivan Linforth, *The Arts of Orpheus* (Berkeley: University of California Press, 1941). Even a moderate position, such as that proposed by Walter Burkert, "Orphism and Bacchic Mysteries: New Evidence and Old Problems of Interpretation," *Protocol of the 28th Colloquy of the Center for Hermeneutical Studies* (Berkeley: Graduate Theological Union, 1977), pp. 1–8, which avoids the extremes of skepticism and credulity alike, stresses the difficulty of working with matters "Orphic." Albert Henrichs, in responding to Burkert's paper (p. 21), uses a striking metaphor: studying the Orphic materials, he observes, is like doing a jigsaw puzzle in which most of the pieces are missing.

34. Several very important studies dealing with these myths have appeared in recent years. Inter alia, see Jean-Pierre Vernant's essays on Prometheus in R. L. Gordon, ed., *Myth, Religion and Society* (Cambridge: Cambridge University Press, 1981), pp. 43–56, 57–79; Jean Rudhardt, "Les mythes grecs relatifs à l'instauration du sacrifice: les rôles corrélatifs de Promethée et de son fils Deucalion," *Museum Helveticum* 27 (1970):1–15; Jean-Louis Durand, "Le rituel du meurtre du boeuf laboureur et les mythes du premier sacrifice animal en Attique," in B. Gentili and G. Paioni, eds., *Il Mito Greco* (Rome: Ateneo & Bizzarri, 1973), pp. 121–134; Cristiano Grottanelli, "Ospitare gli dei: sacrificio e diluvio," *Studi Storici* 25 (1984):847–857.

35. On the *Katharmoi* see Ulrich von Wilamowitz-Moellendorff, *Die Katharmoi des Empedokles, Sitzungberichtungen der preussisches Akademie der Wissenschaften Philosophisch-Historisch Klasse* (Berlin, 1929), 626–661; Walther Kranz,

"Die Katharmoi und die Physika des Empedokles," *Hermes* 70 (1935):111–119; Kirk and Raven, *Pre-Socratic Philosophers,* pp. 348–360; W. K. C. Guthrie, *History of Greek Philosophy* II, 244–265; and Günther Zuntz, *Persephone* (Oxford: Clarendon Press, 1971), pp. 179–274.

36. Zuntz, *Persephone,* pp. 183f. Theophrastos, cited by Porphyry. *De Abstinentia* 2.21, stated that the central themes of Empedokles' works were "theogonies and sacrifices" *(peri tēs theogonias kai tōn thymatōn).*

37. Zuntz, *Persephone,* p. 258. Empedokles was not alone in his opposition to the sacrificial cultus that was the official rite of the Greek *polis.* For a study of others who denounced sacrifice, a denunciation that was at once social, political, and religious, see Marcel Detienne, "Between Beasts and Gods," in Gordon, ed., *Myth, Religion and Society,* pp. 215–228.

38. Inter alia, see Kirk and Raven, *Pre-Socratic Philosophers,* pp. 357–361; Zuntz, *Persephone,* p. 269; Wright, *Empedocles: The Extant Fragments,* pp. 57–76; Herbert S. Long, "The Unity of Empedocles' Thought," *American Journal of Philology* 70 (1949):142–158; C. H. Kahn, "Religion and Natural Philosophy in Empedocles' Doctrine of the Soul," in J. P. Anton, ed., *Essays in Ancient Greek Philosophy* (Albany: State University of New York, 1971), pp. 3ff.; and D. Babut, "Sur l'unité de la pensée d'Empedocles," *Philologus* 120 (1976):139–164.

39. This interpretation derives from Carl Werner Müller, *Gleiches zu Gleichen: Ein Prinzip frühgriechischen Denkens* (Wiesbaden: Otto Harrassowitz, 1965), pp. 64f.

40. I have rejected part of line 4 of this fragment as an interpolation, following the arguments of Zuntz, *Persephone,* pp. 194f.

41. Wright, *Empedocles: The Extant Fragments,* p. 59. See also Ch. 1, n. 57.

42. Molé's position is most fully spelled out in *Culte, mythe et cosmologie dans l'Iran ancien* (Paris: PUF, 1963), esp. pp. 85–147 for the topic of sacrifice. One text, the importance of which he was the first to emphasize, establishes that even within the Zoroastrian tradition every crucial creative act in the history of the world was believed to have been accompanied by sacrifice, these cosmogonic sacrifices establishing a charter and a precedent for all future sacrifice. The text is *PRDD 16B.1–2,* discussed in *Culte, mythe et cosmologie,* pp. 126f.

"In a revealed passage (it is said): Zarathuštra asked of Ohrmazd: "Have you ever performed a sacrifice *(mēzd)?"* Ohrmazd said: "I have performed it. For when I created the world, I performed a sacrifice; when I created breath for Gayōmard, I performed a sacrifice; when you were born from your mother, O Zarathuštra, I performed a sacrifice; when you received the religion from me, I performed a sacrifice. The sacrifice is thus worthy of men. Whenever (men) act justly and righteously, in the beginning [*pad bun,* a phrase with cosmogonic resonances], there should be the performance of sacrifice by them." ' "

43. For the fullest studies of this important text see Emile Benveniste, *The Persian Religion according to the Chief Greek Texts* (Paris: Paul Geuthner, 1929),

pp. 22–32; Molé, *Culte, mythe et cosmologie*, pp. 74–81; Geo Widengren, *Die Religionen Irans* (Stuttgart: W. Kohlhammer, 1965), pp. 124–126; and Mary Boyce, *A History of Zoroastrianism*, vol. 2 (Leiden: E. J. Brill, 1982), pp. 179f. Note also that Schrader-Nehring, II, 136, took this sacrifice described by Herodotos as a model in which traditional IE ritual was most faithfully preserved. For somewhat different reasons from those advanced there, I am led to a similar conclusion.

44. Comparison of the "theogony" to the *Gāthās*, as advanced by Molé *Culte, mythe et cosmologie*, p. 77 and n. 4; and H. H. Schaeder, "Ein indogermanischer Liedtypus in den Gathas," *Zeitschrift der deutschen morgenlandischen Gesellschaft* 94 (1940):399–408, is preferable to comparing it to the Yašts, as do Benveniste, *Persian Religion*, p. 31; Widengren, *Religionen Irans*, p. 126; and Boyce, *History of Zorastrianism*, II, 180.

45. Various attempts have been made to compare the "gods" named by Herodotos either to the Zoroastrian *Aməša Spəntas* or to various *yazata*s but these are rather forced and artificial. See, for instance, Benveniste, *Persian Religion*, p. 27; Boyce, *History of Zoroastrianism*, II, 179. Preferable is the position of Molé, *Culte, mythe et cosmologie*, p. 75.

46. Liddell-Scott, *Greek-English Lexicon*, p. 415. Herodotos was apparently the first author to use the compound form *dia-tithēmi*. The one other passage in which he employs this verb in a sacrificial context (7.39) makes clear that he meant to denote the separation and placement of dismembered bodily parts in carefully chosen and highly significant positions. There he treats a human sacrifice in which the Persian king, Xerxes, ordered the eldest son of Pythios killed, as punishment for his father's disloyal desire to keep him back from the impending invasion of Greece. Accordingly, the boy was cut in two *(dia-temnō)* and the two halves of his body arranged *(dia-tithēmi)* on opposite sides of the road through which the entire Persian army marched on its way to Greece.

47. Private correspondence, 23 April 1983. Gregory Nagy has since called my attention to a similar use of the compound verb *eu-tithēmi* "to arrange well" by Hesiod, *Theogony* 541, with reference to Prometheus's actions performing the first sacrifice and thus establishing the norms for all sacrifice.

48. On treatment of the omentum, see Strabo 15.3.13–14; *Vd* 18.70; *AB* 2.12–14, inter alia. Note also the homology mind/fire in *PRDD* 26.28.

49. The most important analytical works to date on Indian sacrifice are Sylvain Lévi, *La doctrine du sacrifice dans les Brahmaṇas* (Paris: Ernest Leroux, 1898), esp. pp. 13–35, 77–151; Betty Heimann, "The Supra-Personal Process of Sacrifice," *Rivista degli Studi Orientali* 32 (1957):731–739; Jan Gonda, *Die Religionen Indiens*, I (Stuttgart: W. Kohlhammer, 1960), 104–109, 138–197; Madeleine Biardeau and Charles Malamoud, *Le sacrifice dans l'Inde ancienne* (Paris: PUF, 1976), esp. pp. 14–31. Also of tremendous value is Kasten Rönnow, "Zur Erklärung des Pravargya, des Agnicayana und der Sautrāmaṇī," *Le Monde Oriental* 23 (1929):113–173, but here, as in his work on Greek sacrifice (see above, note 32), Rönnow's determination to trace all things back

to an original practice of human sacrifice prejudices his arguments at points. See also Brian Smith, "The Domestication of the Vedic Sacrifice" (Ph.D diss., University of Chicago, 1984).

50. *SNS* 11.4, where the victim's back is assigned to the "Supreme Chief" (Ahura Mazdā) and its belly to Ārmaiti (Earth). For the occurrence of this homologic set in India prior to *BṛhadUp* 1.1, see *AV* 9.5.20 and (with slight modification) *AV* 9.7.2.

51. *AV* 10.10.7. Other important pieces of homologic sacrificial speculation are found in *AV* 9.4.12–16, 9.7.1–18, 10.10.20–21, as well as 9.5.20–21, discussed later in this chapter. Of particular interest is *AV* 9.4.16, where even the refuse of the sacrifice (for classification as such, see *AB* 2.11) is provided with macrocosmic alloforms: hooves/tortoises, chyme/maggots.

52. This development is already begun in *RV* 10.90.6, where the seasons are homologized to aspects of the sacrifice.

53. From the context, it is certain that the *aviśastṛ* here cannot be a "non-dismemberer," however etymologically precise that rendering might be. Rather, he is one who dismembers badly ("ruining the severed limbs with a sword"), hence an "imcompetent dismemberer."

54. The strewing of the *barhiṣ* is particularly reminiscent of the Persian sacrifice described by Herodotos, where "the softest grass" *(poiēn . . . hapalōtatēn)* was strewn to receive the pieces of the victim's flesh.

55. A minor transformation is seen in the treatment of the homology breath/wind, whereby the synonymous term *vāta-* is substituted for the *vāyu-* of *RV* 10.90.13. While both nouns denote the wind as a physical entity, only the latter is capable of referring to a personified wind-deity, Vāyu.

56. The apparent logic of the *Puruṣasūkta* on this point is that, given the homologies head/heaven and feet/earth posited in *RV* 10.90.14, an intermediate point on the body's vertical axis must be found to represent the atmosphere *(antarikṣam)*, which separates heaven and earth. *AB* 2.6, having omitted the homologies of head/heaven and feet/earth (replacing the latter, India-specific homology with the older one of flesh/earth), is free to find an alloform that has some material similarity to the atmosphere rather than one that depends entirely on its relational position vis-à-vis other items in a series. Thus, *asu-* "life-force" or "life-breath" (< **ṇsu-*, from PIE verbal root **an-* "to blow, to breathe") was chosen.

57. The passage reads as follows:

> The father, having lifted up his own son in an altered form,
> Slays the child, exulting greatly, and others are puzzled
> As they sacrifice the pleading (child). And the father, deaf to the cries,
> Having slain (his son), prepares an evil feast in his hall.
> Similarly, the son seizes his father and children (seize) their mother.
> And having torn from them the life-force, they eat their own flesh.

58. See, e.g., *TS* 5.2.5.1, *SB* 1.3.2.1, *SB* 10.2.1.2, and most important, *SB* 6.1.1.5.

59. See the discussions of Lévi, *Doctrine du sacrifice*, pp. 13–35; Biardeau, *Le sacrifice dans l'Inde ancien*, pp. 14–17; Gonda, *Religionen Indiens*, I, 187–197.

60. *SB* 6.1.2.17–19, *SB* 10.1.3.2–7, and—most exhaustively—*SB* 10.5.4.1–12. It is interesting to note that even the smallest offering is ritually endowed with the same five bodily layers (marrow, bone, flesh, skin, and hair); these are symbolically created for offerings of rice and barley in *AB* 2.8 and *SB* 1.2.3.8.

61. On the Agnicayana see Julius Eggeling, trans., *The Śatapatha Brāhmaṇa*, IV (Oxford: Clarendon Press, 1897), xiii–xxvii; and Gonda, *Religionen Indiens*, I, 191f.

62. See J. A. B. van Buitenen, *The Pravargya* (Poona: Deccan College Research Institute, 1968), for description of the ritual. Its flaws notwithstanding, the interpretation of Kasten Rönnow, "Zur Erklarung des Pravargya, des Agnicayana, und der Sautrāmaṇī," remains preferable to that of van Buitenen.

63. See van Buitenen, *The Pravargya*, 1–6, 37, on the non-Vedic origins of the *Mahāvīra*, although I would disagree with his speculation that this section of the ritual may be non-Aryan. With regard to the construction of the firealtar in the Agnicayana, see the remarks of Eggeling, *Śatapatha Brāhmaṇa*, IV, xiii, xviii–xix, and Hyla Stuntz Converse, "The Agnicayana Rite: Indigenous Origin?" *History of Religion* 14 (1974):81–95. Converse argues most persuasively that a ritual involving as many bricks as did the Agnicayana (a minimum, of 10,800) must in its material aspects be related to the Indus valley civilization, for which bricks were the standard building substance, rather than to the brickless Indo-Aryan invaders. She is much less successful, however, in her attempt to separate the "Prajāpati theology" from the invaders' religious ideas, and in this attempt she seriously misrepresents that "theology" (pp. 88–95). In my opinion, it is more accurate to see the priests of the Indo-Aryans as incorporating new physical materials in their rituals, utilizing them in a fashion consistent with their older ideas of the sacrifice.

64. On the derivation of these sources from Posidonios and their relation to one another, see the study of J. J. Tierney, "The Celtic Ethnography of Posidonius," *Proceedings of the Royal Irish Academy* 60, sec. C, no. 5 (1960): 189–275.

65. See, for instance, the puzzled remarks of Jan de Vries, *La religion des Celtes* (Paris: Payot, 1977), p. 230.

66. For Druidic supervision of sacrifices, see Strabo 4.4.5 and Diodoros Sikelos 5.31.4. At 4.4.4, Strabo states that the Druids practice natural philosophy *(physiologia)* and ethics (ēthikē); Diodoros (5.31.2) calls them "philosophers and theologians, who are greatly honored" *(philosophoi te . . . kai theologoi perittōs timōmenoi)*.

67. This text was already compared to Indo-Iranian ideas of creation and sacrifice by D'Arbois de Jubainville, *Introduction à l'étude de la littérature celtique* (Paris: Ernest Thorin, 1883), I, 170.

68. The former position is that of Tierney, "The Celtic Ethnography," esp. pp. 222–223. The latter view is that of Nora K. Chadwick, *The Druids* (Cardiff: University of Wales Press, 1966), which was intended to be a rebuttal of Tierney on this very point; see esp. pp. 45–46, 56–68, 84–92. Conclusions similar to mine are drawn by Mircea Eliade, "Druids, Astronomers, and Head-Hunters," in *Perennitas: Studi in Onore di Angelo Brelich* (Rome: Ateneo, 1980), pp. 173–183. For a fuller discussion, see my essay "The Druids and Human Sacrifice," in Jazayery, ed., *Festschrift for Edgar Polomé* (forthcoming).

69. Mela is here undoubtedly drawing on Poseidonios, to judge from the similarity of this passage to the mention of human sacrifice as the highest ritual of the Druids in Pliny. *NH* 30.4, and the list of topics taught by the Druids in Caesar, *BG* 6.14. Similar conclusions regarding the reliability of Mela have been drawn by Giuseppe Zecchini, *I Druidi e l'opposizione dei Celti a Roma* (Milan: Jaca, 1984), pp. 40 n. 42 and 42 n. 46.

70. Mayrhofer, *Kurzgefasstes etym Wb des Altindischen*, I, 475; Pokorny, *Indogermanisches etym Wb*, pp. 1065f. This verb is used significantly, for instance, in the *Puruṣasūkta* (*RV* 10.90.6): "When the gods stretched forth the sacrifice with Puruṣa as the oblation, / Spring was its butter, summer its fuel, autumn its oblation."

71. On **blōtan* < PIE **bhlād-* "to make large or strong" a (causative?) extension of **bhel-* "to swell, be swollen," see John Loewenthal, "Zur germanischen Wortkunde," *Arkiv for Norsk Filologi* 31 (1919):231f.; Ström, *Germanische Religion*, p. 96; de Vries, *Altnordisches etym Wb*, p. 45.

72. On *mactare*, analyzed as a denominative verb from the past passive participle *mactus* (for **mag-t-us* alongside *mag-n-us*) from earlier **magō*, **magere* "to grow, increase, cause to grow," see Walde-Hofmann, *Lateinisches etym Wb*, II, 4f.; H. J. Rose and O. Skutsch, "Mactare—Macula?" *Classical Quarterly* 32 (1938):220–224; and Benveniste, *Vocabulaire des institutions*, II, 224–225.

All of these discussions share a common problem. For *mactare*, like Germanic **blōtan*, forms three different grammatical constructions, occurring (*a*) with the offering or victim in the accusative and the recipient of the offering in the dative; (*b*) with the offering or victim in the accusative and no mention of a recipient; and (*c*) with the recipient in the accusative and the offering or victim in the dative of instrument. Yet the meaning "to increase" for these two verbs has been successfully demonstrated only for construction *c*: to increase, magnify, or strengthen a deity by means of an offering. Most authors have either ignored constructions *a* and *b* entirely, claimed that they were secondary formations—without either explaining how this could be so or citing evidence in detail—or offered very lame interpretations of how one might go about "increasing" a sacrificial victim.

Yet the above discussion makes clear just how one might go about "stretching" *(tanoti)*, "inflating" *(*blōtan* < **bhel-*), or "magnifying" *(mactare* < PIE **meg'h-*) a victim. Such a verb could well designate precisely the kind of sacrificial action I have described throughout this chapter: the dispersion of bodily parts from a sacrificial victim to their macrocosmic alloforms.

Two Latin passages that have generally been overlooked in previous discussions of *mactare* lend support to this line of interpretation, for they are among the few texts in which a clear picture emerges of the concrete physical action denoted by *mactare*. The first is Lucretius, *De Rerum Natura* 2.352–4:

> For often a slaughtered *(mactatus)* calf lies in decorous temples,
> Close to the incense-burning altars before a god,
> A warm river of blood gushing from its chest.

The second is Vergil, *Aeneid* 10.413–16, a usage of the verb outside the sphere of ritual, which is all the more revealing for its surprising content:

> (Halaesus) slaughters *(mactat)* Ladon, Pheres, and Demodocus;
> He tears off the right hand of Strymonius with his gleaming sword,
> (A hand) which was lifted up at his throat. He strikes the face of
>   Thoas with a rock,
> And scatters the bones about, mixed with bloody brain

In both instances, the victim's body—human or animal—is rent in such a fashion as to release its contents to the world outside. The blood of Lucretius's calf becomes a river *(flumen)*, while those killed by Halaesus—I take the verb *mactat* as governing the whole passage, not just the first line—have their hands lopped off (one is reminded of the Skythian sacrifices to "Ares" described in Herodotos 4.62), or their skulls scattered into the air, accompanied by a spray of brain and blood. In the context of battle, this is mere carnage, but Vergil chose his words carefully, and within a sacral context it seems entirely plausible that one "magnified" *(mactat)* a victim by transforming these bodily parts into cosmic alloforms: skull going to heaven, brain to clouds, and blood to water (here, perhaps rain).

3. The Origin of Food and the Nature of Nutrition

1. On the Roman she-wolf, see my *Priests, Warriors, and Cattle*, pp. 86–87. See also Dominique Briquel, "Les jumeaux à la louve et les jumeaux à la chèvre, à la jument, à la chienne, à la vache," in Raymond Bloch, ed., *Recherches sur les religions de l'Italie antique* (Geneva: Librairie Droz, 1976), pp. 72–97; and A. Alföldi, "La louve du Capitole: quelques rémarques sur son mythe à Rome et chez les Etrusques," in *Hommages à la mémoire de Jerome Carcopino* (Paris: Les Belles Lettres, 1977), pp. 1–7.

2. In *Zad Spram* 2.9, Ēvagdād is said to be a female *(mādag)*, but all other Iranian sources either leave the animal's gender unspecified (Pahl *gāw* can denote any bovine, male or female) or make it a male. Of the sources considered in *Priests, Warriors, and Cattle*, pp. 69–95, all save *Gylfaginning* 6 and the Roman texts make the primordial bovine a male, as do most of the sources considered in this chapter, the exception being the cows in *Adaigh ConRói* 7.

3. The plants created from the hair of a primordial human are regularly identified as inedible, uncultivated grasses, while those created from a primordial bovine are the edible, domesticated grains and/or fruits (see also Chapter 4).

4. Thus *Y* 16.4, *Sirozah* 1.12, 2.12, 2.14, and the Introduction to *Yt* 7.

5. See Arthur Christensen, *Le premier homme et le premier roi dans l'histoire légendaire des Iraniens,* I (Stockholm: Kunglige Boktrycheriet, 1917), 42f. Of the Pahlavi summaries of the lost Nasks, note esp. *Dk* 8.13.1–4, 8.31.30.

6. I have translated *gōspand* "cattle," although the precise sense is something on the order of "domesticated livestock, particularly bovines." Literally it means "beneficent bovines" (< Av *gav- spənta-*), and it denotes all those domesticated species which had their origin from the primordial ox, Ēvagdād. Given this origin, all other domesticated species are seen to be bovines of a sort. *GBd* 13.5 (TD MS. 94.7–9) quotes a lost Avestan passage: "Because of the value of bovines, they were created twice—once in the [Primordial] Ox, and once with all species of livestock."

7. The account of the origin of wine given here should be compared to the Germanic myth of the origin of the mead of poetry from *Skalds* 2:

"Aegir asked: 'From whence did that art which is called Skaldship (i.e., poetry) begin?'

"Bragi (the god of poetry) answered: 'The beginning was like this. The gods had a conflict with that people who are called the Vanir. They arranged for a peace meeting and established a truce in this manner: they both went to one vat and spat their spittle into it. And at their parting, the gods took it and would not let that mark of their truce be lost, and they made a man out of it. He was called Kvasir. He was so wise that no one could ask him their fortune (lit "lot") such that he did not know the answer. He fared far and wide over the world to know men, and he came to a feast (given) for a certain two dwarves, Fjalar and Galar. Then they called him to a private conversation with them and they killed him. They let his blood run into two vats and a kettle, and they called (the kettle) Óðrørir and the vats they called Són and Boðn. They blended honey with the blood, and there was mead from that— that mead which is such that he who drinks of it will become a Skald or a man of knowledge.' "

Several details indicate that Kvasir's death should be understood as quasi-sacrificial, particularly its occurence within a feast (heimboð), which implies the consumption of meat procured through sacrifice, and the gathering of Kvasir's blood in a vat, as was regularly done for the blood of sacrificial victims (see, e.g., *Hákonar Saga inn Góða*, ch. 16). Further, the myth tells not only of the origin of wine from Kvasir's blood but also of the origin of Kvasir from another bodily fluid: the gods' spittle. Finally, it is likely (the skepticism of de Vries, *Altnordisches etym Wb*, p. 336, contradicted by his own remarks in *Altgermanisches Religionsgeschichte,*II, 67, notwithstanding) that Kvasir's name marks him as the personification of another intoxicant: the fermented grain drink denoted by OCS *kvasŭ*, Russ *kvas*, and the Lith loanword *kwōsas* (note also the Dan and Norw verb *kvase* "to crush" and the substantive *kvas* "crushed fruits; juice pressed from crushed fruits"). The various transformations of bodily fluids into intoxicating beverages and intoxicating beverages into bodily fluids as described in Germanic and Iranian sources may be graphed as follows:

Skalds 2:   A bodily → A primordial → A bodily → An
             fluid   being and   fluid   intoxicant
             (spittle)   personified (blood) (mead)
                          intoxicant
                          (Kvasir)

ZS 3.46:   A primordial → A bodily → An → A bodily
                     being   fluid intoxicant fluid
                    (Ēvagdād) (blood) (wine) (blood)

On the strength of this one might reconstruct a theory in which bodily fluids (especially blood) and intoxicants were seem as infinitely interchangeable, sacrifice being the chief means for converting blood into drink and (ritual) consumption being the chief means of converting drink back into blood. The myths of the dismembered Dionysos and of John Barleycorn may also be relevant here, as may the common designation of certain hearty red wines as "Bull's Blood" in Spain and elsewhere in southern Europe to this day.

On the Kvasir myth see Eugen Mogk, *Novelistische Darstellung mythologischer Stoffe* (Helsinki: Suomalainen Tiedeakatemia, 1923), pp. 23–82; Georges Dumézil, *Les dieux des germains* (Paris: Presses Universitaires de France, 1959), pp. 31–37; and Alexander Haggerty Krappe, *Etudes de mythologie et de folklore germaniques* (Paris: E. Leroux, 1928), pp. 65–67.

8. Specifically, *ZS* 3.50–51 and *GBd* 13.4–9 tell that the semen the primordial ox ejaculated at death was carried up to the moon, where it was purified and sent back to the earth to cause the birth of all species of domestic animals. This is introduced into the narrative to parallel the treatment of the primordial man's semen, from which it is said all the races of human beings are descended (*GBd* 14.5). Beyond this, there is a large body of specifically Indo-Iranian speculation on the nature of semen as a universal life-sap with a luminous essence, whence the connection to the celestial bodies (Gayōmard's semen is purified in the sun, Ēvagdād's in the moon). See Herman Lommel, "König Soma," *Numen* 2 (1955):196–205; Gherardo Gnoli, "Lichtsymbolik in Alt-Iran," *Antaios* 8 (1967):528–549; and Mircea Eliade, "Spirit, Light, and Seed," in *Occultism, Witchcraft, and Cultural Fashions* (Chicago: University of Chicago Press, 1976), pp. 93–119.

9. This structure, particularly in its application to herbal healing, is very similar to that in two important Old Irish texts, *CMT* 33–35 and *LG* 7.310. This correspondence, and the understanding of IE healing practices it affords us, will be further explored in Chapter 5.

10. *Pace* the theories of Franz Cumont, see John Hinnells, "Aspects of the Mithraic Bull-Slaying," in *Mithraic Studies*, ed. J. Hinnells (Manchester: Manchester University Press, 1975), esp. pp. 304–309. See also Christensen,

Premier homme, I, 101; and Robert Turcan, "Le sacrifice mithriaque," in *Le sacrifice dans l'antiquité,* pp. 341–380, esp. 369f.

11. See examples such as those described in M. J. Vermaseren, *Corpus Inscriptionum et Monumentorum Religionis Mithriacae,* 2 vols. (The Hague: Martinus Nijhoff, 1956–1960) as entries numbered 158, 172, 173, 181, 212, 245, 310, 321, 321 bis, 335, 350, 357, 366, 368, 397, to list but a few.

12. Although I have been critical of the views of Herman Lommel, "Mithra und das Stieropfer," *Paideuma* 3 (1949):207–219, insofar as he attempted to reconstruct a picture of the pre-Zoroastrian god Mithra from the content of the Mithraic Mysteries (see *Priests, Warriors, and Cattle,* p. 66n), this study now appears to me to be most valuable and perceptive for what it tells us about the Indo-Iranian and IE view of the interrelation of cattle, plants, and fluids, set within the context of sacrificial ritual and cosmogonic speculation, as well as for showing how these ideas were preserved within Hellenistic Mithraism.

13. On the Vṛtra myth see above all Emile Benveniste and Louis Renou, *Vṛtra et Vṛθragna* (Paris: Imprimerie Nationale, 1934). While not initially a cosmogonic myth (see *Priests, Warriors, and Cattle,*pp. 103–124), the Vṛtra myth is elevated to cosmogonic status in later Indian texts, which emphasize the importance of the warrior god Indra within the pantheon and, by extension, the importance of the warrior class within society.

14. The equation of Prajāpati with Puruṣa is established in such texts as *SB* 7.4.1.15 and 6.1.1.5. On the relation of the two figures see, inter alia, Levi, *Doctrine du sacrifice,* pp. 13–35; Gonda, *Die Religionen Indiens,* I, 187–197, esp. 190.

15. For the nature and importance of such wordplay in general, see Jan Gonda, "The Etymologies in the Ancient Indian Brāhmaṇas," *Lingua* 5 (1955):61–68.

16. Note the fact that Vṛtra is regularly portrayed as a serpentine monster, and serpents are never offered as sacrificial victims in Vedic India (or anywhere else in the IE world), domestic animals alone being suitable.

17. A secondary motif enters here, i.e., the homology of hair and plants, for the author takes pains to show that it is only because the libations contain the hair rubbed off Prajāpati's palms that they are able to give rise to plants, the alloform of hair. A similar fusion of the homologies animals/food and hair/plants is encountered in the *Commentary to the Pahlavi Vendidad,* TD MS. 606.7–11, pub. in Kaikhosrow Jamaspasa, "The Ritual of Hair-trimming and Nail-paring in Zoroastrianism," in *Monumentum Georg Morgenstierne* (Leiden: E. J. Brill, 1981), p. 328: "He who (disposes of) hair (in the proper ritual fashion) makes the grass grow, from which each cow that feeds (upon the grass) becomes pregnant twice over, and from the milk of that cow, health and healing from many illnesses arrives for (all) creatures." Here the progression is hair → plants → animals → fluids, and it is the fluids that contain restorative powers.

18. The formula "To the waters, thou, to the plants!" (*adbhyas tvauṣadhibhyaḥ*) is used for the sacrificial animal according to *VS* 6.9; *TS* 1.3.11.1, 3.5.8.1; *KS* 3.5, 26.8, 30.5; *ASS* 7.26.12; and *MSS* 7.2.4.

One is also reminded of the etiological myth of the Athenian Bouphonia ("Cattle-killing") ritual, as related in Porphyry, *DeAbst* 2.28-29. There, the first sacrificial ox was singled out for slaughter because it had eaten cereal offerings set out for the gods. By eating this vegetable matter, it quite literally became "one who has plants as its body," and this identity was later reinforced after the beast's sacrifice, when its hide was stuffed with fodder and the resulting effigy set up as if the animal were alive again (*doran tou boos rhapsantes kai khortōi apogkōsantes exanestēsan*), the ox thus being resurrected as "one who has plants as its body."

Recognition of the homology cattle/food (= fluids + edible plants) also suggests a sweeping new line of interpretation for all Indo-Iranian sacrifices, which existed in two major forms: animal offerings and those of *Sauma (Skt *soma*- Av *haoma*-, OPers *hauma*-), the latter involving a plant regularly regarded as the prototype of all plants, mixed with various fluids (water and/or milk). These two forms of sacrifice thus present alloformic offerings, and it might well be that the purpose of such sacrifices was to transform one alloform into the other. Thus, one would sacrifice cattle or other domestic animals to produce food (i.e., water, milk, butter, grains, and/or vegetables), while sacrificing *Sauma (i.e., plants + fluid) to produce animals that would replenish the herds.

19. In two other, rather brief passages, food plants are associated with the bodies of animals, particularly their pelts. Given this last specification, however, it is difficult to be certain whether these should be grouped within the homology cattle/food or that of hair/plants. Perhaps, like the story of Prajāpati in *SB* 2.2.4.3–5 (quoted above as the Indic "Variant III") or the Iranian text quoted in note 17, the two homologies have been fused to a certain extent.

The first text is part of an Old Bulgarian creation account, found in M. P. Dragomanov, *Notes on the Slavic Religio-Ethical Legends: The Dualistic Creation of the World,* trans. E. W. Count (The Hague: Mouton, 1961), p. 2: "At that time the devil created the goat, and, as he was coming to the Lord, he straddled the billy and gave him a bridle made of a leek; from then on goats have had beards." The second text occurs in Simon Grunau's *Preussische Chronik* 2.4.1, in a passage where the author is relating the wonders of the Prussian landscape, flora, and fauna: "There one finds the wild ox calle 'Aurochs,' which is unbelievably huge. This beast must be slain by an arrow in its mane, for its flesh is such that it is covered with garlic, which in the wilderness blooms into an herb called 'wild lillies.' "

20. On the Erainn and Cu Roi, see T. F. O'Rahilly, *Early Irish History and Mythology* (Dublin: Institute for Advanced Studies, 1946), pp. 75–84.

21. For fuller discussion see Pokorny, *Indogermanisches etym Wb* p. 483; Frisk, *Griechisches etym Wb,* I, 253–255; and Chantraine, *Dictionnaire étymologique de la langue grecque,* pp 185f.

22. This is a correction to the undue stress I earlier placed on the difference between the role played by the primordial animal in Germanic and Roman versions on the one hand and in Irish and Indo-Iranian versions on the other (*Priests, Warriors, and Cattle,* pp. 86–92). I now perceive two broad thematic

patterns within the sitiogonic tradition, one in which the first bovine provides food by giving milk (the "lactational" pattern) and one in which it is killed and transformed into food (the "sacrificial" pattern).

23. This range of meaning is apparent in the semantics of such terms as Skt *paśu-*, Pahl *gōspand* (on which see n.6 above), Lt *pecus*, and Eng *cattle*. On PIE **peku-* see *Priests, Warriors, and Cattle*, p. 65 and n. 98, *pace* Benveniste, *Vocabulaire*, I, 47–61.

Wild animals and the meat taken from wild animals do not seem to play a part in IE thinking about food, all of which was focused on the realm of culture, not nature. Once wild animals are excluded from consideration, the groupings of fluids, plants, animals, and humans into relations of eater and eaten assume a clear and elegant form, as follows:

	Item eaten		
Eaters	Fluids	Plants	Animals
Plants	X		
Animals	X	X	
Humans	X	X	X

When one introduces wild animals—that is, carnivores—into this system, the system collapses, for such animals not only eat meat (the prerogative of humans) while scorning plants (the proper food of animals), they even go so far as to eat humans. Wild beasts thus not only are a physical threat, but also pose a threat to the structures of thought appropriate to cultured existence.

24. For explicit definition of food as plants plus fluids, see *SB* 7.2.3.2 and *Yt* 19.32. In the latter text, water and plants are referred to as "the two foods" (*uye x^{v}arəθe*).

25. See Schrader-Nehring, *Reallexikon*, II, 101–103.

26. For discussions of the complex emotional attitudes and ideological systems regarding the eating of meat, see, inter alia, Marcel Detienne, "La cuisine de Pythagore," *Archives de sociologie des religions* 29 (1970):141–163; idem and J.-P. Vernant, eds., *La cuisine de sacrifice en pays grec* (Paris: Gallimard, 1979); Jean-Pierre Vernant, "Sacrificial and Alimentary Codes in Hesiod's Myth of Prometheus," in R. L. Gordon, eds., *Myth, Religion, and Society* (Cambridge: Cambridge University Press, 1981), pp. 57–79; Cristiano Grottanelli, Niccolo Parise, and Pier Giorgio Solinas, eds., "Sacrificio, organizzazione del cosmo, dinamica sociale," *Studi Storici* 25 (1984):829–956.

27. Similar ambivalence toward meat-eating is evident in such texts as Porphyry, *De Abst* 1.15, 1.26–27, where meat is said to be necessary for athletes and others engaged in an active life, also being used by physicians for the restoration of health, but injurious to philosophers and other elevated souls. Note also, in Iran, *PRDD* 14, which begins by quoting a lost Avestan text in which Ohrmazd states that he has created livestock "so that you men may eat them" (14.1), but which ends with the Wise Lord assuring the cattle, "He who

eats your flesh remains very evil—he becomes all the evil he makes for the cattle" (14.5).

28. A similar point is made by other pastoral peoples. Note, for instance, the following Masai text, recorded by A. C. Hollis, *The Masai: Their Language and Folklore* (Oxford: Clarendon Press, 1905), pp. 289–290: "Now cattle feed on grass, and the Masai love grass on this account . . . The Masai love grass very much, for they say, 'God gave us cattle and grass, we do not separate the things which God has given us.' "

29. The Iranian texts, *ZS* 3.42–51 and *GBd* 13.0–9, differ in this regard. Alone of the texts I have considered, they posit individual alloforms for each of the primordial ox's bodily parts, whereby a specific species of grain or herb grew from each part, gaining thereby the ability to restore that part and only that part.

30. In herbal healing the body is also restored through use of the materials that were created from the first bovine (see Chapter 5).

31. At one time it was fashionable, following the arguments of Götze, "Persische Weisheit in griechischem Gewande," to posit Iranian influence on those aspects of Greek medicophilosophical thought involving the relation of the human body to the universe as microcosm to macrocosm. This view has been refuted, however, by Duchesne-Guillemin, "Persische Weischeit in griechischem Gewande?," who demonstrated the independence of the Greek ideas from Iranian influence. His views have been accepted by most current experts on ancient Greek medicine, e.g. Robert Joly, *Recherches sur le traité pseudo-hippocratique Du Régime, Bibliothèque de la Faculté de Philosophie et Lettres de l'Uliversité de Liège* 156 (1960):37–52; Mansfeld, *The Pseudo-Hippocratic Tract Peri Hebdomadōn*, pp. 22–24; and Gheorghe Bratescu, "Les éléments vitaux dans la pensée médico-biologique orientale et dans la collection hippocratique," in M. D. Grmek, ed. *Hippocratica: Actes du Colloque hippocratic de Paris* (Paris: Editions deu CNRS, 1981), pp. 65–72. H. W. Bailey, *Zoroastrian Problems in the Ninth-Century Texts*, 2nd ed. (Oxford: Clarendon Press, 1971), pp. 78–119, argued for a certain amount of Greek influence, especially Aristotelian, on Middle Persian ideas of the nature of man and the universe including the theory of microcosm and macrocosm (p. 87), but recognized that these were fused with indigenous Old Iranian ideas—ideas that predisposed the Middle Persian authors to be receptive to similar Greek concepts. On the question of possible Greek influence on Iranian theories of nutrition, see note 41 below.

32. I have treated at greater length some of the materials that follow in "Archaic Theories of the Digestive Process," *Journal of Indo-European Studies*, forthcoming.

33. Among other Greek texts, see Plato's *Phaido* 96CD (which may or may not allude to Anaxagoras; I am inclined to believe it does not), and *Tim* 80D–81B; and within the Hippokratic corpus, such works as *Peri Nousōn* 4.33–34 (on which see Müller, *Gleiches zu Gleichem*, pp. 126–137); *Peri Diaitēs* 1.6 (see Joly, *Recherches*, pp. 26–32); *Peri Heb* 15 (see Paul Kucharski, "Anaxagore et les idées biologiques de son siècle," *Revue Philosophique* 154 [1964]:143–145; *Peri Sarkōn* 3 and 13 (see Kucharski, pp. 145–148; *Peri*

Trophēs 7–9; and *Peri Arkhaiēs Iatrikēs* 14. Kucharski, in particular, has shown how widespread these theories were in 5th-century Greece. See also I. M. Lonie, "A Structural Pattern in Greek Dietetics and the Early History of Greek Medicine," *Medical History* 21 (1977):235–260, for rich data and fascinating analyses, although some of the lines of historical development he posits cannot be accepted. It is worth noting that according to Lonie's researches (see esp. pp. 242–258), the primal food fed to patients with serious illnesses was a gruel (*ruphemata*) composed of fluid plus grain, from which they were gradually restored to a full diet.

Among Indo-Iranian sources, see in particular *SB* 3.9.1.1–5, 7.5.1.6–7, and 2.2.4.1–7; *Tandya Māhābrāhmaṇa* 21.2.1; *Tait Up* 3.2; *Praśna Up* 1.14; *M Up* 6.11–12; *Dk* 3.263 (Dresden ed. 211.10–15); and *ZS* 29.1–6. Also note *AitUp* 1.1–2.5, discussed in Chapter 1, in which it was hunger and thirst (*asanāyāpipāse*) that prompted the reassembling of Puruṣa's sundered body. That reassembling, presumably, took place through the act of eating, whereby the elements of the macrocosm re-entered his body, just as they re-enter the body of any eater.

34. See Aetius 1.3.5 (Diels-Kranz A46) and Lucretius, *De Rerum Natura* 1.859–869 (Diels-Kranz A44). Some scholars have also claimed that Plato, *Phaido* 96CD, refers to the theories of Anaxagoras, although the text does not make this claim and its general tone seems to indicate that a widespread view commonly held, rather than that of a single philosopher or philosophical school, is being discussed. Anaxagoras is mentioned by name, however, in a different context some paragraphs later at *Phaido* 97D.

35. Thus, e.g., Werner Jaeger, *The Theology of the Early Greek Philosophers* (Oxford: Clarendon Press, 1947), p. 156; Friedrich Solmsen, "Tissues and the Soul: Philosophical Contributions to Physiology," *Philosophical Review* 59 (1964):441–444; Kucharski, "Anaxagore et les idées biologiques de son siècle," esp. p. 159; and Guthrie, *History of Greek Philosophy*, II, 272. See also Müller, *Gleiches zu Gleichem*, pp. 69–72.

36. One is almost tempted to speculate that a Jewish rabbi in Romanized Judaea was instructing his pupils in Anaxagorean theory when he handed them bread and said "Take, this is my body" (Matthew 26.26, Mark 14.22, Luke 22.19).

37. The homology of fire/mouth is attested as early as *RV* 10.90.13. In general, this precise homology does not figure in cosmogonic speculation outside India, but the specification of fire as an "eater" is widespread, as in *Gylf* 46–47, the story of Loki's eating contest with fire. Note also ON *aldrnari* and OE *ealdornere* "nourisher of life" as kennings for "fire."

38. Note that this "food" is said to have "flowed forth," the verb used being Skt *sru-*, in contrast to *ut-kram-* "to leave, depart, stride forth," which is used for the exit of Prajāpati's breath and semen. Prajāpati's body was thus apparently reduced to a liquid, from which all other food was then produced, as in the other sitiogonic accounts I have considered.

39. According to Plutarch, *Quaestiones Physica* 1.911D (Diels-Kranz A117), Anaxagoras considered plants to be "living beings" (*zōa*) like humans and

animals, an opinion he shared with Plato and Empedokles. For Plato, this close relation of plants to human beings—he even calls them "a kindred to human substance" (*anthrōpines xuggenē physeōs physin, Tim* 77A) made them particularly suitable for use as food. See J. B. Skemp, "Plants in Plato's Timaeus," *Classical Quarterly* 41 (1947):53–60.

40. Note, for instance, the delightful analysis of GBd 28.10 (TD MS. 192.6–12), in which digestion is seen as a thoroughly ethical and dualistic process:

"Since men do good and evil deeds in the material world, when one dies, they calculate their good and evil deeds. One who is pure goes to heaven, and they throw one who is a possessor of the Lie into hell.

"Similarly, men eat food in comparable fashion. That which is good goes to the brain, where it becomes purified blood. It arrives at the heart, and it becomes strength for all the body. That which is mixed with poison, however, goes from the stomach to the intestines, and they throw it outside the body, just as if to hell."

41. The four elements listed here are strikingly close to the four cosmic elements in the Empedoklean system, which became normative in later Greek thought: earth (here clay), air (here wind), fire, and water (here moisture). Together, the four in the *Dēnkart* passage, as in post-Empedoklean Greece, constitute a cosmic totality, being the sole elements present in the entire cosmos (and, a fortiori, the human body). This detail (on which see Bailey, *Zoroastrian Problems*, pp. 88f.) makes it possible that there was Greek influence—perhaps only on this idea or possibly more thoroughgoing—behind the nutritional theories presented in *Dk* 3.157.18. Yet even were this so—and it is by no means certain—there would remain the Indic evidence of *SB* 7.1.2.1–6, written centuries before the birth of Empedokles or Anaxagoras. Diffusion from India to Greece to Iran is possible, if tortuous, but there is not the slightest evidence to suggest that Anaxagoras relied on Indic materials for his theory of nutrition. Rather than argue for direct dependence of one of these texts upon another via some process of diffusion, it thus seems preferable to view them as all drawing upon a common tradition.

42. This is a bit of an oversimplification, for if man is a microcosm of the universe and food is a microcosm of man, then food is also a microcosm of the universe (albeit one at a second remove). Indeed, the picture Anaxagoras presents is one of infinite microcosms nesting one within the other, ranging from the full universe down to the most microscopic speck of matter—although even this is an oversimplification, since even that most microscopic speck could be still further subdivided, and all its subspecks would be microcosms as well.

43. I am grateful to Françoise Bader for calling the importance of this story to my attention, and also for directing me Henri Quellet's stimulating discussion, "L'apologue de Ménénius Agrippa, la doctrine des souffles vitaux (Skr. *prāṇa*) et les origines du stoïcisme," *Travaux Neuchâtelois de Linguistique* 3 (1982):59–167. Quellet's argument for diffusion of certain constructs of mythic physiology from India to Rome via the Stoic philosophers seems unconvincing to me, however.

44. I have treated this side of the legend separately in "Ancora il mondo alla rovescia: Aspetti dell' inversione simbolica," *Annali della Facoltà di Lettere e Filosofia, Università di Siéna* 6 (1985), forthcoming.

45. The role assigned to the blood here is quite similar to that in the *GBd* 28.10, cited in n. 40 above. Also recall the central role Empedokles assigned to blood as the perfect element, in which the four elements (earth, air, fire, and water) are combined in equal proportion (fragments B98, B105).

46. For various versions of this last text see Walther Suchier, ed., *L'Enfant Sage (Das Gespräch des Kaisers Hadrian mit dem klugen kinde Epitus)* (Halle: Max Niemeyer, 1910), pp. 289f., 316f., 340, 409f., 430f. These manuscripts are written in Catalan, Provençal, and French, and date from the end of the 13th century to late in the 15th. Note also that in the *Puruṣasūkta*, before the narration of how the world was created from his body, Puruṣa is said to be "lord of immortality *and that which grows from food*" (*RV* 10.90.2).

47. Also note that when this Irish text gives an account of the creation of food it mentions only plants, not meat.

4. Cures for Baldness, Disposal of Hair

1. The Indic and Iranian myths I have cited both speak of the origin of grain (*SB* 4.2.1.11 *yava-*; *ZS* 3.43 and *GBd* 13.1 *jōrdā*), while in the old Irish version (*Adaigh Con Roi* 7), the term used is OIr *lus*, which has the generalized meaning of "plant" but in more specific contexts denotes particularly "herb" or "vegetable." On this last term see Marstrander, *Dictionary of the Irish Language*, L-247f.

2. See table 3. Of the terms employed for "plants," Pahl *urwar*, OCS *trava*, OFris *gerse*, and Skt *oṣadhi* all primarily denote grasses, while ON *baðmr* and Skt *vanaspati-* denote trees.

3. Pokorny, *Indogermanisches etym Wb*, p. 1139; Buck, *Dictionary of Selected Synonyms*, p. 204; Mayrhofer, *Kurzgefasstes etym Wb des altindischen*, III, 167f.

4. Pokorny, *Indogermanisches etym Wb*, pp. 1139f.; Buck, *Dictionary of Selected Synonyms*, p. 203. Regarding ON *vǫllr*, note its occurrence in the kenning given as the gods' name for trees or wood: *vallar fax* "meadow's mane" (*Alvíssmál* 28).

5. Johann Kirste, "Indogermanische Gebräuche beim Haarschneiden," in *Analecta Graeciensia: Festschrift zum 42 Versammlung deutscher Philologen und Schulmänner in Wien* (Graz: Styria, 1893), pp. 53–59.

6. See, for instance, the immediate dismissal of Kirste's case by Auguste Barth, "Bulletin des religions de l'inde," *Revue de l'histoire des religions* 27 (1893):281f., in favor of a bland analysis in which vegetation did not figure at all, tonsure being merely viewed as "a sort of ransom for the person tonsured" (p. 282).

7. See Durðica Palosija, "Das Brauchtum der Haarschurpatenschaft bei den Südslawen," *Zeitschrift für Balkanologie* 11 (1975):59–65; idem, "Zu

den Haarschurbräuchen bei den Slawen," *Ethnologia Slavica* 8/9 (1976/77): 193–202.

8. Use of folkloric evidence for the reconstruction of older customs and beliefs is always risky. While traditional practices of the rural populations of Europe and Asia have undoubtedly preserved contents of great antiquity into modern times, it is extremely difficult to be certain that this is the case in any specific instance. Yet I believe it would be an error to dismiss all folkloric data as useless for reconstructive research. Rather, it seems desirable that Indo-Europeanists learn to discriminate among the data offered by folk customs. I would offer a few general suggestions, stressing that these are to be taken less as rules of method than as logical probabilities: (1) Public behaviors are more likely to be conservative than are private behaviors, public scrutiny acting as a hedge against change. (2) Ritual behaviors are more likely to be conservative than are nonritualized behaviors, in part because ritual involves the formalized faithful repetition of prescribed behaviors, and also because sacred sanctions may be invoked against breaches of ritual propriety. (3) "Ceremonies of the first time," such as the first tonsure, the first meal in a new house, and so forth, tend to be occasions on which individuals and communities take special care to enact traditional behaviors faithfully. (4) The behaviors of prominent personages, particularly those whose actions are thought to affect the welfare of an entire community, such as kings or priests, are more likely to be conservative than the behaviors of lesser individuals.

As an example of the last point, note that although the prescriptions of *Vd* 17 regarding disposal of hair and nail clippings (to be considered later in this chapter) ought to apply to every Zoroastrian every time his or her hair and nails are cut, in modern practice, only the priests—and indeed, only the most elevated or pious of them—carry out these prescriptions faithfully; J. J. Modi, *Religious Ceremonies and Customs of the Parsees* (Bombay: J. B. Karani, 1937), p. 161.

9. See also *KGS* 2.4.31, *GGS* 2.10.26, *HGS* 2.2.6.13. For a translation of the passage from the *SGS* see Hermann Oldenberg, *The Grihya Sūtras*, 2 vols. (Oxford: Clarendon Press, 1886–1892), I, 55–57.

10. On the expression *arbor felix*, here translated "fruitful tree," associated in Rome with a whole system of classification as to whether trees are fruitful or unfruitful, auspicious or inauspicious, see Jacques André, "Arbor felix, arbor infelix," in Marcel Renard and Robert Schilling, eds., *Hommages á Jean Bayet* (Brussels: Collection Latomus, 1964), pp. 35–46.

11. W. Pötscher, "Flamen Dialis, "*Mnemosyne* 21 (1968):215–239, a discussion centering on the relations of the *Flamen* and the *Flaminica*, seen as a model of the *hieros gamos* between heaven and earth.

12. The passage from Homer that Pliny alludes to is either *Iliad* 14.348, where Zeus prepares a bed of lotus, crocus, and hyacinth for Hera and himself, or *Odyssey* 9.82–104, the incident of the Lotus-eaters.

13. Hanns Bächtold-Stäubli, "Haar," in E. Hoffman-Krayer and H. Bächtold-Stäubli, *Handwörterbuch des deutschen Aberglaubens*, III (Berlin: Walter de Gruyter, 1930/31), 1273, and the literature cited in nn. 297 and 300; Wilhelm

Mannhardt, *Germanische Mythen* (Berlin: Ferdinand Schneider, 1858), p. 630; Adolf Wuttke, *Der deutsche Volksaberglaube der Gegenwart*, 4th ed. (Leipzig: Moritz Ruhl, 1925), p. 330.

14. Palosija, "Das Bauchtum der Haarschurpatenschaft," p. 63.

15. Achende, (pseud.), "Burning Hair," *Notes and Queries*, ser. 3, vol. 10 (1866):146, cited by James Darmesteter, *Le Zend Avesta*, 3 vols. (Paris: Maisonneuve, 1892-93), II, 236. This seems a particularly significant rationale, for reasons we will see in Chapter 6. Briefly, it is a variant upon the more general idea that matter will be returned to the microcosm from the macrocosm at the end of a cosmic cycle, omitting the intermediate step one might expect, i.e., that once buried the severed hair would be transformed into plants, from which form the material substance would be returned to hair at the resurrection.

16. This passage was studied by Jivanji Jamshedji Modi, "Two Iranian Incantations for Burying Hair and Nails," *Journal of the Anthropological Society of Bombay* 8 (1907–1909):557–572; he was, unfortunately, overly influenced by Frazerian ideas on the sorcerous use of hair and nails. Far preferable are the remarks of Darmesteter, *Le Zend Avesta*, II,236 and esp. 238, n. 9, who perceived the underlying system of microcosm and macrocosm behind this simple ceremony.

17. The *Commentary on the Pahlavi Vendidad*, TD MS. 606.7–11, preserves the connection of plants to cattle, as in *Y* 48.6: "He who (treats) hair (thus) makes the grass grow, from which each cow that feeds (upon the grass) becomes pregnant twice over."

18. This follows from four points, the first of which derives from the Avestan text alone, the others from data external to it. First, the discussion in *Vd* 17 continues, verses 7–11 being a separate consideration of the proper means for the disposal of nails. This discussion is far inferior to that of *Vd* 17.1–6; the *maθra* one is told to recite when burying nails (taken from *Y* 34.7b) either has been totally misunderstood in its grammatical construction or has been twisted about for a bit of wordplay (see Darmesteter, *Le Zend Avesta*, II, 238, n. 12). Consideration of nails thus seems to be artificially appended to that of hair. Second, the nouns formed from PIE *wel- denote hair and vegetation only, not nails. Third, the cosmogonic/anthropogonic tradition includes only hair and vegetation, nails appearing in but a very few isolated reflexes (see Chapter 1). Fourth, while the physical similarities of hair and plants are quite clear, those of nails and plants are not. Rather, nails seem to be grouped together with hair because of the similarities of these two body parts (location at extremities, incessant growth, freedom from pain when cut), and to be associated to plants only as the result of the homology hair/plants.

19. This is a daēvic term, identifying the louse as a demonic creature. On *spiš* see E. Benveniste, "Une différenciation de vocabulaire dans l'Avesta," in W. Wüst, ed., *Indo-Iranica: Ehrengabe für Wilhelm Geiger* (Leipzig: Otto Harrassowitz, 1931), pp. 223f.

20. A similar instance, in which nails improperly disposed of turn into antimatter, is found in the *Gylf* 55 account of the "Nail-Ship" *Naglfar*; see my

"Treatment of Hair and Fingernails among the Indo-Europeans," *History of Religions* 16, no. 4 (May 1977):360f. Note, however, that the etymology of ON *Naglfar* remains subject to debate. Most recently, see Edgar Polomé, "Two Etymological Notes," in *Festschrift J. Knobloch* (forthcoming).

Hair might also be transformed into antimatter, predictably, through the improper performance of sacrificial dismemberment; note *SNS* 10.8: "Another (precept) is this: the strong avoidance of illicitly slaughtering the species of domestic animals. For in the *Sūdkar (Nask)*, it is said regarding those who illicitly slaughter livestock, that the hair of those animals becomes like sharp arrows, and the one who has slaughtered illicitly is killed."

21. On the Ahuna Vairya see Molé, *Mythe, culte et cosmologie*, pp. 154–156; E. Benveniste, "La prière Ahuna Varya dans son exégèse zoroastrienne," *Indo-Iranian Journal* 1 (1957):77–85.

22. Text given in Bächtold-Stäubli, *Handwörterbuch des deutschen Aberglaube*, III, 1245. See also Jacob Grimm, *Deutsche Mythologie*, III, 446, item 376.

23. Full text given in Bächtold-Stäubli, *Handwörterbuch des deutschen Aberglaubens*, III, 1245.

24. In the Indian epic tradition, the homology of hair and plants is also employed without either anthropogonic or cosmogonic directionality, particularly in scenes wherein the luxuriant hair of the heroine (Sītā in the *Rāmāyaṇa*, Draupadī in the *Mahābhārata*) represents the earth's vegetation, the heroine herself representing the earth. See Daniel Dubuisson, "La déesse chevelue et la reine coiffeuse: recherches sur un thème épique de l'inde ancienne," *Journal asiatique* 266 (1978):291–310; and Alf Hiltebeitel, "Draupadi's Hair," *Puruṣārtha* 4 (1980).

25. Bächtold-Stäubli, *Handwörterbuch des deutschen Aberglaubens*, III, 1242, and the sources cited there in nn. 19–26.

26. The same basic story is given in the *Book of Leinster* version of the *Tain*, ll. 1973–1979, although there only mulberry juice is employed. The significance of this passage was first called to my attention by William Sayers, whose study of "Early Irish Attitudes Toward Hair and Beards, Baldness and Tonsure," is forthcoming in *Zeitschrift für celtische Philologie* (1986).

27. See A. Ernout, ed., *Pline l'ancien, Histoire Naturelle*, XII (Paris: Les Belles Lettres, 1949), 89.

28. Pliny, *NH* 12.37.

29. Certain Indic texts make interesting use of this complementarity by describing the earth as being "bald" (Skt *kālvālikr̥tā*, *r̥kṣā*, or *alomakā*), the creation of plants (often from Prajāpati's hair) being thus a cure for macrocosmic "baldness." See, for instance, *SB* 2.2.4.3–5 (studied in Chapter 3) or *TS* 7.4.3.1.

5. *Magical Healing*

1. See my discussion in "The Ferryman of the Dead," *Journal of Indo-European Studies* 8 (1980):45 and n. 17.

2. See Pokorny, *Indogermanisches etym Wb*, p. 706; Buck, *Dictionary of Selected Synonyms*, p. 307; and Schrader-Nehring, *Reallexikon*, I, 60.

3. Emile Benveniste, "La doctrine médicale des indo-européens," *Revue de l'histoire des religions* 130 (1945):5–7. The broader sense of IE *med- is apparent in such derivates as Gk *medōn* ~ *medeōn* "ruler, leader," Osc *med-dīss* (< *medo-dik̂-s*) "judge," Arm *mit* "thought," OIr *midiur* "I think, I judge," and Lt *meditor, -ārī* "to think over, ruminate on."

4. Pokorny, *Indogermanisches etym Wb*, p. 520; Buck, *Dictionary of Selected Synonyms*, p. 301; Feist, *Etym Wb des gotischen Spraches*, pp. 232f.

5. *Kai-lo- occurs as a formulaic greeting or drinking toast, as in Goth *hails* or OE *hāl* (Eng *hail;* see *Beowulf* 407 for the OE usage), OBulg *cĕlujǫ* and Russ *čelovat'* "to greet, to kiss (in greeting)," and OPruss *kails*, which occurs in three separate drinking formulas, on which see William R. Schmalstieg, *Studies in Old Prussian* (University Park: Pennsylvania State University Press, 1976), pp. 87, 92–93. On the Germanic terms see Walter Baetke, *Das Heilige im Germanischen* (Tübingen: J. C. B. Mohr, 1942).

The IE adjective *solwo- "whole, total, healthy," also is used as a saluation in Gk *oule* (< *holwos*) and Lt *salvē* (< *salve*, with an imperative replacing the earlier vocative under the influence of *valē*). The application of this term to the sphere of physical well-being is evident in Av *haurva-tāt-* and Skt *sarva-tāti-* (the latter feminine), "wholeness, health," Alb *gjalë* "powerful, fat, lively," Arm *olĵ* (*solyo-*) "healthy, whole," and numerous related Italic forms such as Lt *salūs* "health, safety, deliverance," *salū-bris* "health-giving," and *salvus* "safe, saved, unharmed." On these, see Schrader-Nehring, *Reallexikon* I, 416–417, and Pokorny, *Indogermanisches etym Wb* pp. 979f.

6. James Darmesteter, *Ormazd et Ahriman* (Paris: F. Vieweg, 1877), p. 293; Benveniste, "La doctrine médicale des indo-européens," pp.5–12; Jaan Puhvel, "Mythological Reflections of Indo-European Medicine," in George Cardona et al., eds., *Indo-European and Indo-Europeans* (Philadelphia: University of Pennsylvania Press, 1970), pp. 369–382.

7. *Yt* 3.6 also contains a variant of the passage from *Vd* 7.44, which Puhvel, "Mythological Reflections of Indo-European Medicine," p. 375, considered to be older and more authentic in its listing and order of medical specialties, a conclusion with which I would differ. The passage reads as follows: "Among sacred formulas—that which cures by Right, that which cures by the law, that which cures by the knife, that which cures by plants, and that which cures by sacred formulas (alone)—the most curing of cures is that which cures by the beneficent sacred formula." In assessing the importance of this variant, first note that the elevation of "that which cures by Right" (*ašō.baēšaza-*), unknown elsewhere, to first position is due entirely to the occurrence of this verse within a hymn dedicated to Right (*Aša*), the *Ardwahišt Yašt*. Second, the order of *Yt* 3.6 is quite different from that of either Gk reflex, whereas that of *Vd* 7.44 corresponds closely to that of the Gk testimonies. Third, for all that healing by sacred formulas (*mąθrō.baēšaza-*) has been reduced to final position in the list, it is still stressed as "the most curing of cures" (*baēšazanąm baēšazyōtəmō*), and, moreover, all

the modes of curing are listed as subtypes of sacred formulas, given the inital *mąθranąm* of the passage.

8. Arthur Christensen, *L'Iran sous les sassanides* (Copenhagen: Einar Munksgaard, 1944), p. 420. Benveniste, "La doctrine médicale des indo-européens," pp. 10–11, also adduced *RV* 10.39.3 as a correspondence to Pindar's list of illnesses—the Aśvins are there called healers of the blind (*andha-*), the emaciated (*kṛśa*), and those whose bones are broken (*ruta-*)—but the specific terms of the comparison strike me as too weak to afford certainty of common origin.

9. On the importance of fire see, inter alia, Johannes Maringer, "Fire in Prehistoric Indo-European Europe," *Journal of Indo-European Studies* 4 (1976):161–186.

10. Adalbert Kuhn, "Indische und germanische Segensspruch," *Zeitschrift für vergleichende Sprachforschung* 13 (1864):49–74, 113–156, from which the initial discussion of the Second Merseburg Charm is rpt. in Rüdiger Schmitt, ed., *Indogermanische Dichtersprache* (Darmstadt: Wissenschaftliche Buchgesells-chaft, 1968), pp. 11–25. Recent summaries of the materials treated by Kuhn, which support his views and add to them, are Rüdiger Schmitt, *Dichtung und Dichtersprache in indogermanischer Zeit* (Wiesbaden: Otto Harrassowitz, 1967), pp. 285–294; Rolf Ködderitzsch, "Der zweite Merseburger Zauberspruch und seine Parallelen," *Zeitschrift für celtische Philologie* 33 (1974): 45–57; and Enrico Campanile, *Ricerche di Cultura Poetica Indoeuropea* (Pisa: Giardini, 1977), pp. 88–96.

11. For the best treatments of the mythic frame-story, see Siegfried Gu-tenbrunner, "Der Zweite Merseburger Spruch im Lichte nordischer Überlie-ferungen," *Zeitschrift für deutsches Altertum und deutsche Literatur* 80 (1943):1–5; Felix Genzmer, "Die Götter des zweiten Merseburger Zauberspruchs," *Arkiv for Norsk Filologi* 63 (1948):55–72; idem, "Germanische Zaubersprüche," *Germanisch-Romanische Monatschrift* 32 (1950):29–32; and Franz Rolf Schröder, "Balder und der zweite Merseburger Spruch," *Germanisch-Romanische Mon-atschrift* 34 (1953):161–182.

12. For the Finno-Ugric variants see Kaarle Krohn, "Wo und wann ents-tanden die finnischen Zauberlieder?" *Finnisch-Ugrische Forschungen* 1 (1901):148–158; and Reidar Th. Christiansen, *Die finnischen und nordischen Varianten des zweiten Merseburgerspruches*, Folklore Fellows Communication 18 (Hamina, 1914).

13. Matthew 21.1–9; Mark 11.1–10; Luke 19.28–38; John 12.12–16. There is some ambiguity in these sources as to whether Jesus rode an ass or a colt (Matthew and John hold to the former, the others to the latter). This has been regularized as a horse in the Germanic version, to facilitate Jesus' replacing Wodan in the charm.

14. Note the connection of this text to themes of resurrection discussed in Chapter 6.

15. The most important text is cited by Kuhn, "Indische und germanische Segensspruch," pp. 151f.: "For the Lord, for the good deed, for Sts. Peter and Paul, Archangel Michael, and for the Angel of Christ, for this servant

of god, by name N.N. Place the two heights together, join them together . . . Grow together body with body, bone with bone, vein (or: sinew) with vein (or: sinew). Christ sealed himself to seal all men. Closed be this wound of the servant of God, by name N.N. In three days and three hours, may there be neither pain nor itching, without blood, without wound for the century. Amen." Again, as in *Codex Vat* 4395, the raising of Christ from the dead is the mythic prototype that guarantees the success of the charm, this being signaled by the provision that the healing will be accomplished in three days, the time elapsed between the crucifixion and the resurrection.

16. For two interpretations of the significance of the Arundhati see Victor Henry, *La magie dans l'Inde ancienne* (Paris: E. Leroux, 1904), p. 180; and Jean Filliozat, *La doctrine classique de la médecine indienne* (Paris: Imprimerie nationale, 1949), pp. 110f.

17. The major exception to this is Bernfried Schlerath, "Zu den Merseburger Zaubersprüchen," rpt. in Schmitt, ed., *Indogermanische Dichtersprache*, pp. 325–333, and rebutted by Schmitt, *Dichtung und Dichtersprache*, pp. 285–290.

18. Pokorny, *Indogermanisches etym Wb*, p. 750. Note also OHG *mar(a)g*, *mar(a)k*, ON *mergr*, OPruss *musgeno*, all of which mean "marrow"; Lt *medulla* "marrow, pith"; Av *mazga-* "marrow, brain"; and OCS *mozg* "brain," alongside *moždan* "marrow."

19. Wolfgang Krause, *Die Kelten* (Tubingen: J. C. B. Mohr, 1929), p. 42. Krause actually cited *CMT* 33–35, although he did not discuss the text in full.

20. See discussion in W. H. S. Jones, ed., *Hippocrates*, 4 vols. (London: William Heinemann, 1931) IV, 184f.

21. Pokorny, *Indogermanisches etym Wb*, p. 783, noting also Alb *asht, ashtë*, Hitt *hastāi-*, and Lt *os* (more correctly *oss* < **ost*), genitive *ossis*.

22. The tremendous complexity of ideas that may be encoded in the simple gestures of healing ritual has been ably suggested by Herbert Fischer, "The Use of Gesture in Preparing Medicaments and In Healing," *History of Religions* 5 (1965):18–53.

23. Note the charms from Scotland and from Orkney Island cited in Kuhn, "Indische und germanische Segensspruch," pp. 53–54.

24. See the materials cited in Oskar Ebermann, "Blut- und Wundsegen," *Palaestra* 24 (1903):13–15.

25. Ibid., p. 16. A Swedish variant preserves the rhyme—*Mallt och Sallt* (p. 16)—and where the term *Schmär* is used to denote grease, the charm is adapted to preserve a rhyme, e.g., "Nimm Schmär und Salz klein, / und schmier dem Rösslein sein Gebein" (p. 13).

26. With regard to the gestures used in association with *AV* 4.12, *KS* 28.5–6 tells that the injured limb is to be washed with an infusion made from the Arundhati plant. See Henry, *La magie dans l'Inde antique*, p. 195.

27. His name, moreover ("Twin" < **Yemo-*), connects Yama to such other first-man figures as ON Ymir, Av Yima, and Lt Remus. On the linguistics of these comparisons, see note 3 to Chapter 1 and, more broadly, *Priests, Warriors, and Cattle*, pp. 69–95.

28. Similarly, the leaf used in the Norwegian charm is placed on the injured limb "so that these (i.e., bone, marrow, and flesh) should stay in their place." It thus seems to become a sort of sinew or connective tissue, and it may be that there existed a mythic prototype for such a transformation along lines like those of *AV* 5.5.8–9.

29. OIr *luib* is glossed as *herba (Irish Glosses* 114) and predominantly used to denote herbs with curative properties. See Carl Marstrander, gen. ed., *Contributions to a Dictionary of the Irish Language: L* (Dublin: Royal Irish Academy, 1966), pp. 237f., and the texts cited therein.

30. This number also homologizes Miach's bodily parts to the number of days in the years establishing both year and body as total entities. Similarly, in India Prajāpati is regularly identified with the year via a mystic numerology. See, e.g., *SB* 6.2.2.8–9, 8.4.1.11, 8.4.4.20.

31. Similar ideas are found in *SB* 7.2.4.19–20, where it is said that the body of Prajāpati is put back together with all herbs and medicines.

32. Text from Ebermann, "Blut- und Wundsegen," p. 21.

33. Note also that the charm specifies that the stone must be replaced exactly in the spot from which it was taken; presumably the earth would suffer a wound if it were not so restored.

34. Text in Ebermann, "Blut- und Wundsegen," p.7.

35. Kuhn, "Indische und germanische Segensspruch," pp. 66–69. More recently, see Genzmer, "Germanische Zauberspruch," pp. 22–24; Schmitt, *Dichtung und Dichtersprache*, pp. 291–294; and Gerhard Eis, *Altdeutsche Zaubersprüche* (Berlin: Walter de Grutter, 1964), pp. 7–30.

36. Eis, *Altdeutsche Zaubersprüche*, pp. 10–19.

37. On *yakṣma* see Filliozat, *La doctrine classique de la médecine indienne*, pp. 83f.

38. Eis, *Altdeutsche Zaubersprüche*, pp. 24f. This notwithstanding, Eis—who is no specialist in Indo-European matters—preferred to think in terms of diffusion from India to Germany, a view that has been thoroughly rebutted by Schmitt, *Dichtung und Dichtersprache*, pp. 293f.

Also note the oath sworn by Fergus mac Róich just prior to his entry into battle near the culmination of the *Táin Bó Cúailnge*, which William Sayers, in "Fergus and the Cosmogonic Sword," has shown to preserve extremely ancient sacrificial, cosmogonic, and physiological materials. In the version given in *YBL* ll. 4009–4016, Fergus swears to strike "men's jaws from their necks, men's necks from their upper arms, men's upper arms from their elbows, men's elbows from their forearms, men's forearms from their fists, men's fists from their fingers, men's fingers from their nails." He goes on to threaten the same severance for "the top's of men's heads from their middles, men's middles from their thighs, men's thighs from their knees, men's knees from their calves, men's calves from their feet, men's feet from their toes, men's toes from their nails." In both of these series the final item is nails *(ingne)*, which mark the body's outermost extremity.

39. Comparing the terms encountered in the various versions of the charm for injury to limbs and in that against infestation yields yet another phonologic correspondence. Thus, Skt *snāvan-* and Gk *neuron*, the latter term occurring

in Hippokratic *Aphorisms* 6.19 and 7.28, both derive from an archaic heteroclite-stem noun from PIE *$sneH_1$ "to spin," as do also Arm *neard* "sinew, fiber," Tokh B. *ṣñaura* "nerve, sinew," and Av *snāvarə* "sinew." See Mayrhofer, *Kurzgefasstes etym Wb*, III, 533f.

40. Thus, verse 1 of *AV* 2.33 (= *RV* 10.163.1 and *AV* 20.96.17) drives the infection out of all the organs of the head (eyes, nose, ears, chin, tongue, brain); verse 2 (= *RV* 10.163.2 and *AV* 20.96.18) moves via the neck and throat to the upper torso (breastbone, backbone, shoulders, arms, forearms); verse 3 (cd of which = *RV* 10.163cd and *AV* 20.96.19cd) takes care of the internal organs of the upper chest cavity (heart, lungs, gall bladder(?), ribcage, kidney, liver); verse 4 (ab of which = *RV* 10.163.3ab and *AV* 20.96.19ab) passes down to the organs of the lower abdomen (intestines, bowels, rectum, belly, spleen, navel); and verse 5 (ab of which = *RV* 10.163.4ab and *AV* 20.96.20ab; cd of which is quite similar to, but with significant differences from, *RV* 10.163.4cd and *AV* 20.96.20cd) drives the infection out of the lower torso and limbs (back, hips, thighs, knees, heels, feet). It is at this point that *AV* 2.33 inserts the anomalous verse 6. *RV* 10.163.5 (= *AV* 20.96.21) goes on to drive the infection out from the urinary system (bladder and urethra) as well as from the outermost extremities of dead tissue (hair and nails). Johannes Hertel rightly compared these charms to the purification ceremony of *Vd* 8.35–72 (see also *Vd* 9.15–26) in an appendix to R. F. G. Müller, "Die Medizin im Ṛg Veda," *Asia Major* 6 (1930):377–385. In that ceremony the pollution of death, occasioned by touching a corpse, is washed away, starting at the top of the head and working downward to the soles of the feet, moving right to left in any instance of paired limbs or organs (ears, shoulders, thighs, knees, etc.).

41. Text from Vasily Nikolaevic Dobrovolsky, *Smolenskij Etnografičeskij Sbornik"*, I (St. Petersburg: 1891), 174. Trans. following M. Sokolov, *Russian Folklore* (New York: Macmillan, 1950), p. 251.

42. Thus, e.g., OIr *feith* "fiber, sinew, vein, nerve"; Lith *gýsla* "vein, sinew"; OCS *žila*, Russ *žíla*, and SCr *žȉla* "vein, sinew"; and Skt *snāvan-*, Av *snāvarə*, Sogd *sn'w*, all of which mean "sinew," beside Ossetic (Iron) *nvar* "vein."

43. This system of physiological organization from core to periphery is explicit in the Old Irish accounts of Miach's death, and in the Pahlavi literature, as for instance in *ZS* 30.4: "The material body is complete in seven layers. The innermost is the marrow. Around the marrow is the bone; around the bone is the flesh; around the flesh is the sinew (or: fat); around the sinew (or: fat) are the veins; around the veins is the skin; around the skin is the hair."

Indic sources also make explicit use of the same general system, as in *SB* 6.1.2.17 and 10.1.3.4 or, most concisely, *AB* 2.14: "Man (Puruṣa) is established out of five parts: hair, skin, flesh, bone, and marrow."

44. *Yašt* 8.43 reads as follows: "We sacrifice to the star Tištrya, possessing riches, possessing glory. He washes away all evils with water; traversing (the sky), he causes all to grow; most strong, he heals creation when he has received sacrifice, been sated, celebrated, welcomed."

45. For lists of the xrafstars see *Vd* 14.5, 18.65; *Sad Dar Bundahišn* 43; Herodotos 1.140. On their creation in order to attack the earth see *GBd* 4.15, 5.3, noting also that Ahriman himself assumed the form of a snake in his first assault on the good creation (*GBd*, 4.10). For the etymology of *xrafstra-* < PIE *skrep-* "to bite, sting, cut," see H. W. Bailey, "A Range of Iranica," in M. Boyce and I. Gershevitch, eds., *W. B. Henning Memorial Volume* (London: Lund Humphries, 1970), pp. 25–28.

46. On the myth of Tištar and Apaoša, with emphasis on the interpretation of their names, see B. Forssman, "Apaoša, der Gegner des Tištriia," *Zeitschrift für vergleichende Sprachforschung*, 82 (1968):37–61.

47. *GBd* 10.7–15; 3.19.

48. Thus Nyberg, *Manual of Pahlavi*, II, 163. Equally possible, however, is derivation from Av *pūti-* "putrefaction." The possibility that this ambiguity is intentional is most suggestive.

49. The two lakes are the Cecist (< Av *Caēcasta-*) and the Sōbar, on which see *GBd* 12.3–4 and *ZS* 3.24. The latter "throws off all coarseness in (all) directions, and keeps itself strong, bright, and pure." Of the former it is said that because of its unduly warm water "nothing comes into being in it" (TD MS. 92.3). The chief Av mention of this lake (*Yt* 5.49) contains the puzzling adjective *urvāp-*, for which James Darmesteter, *Études iraniennes* (Paris: F. Vieweg, 1883), II, 179–180, suggested the translation "of salty water." His case, accepted by Karl Friedrich Geldner, "Zur erklärung des Avesta," *Zeitschrift für vergleichende Sprachforschung* 28 (1887):187n., and rejected by Bartholomæ, *Altiranisches Wörterbuch*, p. 404, remains highly suggestive but not fully conclusive. More recently, see H. W. Bailey, "Irano-Indica," *Bulletin of the School of Oriental and African Studies*, 12 (1947/48):331, who holds open the possibility that Darmesteter was correct, in light of the Middle Parthian form *wl* for "salty."

50. The rivers are the Arang (< Av *Raŋha-*) and the Weh (< Av *Vaŋuhi-Dāitya-*), on which see GBd 11.1–7. They are said to have been totally peaceful before Ahriman's onslaught, their flowing motion having been precipitated by his attack; at the Renovation they will be still once more (*GBd* 11.7). But according to an Av source, *Vd* 1.2: "The first place and best dwelling which I, Ahura Mazdā, created was Airyana Vaējah, with the Vaŋuhi Dāitya (river). Then, in opposition to that, Aŋra Mainyu, the extremely deadly one, made the red serpent and the winter, created by demons." Later interpreters of the text clearly misunderstood the meaning of "the red serpent," for the Av *ažimca yim raoiδitəm*, where *raoiδita-* "red," derived from PIE *reudh-*, like Gk *ereuthos*, Lt *rūbidus*, OIr *rúad*, etc. is translated into Pahl as *az ī rōd* "serpent of the river," with Pahl *rōd* "river" (< OPers. *rautah-*, Av *raδah-*) in place of *raoiδita-*. It thus appears that the serpent was taken as the creation of Ahriman against the river Vaŋuhi Dāitya and the winter as his creation against the province Airyana Vaējah. Note also the tradition regarding the Dāitya, named without its standard Av adjective *vaŋuhi-* ("good"), in *GBd* 11A.7–8 (TD MS. 87.8–9): "(The Dāidī) has more xrafstars than all other rivers. As it says (in the Avesta): 'The river Dāidī is full of xrafstars'." One other fact should be

observed regarding the significance of the Weh in this passage: its homography with another Pahl term that figures prominently in the same chapter of the *GBd*. For both *weh* ("good" < Av *vohu-* [masc], *vaŋuhi-*[fem]) and *wiš* ("poison, venom" < Av *viša-*) are written with the characters *wyš*. The written form of the river's name thus introduces an ambiguity: the reader may take it as "venom" or "good," or—what I think is intended here—"the river that transforms venom into good."

51. See *GBd* 10.5. This process is explicitly compared to the circulation of blood within the body in *GBd* 28.8.

52. Compare *Gylf* 14, where we are told that, as part of the cosmogonic drama, the worms investing the body of the primordial victim were transformed into other pests along the lines of a six part homologic set:

Flesh	:	Earth
(Bones)	:	Stones
Worms	:	Dwarves

"The dwarves were first placed and came alive in Ymir's flesh, where they were maggots. But by the gods' decree, they acquired human wisdom and a human body, and they lived, moreover, in earth and in stones."

This should be compared to the story of the origin of xrafstars from the dismemberment of Dahāg, the arch-villain of Iranian national mythology, as related in *Dk* 9.21.8–10, where it is explicitly set parallel to the dismemberment of Yima (*Dk* 9.21.2) and implicitly to that of Gayōmart. The text reads as follows: "Upon Frēdōn's victory, he wished to kill Dahāg, and he beat him with his club on his side, heart, and skull, but Dahāg did not die from that beating. So (Frēdōn) struck him with his sword, and upon the first, second, and third blows many species of xrafstar poured out from the body of Dahāg. And the Creator, Ohrmazd, said to Frēdōn: 'Do not dismember Dahāg, for if you dismember Dahāg, you will make this earth full of serpents, otters, scorpions, lizards, tortoises, and frogs.' " This passage is discussed further in Marijan Molé, "La guerre des géants d'après le Sūtkar Nask," *Indo-Iranian Journal* 3 (1959):284.

53. See the interesting discussion by K. A. Wipf, "Die Zaubersprüche im Althochdeutschen," *Numen* 22 (1975): esp. 43–45 and (with direct reference to the Second Merseburg Charm) 48–49.

6. Death and Resurrection, Time and Eternity

1. See Chapter 5 and my "The Ferryman of the Dead," pp. 45–46 and n. 17.

2. Pokorny, *Indogermanisches etym Wb*, pp. 390f.

3. Ibid., pp. 735f.; see also Buck, *Dictionary of Selected Synonyms*, p. 286; Ernout-Meillet, *Dictionnaire étymologique de la langue latine*, pp.631f.

4. See, for instance, *Il* 16.856, 22.362; *Od* 11.214; *RV* 10.16.1–3, 10.13.4; *Y* 55.2; *Vd* 8.81, 19.7; *Gylf* 3; *Beow* 422–424; *Slovo* 157.

5. Processes of bodily decay figured prominently in IE thought regarding death, and in funerary rituals. See Kurt Ranke, *Indogermanische Totenverehrung* (Helsinki: Academia Scientiarum Fennica, 1951), esp. pp. 337–338, 342–346.

6. On this text see Erwin Rohde, *Psyche: Seelencult und Unsterblichkeitsglaube der Griechen*, 6th ed. (Tübingen: J. C. B. Mohr, 1910), II, 257–261; L. Farnell, *Greek Hero Cults and Ideas of Immortality* (Oxford: Clarendon Press, 1921), p. 398; Müller, *Gleiches zu Gleichem*, p. 169; and W. K. C. Guthrie, *In the Beginning: Some Greek Views on the Origins of Life and the Early State of Man* (London: Methuen, 1957), pp. 49–52. More broadly, see Gregory Nagy, "Patroklos, Concepts of Afterlife, and the Indic Triple Fire," *Arethusa* 13 (1980):161–195, esp. 183–184.

7. *Inscriptiones Graecae²*, I (Berlin: G. Reimer, 1883), 945.

8. Frisk, *Griechisches etym Wb*, II, 1141f. See also the famous scene of Sarpedon's swoon, *Il* 5.696–698, where Sarpedon breathes out his life-breath (*psykhē*), only to have it restored by its macrocosmic alloform, the wind:

> And his *psykhē* left him, and a mist poured down over his eyes.
> But he reawakened, and the breath of the north wind
> Blowing led him back to life—he who had evilly breathed forth his
> life-force (*kakōs kekaphēota thymon*).

9. See Guthrie, *In the Beginning*, pp. 11–45. The myths in which the first inhabitants of a given city are said to spring from the soil have been studied by François Vian, *Les origines de Thèbes* (Paris: Etudes et commentaires, 1963); and Enrico Montanari, *Il Mito dell' autoctonia: Linee di una dinamica mito-politica ateniese* (Rome: Bulzoni, 1981).

10. On this and similar passages in Euripides see Müller, *Gleiches zu Gleichem*, pp. 167–173.

11. This question and the entire chapter are introduced by a formulaic phrase indicating that this Pahl version draws on a now-lost Av original: "In the Religion, it is revealed that . . ."

12. On this internal fire, see such texts as *GBd* 18.3 and 7, *ZS* 29.3–5. The homology fire/light is of no real consequence in the analysis of death as presented at *ZS* 34.7, however, as is apparent from the fact that when the author considers resurrection in *ZS* 34.8–15 he makes no mention of fire/light, nor does it figure in any of the other Pahl discussions of death and resurrection.

13. The question of the relation between burial and cremation in Indo-European treatment of the dead remains vexed. For a general summary, see Schrader-Nehring, *Reallexikon* I, 102–118, 123–136. But even with cremation, the bones—which would not be consumed by the heat of a wood fire— would have been buried. Although the later Zoroastrian tradition rejected both cremation and burial as polluting the sacred fire and sacred earth respectively, it now appears that burial was a regular part of earlier Iranian funerary practice, as evidenced by the etymology of Av *daxma-* "place for the

corpse's exposure" in attested usage, but originally "grave, tomb," as demonstrated by Karl Hoffmann, "Av. daxma-," *Zeitschrift für vergleichende Sprachforschung* 79 (1965):238.

14. I am grateful to Hanns-Peter Schmidt for pointing out errors in my earlier line of interpretation, "Death and Resurrection in Indo-European Thought," *Journal of Indo-European Studies* 5 (1977): 249–250.

15. See such a usage in *AV* 1.17.4, where the patient is asked to rest quietly (*ilayati*) for a while as part of his treatment.

16. Whereas *BṛhadUp* 3.2.13 has two separate homologies—breath(*prāṇa-*)/wind and self(*ātman-*)/atmosphere(*ākāśa-*), these two fall together here. Etymologically, Skt *ātman-* is akin to OHG *ātum* (modern German *Atem*) "breath." See Mayrhofer, *Kurzgefasstes etym Wb*, I,73, and Pokorny, *Indogermanisches etym Wb*, p. 345.

17. The phrase "heaven and earth" (*dyām ca . . . pṛthivīm*) is simply formulaic.

18. Thus, Keith, *Religion and Philosophy of the Veda and Upanishads*, p. 405; Gonda, *Religionen Indiens*, I, 138.

19. See, in particular, the "Epistle Didicatorie" of the *Devotions* and the heading to the 21st Meditation.

20. See Mary Paton Ramsay, *Les doctrines médiévales chez Donne*, 2nd ed. (London: Oxford University Press, 1924), pp. 246–253; Milton Allan Rugoff, *Donne's Imagery: A Study in Creative Sources* (New York: Russell and Russell, 1962), pp. 43–45; and Eluned Crashaw, "Hermetic Elements in Donne's Poetic Vision," in A. J. Smith, ed., *John Donne: Essays in Celebration* (London: Methuen, 1972), pp. 324–348, esp. 333–335.

21. Other figures of the English Renaissance were also receptive to the ancient theories of microcosm and macrocosm, preserved and transmitted through Neoplatonic, Hermetic, and Alchemical sources. I considered Sir Walter Raleigh's treatment of the theme in Chapter 1. Note also Ariel's song from *The Tempest*, act I, sc. 2, in which Shakespeare viewed death as the transmutation of bodily matter into macrocosmic alloforms:

> Full fathom five thy father lies;
>   Of his bones are coral made;
> Those are pearls that were his eyes;
>   Nothing of him that doth fade,
> But doth suffer a sea-change
> Into something rich and strange.
> Sea-nymphs hourly ring his knell.

Nor does the tradition end here, for it was the failure of such processes in the modern world—the inability of individual death to attain sacrificial significance, sustaining the cosmos while conveying dignity and meaning to mortal existence—that prompted T. S. Eliot's The *Wasteland*, which alludes to many of the passages I have discussed. On the popularity of the microcosm theory in 16th- and 17th- century England see Leonard Barkan, *Nature's Work of Art: The Human Body as Image of the World* (New Haven: Yale University Press, 1975).

22. Also note the account given in *Boroma* 40 of the death of the Irish king Loegaire mac Neill. Having violated an oath he had sworn by the elements, Loegaire was brought to judgment accordingly, "so that the elements laid a doom of death upon Loegaire alongside of Casse: the earth to swallow him and the sun to burn him and the wind to depart from him." This passage has been discussed by G. F. Dalton, "The Ritual Killing of the Irish Kings," *Folklore* 81 (1970):11. Other Irish kings die under circumstances whereby their bodies fall to the elements fire, wind, and water, as for instance Muircertach mac Erca, who drowns in a vat of wine into which he fell while trying to escape a burning house, fleeing also a troop of phantoms led by a woman named Sín ("Storm Wind"). On this and other related texts, see ibid., pp. 1–22, and Clémence Ramnoux, "La mort sacrificielle du Roi," *Ogam* 6 (1954):209–218.

23. One is tempted to say that there is no creation without a destruction, but this formulation is a serious oversimplification. In truth, every act of creation is simultaneously an act of destruction: when a living organism is created, the cosmos is in that measure destroyed or de-created, and conversely, when the cosmos is created or its material substance renewed, a living organism is destroyed or de-created.

24. Based on such texts as Hesiod *WD* 106–201, *BYt* 1.1–5, *Dk* 9.8, *Manu* 1.81–86, *Vsp* 45, Strabo 4.4.4, *Tain Bó Cuailnge*, *BL* 4732–4738, and the "Song of the Little World" from the Welsh *Book of Taliesin*, one may perceive a traditional analysis of temporal cycles common among the IE peoples, in which creation is followed by a sequence of four world ages, each of which is morally and physically worse than its predecessor. This sequence ends in cosmic catastrophe, usually involving fire, earthquake, and/or flood (that is, destruction by action of the macrocosmic elements), after which creation begins anew. We can now perceive the finer mechanics of this cataclysm and renovation: the destruction of the cosmos produces the resurrection of the dead, and the sacrifice of one or more of those who have just arisen re-creates the cosmos. A thorough consideration of these themes lies beyond the scope of the present work, demanding a book unto itself. On the system of world-ages and cycles of creation and destruction, see Rudolf von Roth's classic treatment, *Der Mythus von den fünf Menschengeschlechtern bei Hesiod* (Tübingen: L. T. Fues, 1860); and Christensen, *Premier homme*, I, 57–62. Others who have dealt with this theme are Reitzenstein, *Studien zum antiken Synkretismus*, pp. 45–68; Jula Kerschensteiner, *Platon und der Orient* (Stuttgart: W. Kohlhammer, 1945), pp. 161–179; B. L. van der Waerden, "Das Grosse Jahr und die ewige Wiederkehr," *Hermes* 80 (1952):129–155; Guthrie, *In the Beginning*, pp. 63–79; Arthur O. Lovejoy and George Boas, *Primitivism and Related Ideas in Antiquity* (Baltimore: Johns Hopkins Press, 1935); Charles Mugler, "Le retour éternel et le temps linéaire dans la pensée grecque," *Bulletin de l'association Guillaume Budé* (1966):405–419; and Natrovissus (pseud.), "Le chant du petit monde d'après Taliesin," *Ogam* 3 (1951):167–171.

On the Greek data, note the novel lines of interpretation proposed by Jean-Pierre Vernant, *Mythe et pensée chez les grecs* I (Paris: Maspero, 1974), 13–41, 42–79, and the criticisms offered by J. Defradas, "Le mythe hesiodique des races: essai de mise au point," *L'information littéraire* 4 (1965):152–156; and K. Matthiessen, "Form und Funktion des Weltaltermythos bei Hesiod," in G. W. Bowersock et al., eds., *Arktouros: Hellenic Studies Presented to Bernard M. W. Knox* (Berlin: Water de Gruyter, 1979), pp. 25–32. I understand that William Sayers has recently completed a study of the Celtic materials that will soon be scheduled for publication.

25. See *Yt* 19.11, 19.89, and *Fragment Westergaard* 4.3, which states: "The deceased rise up again; corporeal life is placed back into lifeless bodies, from which life had been separated." Lommel, *Religion Zarathuštras*, pp. 232f., maintained that the idea of the resurrection was already implicit in such passages of the Gathic Avesta as *Y* 30.7 and 34.14, but while I am in sympathy with his general point, I find neither citation convincing.

26. On *frašagird* see Bailey, *Zoroastrian Problems*, pp. vii-xv. For useful discussions of Zoroastrian eschatology see Lommel, *Religion Zarathuštras*, pp. 219–236; Widengren, *Religionen Irans*, pp. 105–108, Boyce, *History of Zoroastrianism*, I, 242–246; and above all Molé, *Culte, mythe, et cosmologie*, pp. 86–100, 412–418. Note that the attempt to fit traditional ideas, originally part of a system that stressed the infinity and cyclicity of time, into the Zoroastrian system, in which the duration of the material world was rigidly limited to 12,000 years, produced many transformations of the common IE themes, and also many difficulties for the Zoroastrian theologians.

27. The resurrection is also treated at some length in the *GBd*, ch. 34 (TD MS. 220.15–223.2); see my "Death and Resurrection," pp. 254–257.

28. Text in Elsa Mahler, *Die Russische Totenklage* (Leipzig: Otto Harrassowitz, 1935), pp. 466, 468.

29. Roman Jakobson, "Kompozicija i kosmologija plača Jaroslavny," *Trudy Otdela drevnerusskoj literatury* 24 (1969):32ff.

30. Jaroslavna's lament (*Plač" Jaroslavnyn"*) comes at the end of the second major section of the *Slovo*, and Igor's escape is related in the third section. This arrangement led some early authorities to posit a different date of composition for these sections, arguing that Igor's escape was unforeseen when section 2 was written, and that section 3 was added later; see, e.g., Leonard A. Magnus, ed., *The Tale of the Armament of Igor* (London: Oxford University Press, 1915), p. xxxix. But this thesis seems quite artificial. Rather, I am inclined to see this "unforeseen" restoration of the supposedly "dead" Igor as a presentation in historical terms of a religiocosmological theory of death and resurrection.

31. Note also that Jaroslavna's lament hearkens back to an earlier passage in the *Slovo*, ll. 175–180, where similar cosmic elements—the wind, the earth, and waters in the form of rivers—assault Igor and his army. His "death" being at the hands of the elements, Jaroslavna thus calls upon the elements to effect Igor's "resurrection." On the formal qualities that lead to classification of Jaroslavna's plea as a lament, see Mahler, *Russische Totenklage*, pp. 32–33.

32. See, in particular, Pomponius Mela 2.2.18; Photius, *Lexicon*, on "Zamolxis," and the *Suda* on "Zalmoxis" and "Terizoi."

33. See Caesar, *De Bello Gallico* 6.14; Diodoros Sikelos 5.28.6; and Strabo 4.4.4. The last passage, while maddeningly brief, is extremely interesting, for

it connects the indestructibility of human beings to that of the entire universe, while at the same time making mention of periodic eschatological cataclysms (on this last feature see also Strabo 7.3.8): "These ones (the Druids, Bards, and Vates) and others say that souls and the cosmos are impervious to decay, although at certain time(s) fire and water will prevail over them."

34. See, for the Thracians, Mircea Eliade, *Zalmoxis: The Vanishing God* (Chicago: University of Chicago Press, 1972), pp. 21–75; and Ioan G. Coman, "L'immortalité chez les Thraco- Géto-Daces," *Revue de l'histoire des religions* 198 (1981):243–278; for the Celts, Jan de Vries, *Keltische Religion*, pp. 248–252.

35. To take but one example, Pomponius Mela 2.2.18—one of the most important sources for Thracian funerary ideas—seems either confused, indecisive, or badly informed when he reports a wide variety of beliefs among the Thracian Getae: some of whom, he says, believe that the dead return, some that they go to a happier realm, and some that they go nowhere but are better off dead.

36. As, for instance, in Caesar *BG* 6.14, Ammianus Marcellinus 15.9, Pomponius Mela 3.2, or the various writers of the Alexandrian School, discussed by Chadwick, *The Druids*, pp. 58–61.

37. The chief sources for German eschatology are *Vsp* 41–66 and *Gylf* 51–53, along with some scattereed references in other works of the Poetic Edda (esp. *Vaf* and *Lok*). Also note the OHG poem "Muspell" and the iconographic evidence discussed in John Stanley Martin, *Ragnarok: An Investigation into Old Norse Concepts of the Fate of the Gods* (Assen: van Gorcum, 1972), pp. 72–75.

38. See Stig Wikander, "Germanische und indo-iranische Eschatologie," *Kairos* 2 (1960):83–88; idem, "Från Bråvalla till Kurukshetra," *Arkiv för Nordisk Filologi* 75 (1960):183–193; Georges Dumézil, *Les dieux des Germains* (Paris: PUF, 1959), pp. 78–105; idem, *Mythe et epopée*, 2nd ed. (Paris: Gallimard, 1968–1973), I, 208–237; Steven O'Brien, "Indo-European Eschatology: A Model," *Journal of Indo-European Studies* 4 (1976):295–320; and Dominique Briquel, "Mahābhārata, crépuscule des dieux, et mythe de Prométhée," *Revue de l'histoire des religions* 193 (1978):165–185; *pace* such earlier attempts as Axel Olrik, *Ragnarök: Die Sagen vom Weltuntergang* (Berlin: Walter de Gruyter, 1922); Richard Reitzenstein, "Weltuntergangsvorstellungen," *Kyrkohistorisk Årsskrift* (1924):129–212; and Will-Erich Peuchert, "Germanische Eschatologie," *Archiv für Religionswissenschaft* 32 (1935):1–37.

39. Thus, e.g., de Vries, *Altgermanische Religionsgeschichte*, II, 397f.; Ström, *Germanische Religion*, pp. 246–248; Karl Helm, "Weltwerden und Weltvergehen in altgermanische Sage, Dichtung und Religion," *Hessische Blätter für Volkskunde* 38 (1940):29–34; and Ursula Dronke, "Beowulf and Ragnarok," *Saga-book of the Viking Society* 17 (1969):303–310; *pace* the earlier views, e.g., of Sophus Bugge. Two studies in particular have made the old theory of Christian influence untenable. First, Martin, *Ragnaṛok*, pp. 41–48, has found the work and teaching of Christian missionaries to the Germans quite lacking in eschatological themes that could have contributed to the Ragnaṛok mythology as we know it. Second, Paul Bauschatz, *The Well and the Tree* (Amherst: University of Massachusets Press, 1982), esp. pp. 142–143, has shown that

given the fundamental pre-Christian Germanic ideas of time and causality the Ragnarǫk cataclysm must be followed by a renovation and new beginning, Christian influence hardly being necessary for such a conclusion.

40. On this motif see Kurt Schier, "Die Erdschöpfung aus dem Urmeer und die Kosmogonie der Völuspá," in H. Kuhn and K. Schier, eds., *Märchen, Mythos, Dichtung: Festschrift für Friedrich von der Leyen* (Munich: C. H. Beck, 1963), pp. 303–334.

41. See A. G. van Hamel, "The Game of the Gods," *Arkiv för Nordisk Filologi* 50 (1934):218–242, with whom I would differ only on certain details.

42. These "sacrificial wands" have been compared to the Skt *barhiṣ* and the Av *barəsman* by Ake Ström, "Indogermanisches in der Völuspa," *Numen* 14 (1967):179, 194. The renewal of sacrifice also plays an important part in Iranian accounts of the Renovation (*GBd* 34.23, *ZS* 35.15–17), and in Greek accounts of Deukalion and the flood (Apollodoros, *Bibl* 1.7.2). As suggested in n. 24 above, the fact that sacrifice was necessary for the re-creation of the world after the cosmic catastrophe would seem to be a part of the general IE eschatological tradition.

43. As first recognized by Güntert, *Arische Weltkönig*, pp. 338f. See also de Vries, *Altnordisches etym Wb*, p. 601.

44. Hesiod, fragment 234, in R. Merkelbach and M. L. West, eds., *Fragmenta Hesiodea* (Oxford: Clarendon Press, 1967), p. 114, preserved in Strabo 7.7.2; Pindar, *Olympia* 9.41–46.

45. Apollodoros, *Bibl* 1.7.2. While Pandora is explicitly said to be the first woman, Pyrrha is the first woman who is *born*, her mother having been constructed by the gods. The creation of humans by Prometheus from earth plus water and/or air is related in *Bibl* 1.7.1; Ovid, *Met* 1.86–96, 363–364. On these myths in general see Guthrie, *In the Beginning.* pp. 24–27; on Deukalion as a first-man figure see J. Rudhardt, "Les mythes grecs relatifs á l'instauration du sacrifice: les rôles corrélatifs de Prométhée et de son fils Deucalion," *Museum Helveticum* 27 (1970):1–15.

46. On this text, with comparison to Indic materials, see Franco Crevatin, *Ricerche di Antichità Indeuropee* (Trieste: Edizioni LINT, 1979), pp. 29–31.

47. See also Apollodoros, *Bibl* 1.7.1. Also note a local legend from Ikonion, recorded in the *Etymologicon Magnum*, in which after the flood it is Prometheus, along with Athene, who re-creates human beings at Zeus's direction. People are shaped from clay (a mixture of earth and water), into which Prometheus blows the breath of life. This anthropogony thus involves three macrocosmic elements—earth, water, and air, the alloforms of flesh, blood, and breath respectively—and precisely repeats the earlier anthropogony described in *Bibl* 1.7.1 and *Met* 1.86–96, 362–364.

48. On death and rebirth also note *Phaidō* 70C–72D, *Parmenides* 155E–157B, and *Tim* 42B–D. On cosmic cycles see *Laws* 677A–683A, *Tim* 22C, and *Kritias* 109D. For a similar treatment of death and rebirth in a pre-Platonic source, see the Hippokratic *Peri Diaitēs* 1.4.

49. Thus Reitzenstein, *Studien zum antiken Synkretismus*, pp. 34–35, 66–68; idem, "Plato und Zarathustra," *Vörtrage der Warburg Bibliothek* 1924/25

(1927):32–34; J. Bidez, *Eos, ou Platon et l'Orient* (Brussels: M. Hayez, 1945), pp. 66–77. More cautious, but open to the suggestion, is Pierre-Maxime Schuhl, *La fabulation platonicienne* (Paris: PUF, 1947), pp. 102–104. Also on this myth see H. Herter, "Gott und die Welt bei Platon: Eine Studie zum Mythos des Politikos," *Bonner Jahrbuch* 158 (1958):106–117; and Pierre Vidal-Naquet, "Le mythe platonicien du *Politique*," in Julia Kristeva et al., eds., *Langue, discours, société: pour Emile Benveniste* (Paris: Editions du Seuil, 1975), pp. 374–390.

50. Plato states (*Politikos* 268E–269B) that he means to draw together three bodies of legend: (1) the story that the celestial bodies reversed their directions during a quarrel between Atreus and Thyestes (preserved in Euripides, *Elektrē* 690–746 and scholia thereto; also in his *Orestes* 1001–1004); (2) the stories of the golden age of Kronos (as in Hesiod, *WD* 109–120); and (3) the various myths of autochthonous races (*gēgeneis*) (the people created by Deukalion and Pyrrha, the Thebans who sprang from dragons' teeth sown in the earth, etc.). In all likelihood he also had in mind Herodotos 2.142, and Empedokles' system as outlined in *Peri Physeōs*.

51. Thus, most aggressively argued by W. J. W. Koster, *Le mythe de Platon, de Zarathoustra, et des Chaldeens* (Leiden: E. J. Brill, 1951) pp. 39–47; see also Perceval Frutiger, *Les mythes de Platon* (Paris: PUF, 1930), pp. 241–244; and Kerschensteiner, *Platon und der Orient*, pp. 101–105.

52. On the intermixture of cosmic elements to form bodily tissues, see fragments B96 and B98 and Solmsen, "Tissues and the Soul," pp. 436–441.

53. Metempsychosis is an important part of Empedokles' system, and given the evidence of similar theories among the Indians, Celts, and Thracians, as well as in Empedokles' mysterious predecessor Pythagoras, it may conceivably be part of the IE heritage. This issue is far too complex for treatment in the present context. For Empedokles' theories of the cycle of rebirths, see fragments B115, B117, and B146, and, e.g., Herbert S. Long, "The Unity of Empedocles' Thought," *American Journal of Philology* 70 (1949):142–158.

54. The text of this fragment is defective in the first, third, and fifth lines. While the last two are easily restored, the first line is not so simple, and Diels-Kranz sets a question mark after the proposed *hikōntai*. I have accordingly left the last phrase of this line untranslated, an omission that does not seem to interfere with the sense of the fragment as a whole. Empedokles is describing in the first three lines the various possible (re)births into organisms that represent the four elemental realms—birds representing air, bushes representing earth, men representing fire (as in B117), and wild animals, somewhat surprisingly, doing service for fish in representing water.

55. See, inter alia, Lévi, *Doctrine du sacrifice*, pp. 77–151; Gonda, *Religionen Indiens*, I, 174–180, 190–191; Biardeau, *Le sacrifice dans l'Inde ancienne*, p. 21; and Betty Heimann, "The Supra-personal Process of Sacrifice," *Rivista degli Studi Orientali* 32 (1957):731–739. On the Druids, see the passage from the *Senchus Mór* cited in Chapter 2 above.

7. Reflections on Myth and Society

1. The nature of the IE social system has been explored primarily by Georges Dumézil and Emile Benveniste. Of Dumézil's work see esp. "La préhistoire indo-iranien des castes," *Journal asiatique* 216 (1930):109–130; *Jupiter Mars Quirinus* I–IV (Paris: Gallimard, vol. IV PUF, 1941–1948); and *L'idéologie tripartie des indo-européens* (Brussels: Latomus, 1958), esp. pp. 7–33. Of Benveniste's see "Les classes sociales dans la tradition avestique," *Journal asiatique* 221 (1932):117–134; "Traditions indo-iraniennes sur les classes sociales," *Journal asiatique* 230 (1938):529–549; and *Vocabulaire des institutions indo-européenes*, I, 279–292.

2. A certain variation is evident in the major reflexes of the sociogonic myth. While the Old Russian "Poem on the Dove King," Plato's *Timaios*, and the Irish story of Lugaid Red-Stripes posit origin from the head for representatives of the highest class, the Indic sources consistently specify Purusa's mouth as the point from which the priests emerged, to which might be compared Diodoros Sikelos's observation (5.31.4) that the Druids were understood to be persons "having the same voice as the gods" (*homophōnōn . . . tois theois*).

3. On the "heat of the warrior" see Georges Dumézil, *Horace et les Curianes* (Paris: Gallimard, 1942) pp. 11–46.

4. I interpret the third class somewhat differently from Benveniste and Dumézil; see *Priests, Warriors, and Cattle*, pp. 134–140. Two interesting studies of attitudes toward the commoner class (Dumézil's "troisième fonction") have appeared in recent years: Daniel Dubuisson, "The Apologues of Saint Columba and Solon, or the 'Third Function' Denigrated," *Journal of Indo-European Studies* 6 (1978):231–242; and Dominique Briquel, "Tarente, Locres, les Scythes, Théra, Rome. Précédents antiques au thème de l'amant de Lady Chatterly?" *Mélanges d'archéologie et d'histoire de l'école française de Rome* 86 (1974):673–705.

5. See Biardeau, in *Sacrifice dans l'Inde ancienne*, pp. 26f.

6. Louis Dumont, *Homo Hierarchicus: The Caste System and Its Implications* (Chicago: University of Chicago Press, 1970).

7. Mayrhofer, *Kurzgefasstes etym Wb*, I, 247.

8. For an excellent discussion of the socioeconomic realities of the *dakṣiṇā*, the "gift" or stipend given to priests in return for their performance of sacrifice, see Charles Malamoud, in *Sacrifice dans l'Inde ancienne*, pp. 155–204.

9. The literature on the meaning of Skt *bráhman-* and its relation to the priestly title *brāhmaṇa-* is enormous. For a summary and references see Mayrhofer, *Kurzgefasstes etym Wb*, II, 452–456; III, 769. For the best discussion of Indic speculation on the powers of sacred speech see Louis Renou, *Etudes Védiques et Paninéennes, I, Les pouvoirs de la parole dans le Ṛgveda* (Paris: E. de Boccard, 1955).

10. See, inter alia, J. Loth, "Le mot désignant le genou au sens de génération chez les Celtes, les Germains, les Slaves, les Assyriens," *Revue celtique* 40 (1923):143–152; and E. Benveniste, "Un emploi du mot 'genou' en viel irlandais et en sogdien," *Bulletin de la société de linguistique de Paris* (1926): 51–53.

11. The passage continues, correlating four cardinal virtues to the social classes: good character to the priests, manliness to the warriors, wisdom (that involved in "the wise work of cultivation") to the commoners, and diligence to the artisans (SGW 1.25–29). On translation of Pahl *wāstryōsīh* as "commoners," see n. 17 below.

12. On this text, see *Priests, Warriors, and Cattle*, pp. 77–79 and the literature cited therein.

13. Note, for example, the enclosure built by Yima to save his people from an apocalyptic winter (*Vd* 2.30). As Benveniste argued in "Les classes sociales dans la tradition avestique," pp. 120f., the three sections of this enclosure may be associated to the three social classes: the largest and lowest being that of the commoners; the smallest and highest, that of the priests; and the middle section, that of the warriors. More broadly on Yima, see *Priests, Warriors, and Cattle*, pp. 76–79, and the classic work of Christensen, *Premier homme*, II.

14. On this text, see Marijan Molé, "Le partage du monde dans la tradition des iraniens," *Journal asiatique* 240 (1952):456–458.

15. The most important Greek myth in which a first king divides his realm and the social classes among his sons (here four rather than three) is that of Iōn, the ancestor of the Ionians, mentioned in Strabo 8.7.1; Plutarch, *Life of Solon* 23.5; Herodotos 5.66; and Aristotle, *Athēnaiōn Politeia* 41.2, most of which are discussed by Dumézil, *Idéologie tripartie*, p. 16. Also of interest is Plato, *Rep* 435A–436A, in which the essential characteristics of the social classes are distributed geographically, the Thracians and Skythians to the north being said to have the most bravery; the Egyptians and Phoenicians to the south, love of wealth; and the Greeks—who like the Iranians saw themselves as the best of peoples, at the center of the world—love of wisdom.

The most important Germanic correspondence to this pattern is found in Tacitus, *Germania* 2, a text discussed in Chapter 2.

16. On the general problem of a fourth class being added to the IE three-class system, see Georges Dumézil, "Métiers et classes fonctionnelles chez divers peuples indo-européens," *Annales E.S.C.* 13 (1958):716–724.

17. The term here translated "commoner" literally means "pastoralist-herdsman," being derived from Av *vāstrya.fšuyant-*. Obviously the duties of this class had expanded to include agriculture, as attested in this passage. They thus must be considered a generalized class whose activities were primarily concerned with the production of food and wealth, herds being the standard measure of wealth among the Iranians as throughout the IE world.

18. This development may also be facilitated by the fact that in the Old Russian variant the first man—the Christianized Adam—lacks any possible identification as a mythic king, this being absent from the Adam of Genesis 1–5. Kings thus would be absent from the Russian sociogony altogether did they not replace priests as representatives of the highest class.

19. On society being constituted on the basis of sacrifice in India, see Biardeau, *Sacrifice dans l'Inde ancienne*, pp. 26–27. On the religiosocial nonbeing of the outlaw, see Hans-Peter Hasenfratz, *Die Toten Lebenden: Eine Religionsphänomenologische Studie zum sozialen Tod in archaischen Gesellschaften* (Leiden:

E. J. Brill, 1982); and Mary Gerstein, "Germanic Warg: The Outlaw as Were-wolf," in Gerald Larson et al., eds., *Myth in Indo-European Antiquity* (Berkeley: University of California Press, 1974), pp. 131–156.

20. See Georges Dumézil, "La tradition druidique et l'écriture: le vivant et le mort," *Revue de l'histoire des religions* 122 (1940):125–133.

21. This point is also implied at the outset of the passage, where the two "noble" classes—those which have "any rank and honor at all" are set in constrast to the plebes.

22. On Caesar's dependence on Posidonios see Tierney, "The Celtic Ethnography of Posidonius," pp. 211ff.

23. An Irish source that shows this same disdain for the lower class is treated in Dubuisson, "The Apologues of Saint Columba and Solon" exp. pp. 232–235.

24. The socioeconomic functioning of warrior bands is more thoroughly reported for the Germans—esp. in Tacitus, *Germania* 13–15—than for the Celts, but the two seem to be quite similar in this regard; see John Lindow, *Comitatus, Individual, and Honor* (Berkeley: University of California Press, 1976); and Anne K. G. Kristensen, *Tacitus Germanische Gesellschaft* (Copenhagen: E. Munksgaard, 1983).

25. See Georges Dumézil, *Jupiter Mars Quirinus I* (Paris: Gallimard, 1941), pp. 257–260; idem, *Mythe et epopée*, I, 493–496; Bernard Sergent, "L'utilis-ation de la trifonctionalité d'origine indo-européenne chez les auteurs grecs classiques," *Arethusa* 13 (1980):233–278; idem, "Les trois fonctions des indo-européens dans la Grèce ancienne: bilan critique," *Annales E.S.C.* 34 (1979):1155–1186. See also R. Bodeüs, "Société athénienne, sagesse grecque et idéal indo-européen," *L'Antiquité classique* 41 (1972):455–486.

26. The listing of the classes in *Republic* 415A gives fuller descriptions, mentioning "those who are fitted to rule" (*hosoi . . . hikanoi arkhein*), "those who are defenders" (*hosoi d'epikouroi*), and "the peasants and other artisans" (*tois te georgois kai tois allois dēmiourgois*).

27. See, for instance, *Rep* 415D–417B, where Plato discussed the danger of the defensive class—which ought ideally to serve as a sort of watchdog—turning into wolves that prey on the state. More broadly on this theme, see Marcel Detienne and Jesper Svenbro, "Les loups au festin ou la Cité impossible," in Vernant and Detienne, *La cuisine du sacrifice*, pp. 215–237.

28. Note that Plato classifies and ranks the soul via categories of mortality and gender. Thus, the rational soul is immortal and not gender specific ($+/+$); the spirited soul, mortal and male ($-/+$); the appetitive, mortal and female ($-/-$).

29. On the class basis of Plato's political theory, see Ellen Meiksins Wood and Neal Wood, *Class Ideology and Ancient Political Theory: Socrates, Plato, and Aristotle in Social Context* (New York: Oxford University Press, 1978), esp. pp. 137–143.

30. Plato presents another sogiogonic myth at *Republic* 414D–415A, saying that the three classes were born from the earth (*gēgeneis*) and are thus brothers

(*adelphōn*), who are different because gold was mixed into the substance of the highest clas (those fit to rule), silver into the intermediate class (defenders), and iron plus bronze into the lowest class (peasants and artisans). This, like the sociogonies of the dynastic type (e.g. the myth of Frēdōn's sons and the materials discussed in note 15 above) shows the origin of the classes as the result of divisions effected within the earth.

31. Thus note the roles of Yama in India, Yima in Iran, Iōn in Greece, Romulus in Rome, Witowudi in Prussia, and—following the analysis of Dieterle, "The Hidden Warrior"—the sons of King Niþuð in the ON *Vǫlundarkviða*. In Christianized texts like the "Poem on the Dove King," Adam often inherits the role of the individual in whom all classes are contained. For discussion of several medieval examples, see Joel H. Grisward, "Triades de calamités et médecine tripartite (suite)," in J. Taillordat et al., eds., *E. Benveniste aujourd'hui* (Louvain: Editions Peeters, 1984), II, 72–75.

32. See Dumézil, *L'ideologie tripartie des indo-européens*, pp. 32–33.

33. Daniel Dubuisson, "L'équipement de l'inauguration royale dans l'Inde védique et en Irlande," *Revue de l'histoire des religions* 193 (1978):153–164; idem, "Le roi indo-européen et la synthèse des trois fonctions," *Annales E.S.C.* 33 (1978):21–34, following lines suggested by Georges Dumézil, "Le Rex et les Flamines Maiores," in *La Regalità Sacra* (Leiden: E. J. Brill, 1959), pp. 407–417. The rituals studied by Dubuisson in the first article cited show the future king receiving a garment that is imbued with the power of the sacred (e.g., the Indic *tārpya*, which is soaked in ghee to hold within its fibers the essence of sacrifice), a weapon, and a pair of shoes associated with wealth (e.g., filled with money in the Irish reflex). Although little is known about how the garments were worn, if they were placed upon the head, then the item associated with priesthood would be correlated to the spot on the first king's body from which priests emerged (the head), the item associated with the warrior class (the weapon) to the place from which warriors emerged (the arms), and the item associated with the commoners (the shoes) to the place from which they emerged (the feet).

Beyond the data adduced by Dubuisson, Dominique Briquel, "Sur l'équipement royal indo-européen," *Revue de l'histoire des religions* 200 (1983):67–74, has sought corroborating Greek and Roman examples, with results that are more suggestive than conclusive.

34. Greek *phialē* often denotes a libation cup, and that such a usage is intended here is confirmed by the testimony of Curtius Rufus 7.8.17–18; see note 41 below.

35. That the "daughter of the river Borysthenes" was the goddess Earth has been established by Wilhelm Brandenstein, "Die Abstammungssagen der Skythen," *Wiener Zeitschrift für die Kunde des Morgenlandes* 52 (1953–1955):189.

36. The significance of the name *Paralatai* was first recognized by Christensen, *Premier homme*, I 136–137, 140, and has been accepted by virtually all experts since. Regarding Haošyaŋha, see Georges Dumézil, "La société scythique avait-elle des classes fonctionelles?" *Indo-Iranian Journal* 5 (1962):200,

and my summary treatment, "Haošyangha Paraðāta," in Carsten Colpe, ed., *Wörterbuch der Mythologie: Altiranische und Zoroastrische Mythologie*, H. W. Haussig, gen. ed. (Stuttgart: Klett-Cotta, 1974–1982), pp. 363f.

37. On **kavi-* see *Priests, Warriors, and Cattle*, p. 61 and n. 67; Mayrhofer, *Kurzgefasstes etym. Wb.*, I, 187–188. On the phonetics of the comparison between Av *paraðāta-* and Skt *purohita-*, see Bartholomae, *Altiranisches Wörterbuch*, p. 854; Mayrhofer, *Kurzgefasstes etym Wb*, II, 310, however, expresses some hesitation. On the Indian Purohita and his relation to the king see Jan Gonda, *Ancient Indian Kingship from the Religious Point of View* (Leiden: E. J. Brill, 1969), pp. 65–67; idem, "Purohita," in O. Spies, ed., *Studia Indologica: Festschrift für Willibald Kirfel* (Bonn: Universität Bonns, 1955), pp. 107–124.

38. Dumézil, "La société scythique," p. 202.

39. Different attempts to interpret the first element in this compound are found in Brandenstein, "Abstammungssage," pp. 195f.; and Dumézil, "La société scythique," p. 201.

40. Dumézil, "La société scythique," pp. 201–202. His attempt to derive the first element of the compound, *Ka-*, from Iranian *gau-* (< PIE **gʷou-*), "bovine," is quite tortured, however.

41. Skythian ambassadors are warning Alexander the Great against invading their country (Curtius Rufus 7.8.17–18): "We are not able to serve anyone, nor do we wish to rule. There are gifts given to us—you are not ignorant of the Skythian tribe (*gentem*)—a yoke of oxen and a plow, an arrow, a spear, a libation cup (*patera*). These we use, both with friends and against enemies. We give the fruits obtained by the labor of our oxen to friends, and with the cup we pour libations of wine to the gods with our friends; we assail our enemies with the arrow from afar, and with the spear close at hand."

42. His name, Kolaxais, is best analyzed as < Iranian **(s)kolo-xšaya-* "ruler of the Skolotoi," Skolotoi (with a plural formation in *-t-*) being the name the Skyths use to designate themselves "descendants of Skolo," according to Hdt 4.6; see Christiansen, *Premier homme*, I, 138 inter alia.

43. Ibid., 137f.; Dumézil, "Préhistoire indo-iranien des castes," pp. 119–121; Benveniste, "Traditions indo-iraniens sur les classes sociales," pp. 534–537; Brandenstein, "Abstammungssage," p. 185; Widengren, *Religionen Irans*, p. 156. Note also E. Grantovskij, "Indoiranische Kastengliederung bei den Skythen," *Twenty-fifth International Congress of Orientalists* (Moscow: Verlag für orientalische Literatur, 1960), esp. pp. 17–20; François Hartog, "Les Scythes imaginaires: espace et nomadisme," *Annales E.S.C.* 34 (1979):1137–1154, esp. 1146; and above all A. M. Xazanov, *Sošial"naja Istorija Skifov* (Moscow: 1975), esp. p. 335.

Also note that the fiery gold is probably a Skythian motif parallel to the Av *xᵛarɘnah-* "royal (solar) glory"; see *Priests, Warriors, and Cattle*, pp. 77–79 and the literature cited in notes 132 and 134, also G. Gnoli, "Lichtsymbolik in Alt-Iran," *Kairos* 8 (1967):528–549.

44. The fullest study of these materials to date is Georges Dumézil, *Mythe et epopée*, II, 345–353, although he treats only a portion of the available evidence.

45. *Cath Boinde* 1, the one other text that gives the story of the Find-eamna in fullest detail, offers only one etymology of their name: that from *eamain*.

46. See Carl Marstrander, "Ir. Emun, Emuin," *Eriu* 5 (1911):160; and Christian Guyonvarc'h, "Vocabulaire vieux-celtique, *(I)EMNOS 'jumeau,'" *Ogam* 10 (1958):103.

47. Whitley Stokes, "The Rennes Dindsenchas," *Revue Celtique* 16 (1895):150. Dumézil, *Mythe et epopée*, II, 347, followed Stokes's translation faithfully, rendering the three names "Tumulte, Honte, Pétrin," and was thus led to deny the possibility of interpreting these three figures along the lines of social class or "function" (351–352).

48. See Marstrander, *Dictionary of the Irish Language*, B-179; Vendryes, *Lexique étymologique*, B-85f.; and Pokorny, *Indogermanisches etym. Wb.*, p. 166.

49. Marstrander, *Dictionary of the Irish Language*, N-O-P-13f. See also Pokorny, *Indogermanisches etym Wb*, pp. 765f.; otherwise, Vendryes, *Lexique étymologique*, N-3.

50. Marstrander, *Dictionary of the Irish Language*, L-214; Pokorny, *Indogermanisches etym Wb*, p. 692.

51. The birth of Lugaid Red Stripes from the incestuous union of Clothru and the Find-eamna is also recorded in the *Rennes Dind* 140; *Cath Boinde* 1; the *Ban Shenchus* (text in *Revue celtique* 47[1930]:296, trans. pp. 321–322); and the *Aided Meidbe* (in *BL* 124b41–55).

52. This basic pattern is also preserved in the *Vǫlundarkviða*, as shown by Richard Dieterle, "The Hidden Warrior: The Social Code of the Vǫlundarkviða," and in the version of the Apologue of Menenius Agrippa presented by Dionysius of Halicarnassus 6.86—albeit with some minor variations in both instances. Also compare the description of Agamemnon in *Iliad* 2.477–79, another king whose body is divided into three different bands on a vertical axis. The functional identities assigned these bands, however—with the exception of the uppermost—do not correspond well to those attested in other variants.

> . . . and among them was resplendent Agamemnon—
> His eyes and head resembling Zeus who delights in thunder,
> His loin (or: girth) to Ares, and his chest to Poseidon.

53. See *Serglige Conculaind* 21–27 (a passage that seems to ben an interpolation to the bulk of the text) and the *Cottonian Annals* 99–101. The text to the former is found in Ernst Windisch, *Irische Texte*, I (Leipzig: S. Hirzel, 1880), 212–214; the latter, in *Revue celtique* 41(1924):314. Cu Chulainn's tutorage of and high regard for Lugaid is also attested in the *Aided Lugdach ocus Derbforgaille*, the text of which is in *Eriu* 5[1911]:208.

54. See *Bemmend Branduib for Brega* (from *BL* 48b17–19), noting also *Dubthach hua Lugair cecinit* (*BL* 45a9–10), and *Do chomramaib Laigen inso sis* 10–11 (text in *Zeitschrift für celtische Philologie* 8[1912]:117).

55. Within these reflexes, it is the Iranian Yima who best preserves his PIE identity as first king. Also note here the myth of Romulus's dismember-

ment, treated in Chapter 2. This too is a sociogonic myth, in which society—if not the three social classes—was created from the dismembered body of the first king. Dieterle's discussion of the *Vǫlundarkviða* narrative is also relevant.

56. Note also a variant of the regiogonic myth in *Manu* 7.1–7, in which the eight deities who guard the cardinal directions (the *lokapālas*) are placed into the body of the would-be king. It was thus, according to this text, the fusion of all cosmic space rather than that of all social classes that made a man a king. The medieval descriptions of Adam as a man in whom the three classes were conjoined also fit the regiogonic pattern, although "Adam" is obviously no king. On these see Grisward, "Triades de calamités," pp. 72–75.

57. Since at least 1958, Dumézil has consistently used the term *ideology* to describe the object of his Indo-European researches. He uses this term in an idiosyncratic, depoliticized fashion, however, denoting—if I read him rightly—the fundamental tripartite structural pattern that, as he sees it, informed not only the organization of IE society but virtually all realms of life and thought. I use *ideology* in a more conventionally Marxist sense, to denote the body of ideas, claimed to be objective or even eternal truths, that are propagated by members of certain classes and serve to legitimate a state of affairs beneficial to their own class interests. Further on the relation of social realities to ideological expressions see Daniel Dubuisson, "Structure sociale et structure idéologique: l'apport de Georges Dumézil," in J. Bonnet, ed., *Georges Dumézil* (Paris: Centre Georges Pompidou, 1981), pp. 147–158. On this issue, I agree with Cristiano Grottanelli, "Temi Dumeziliani fuori dal mondo indo-europeo," *Opus* 2 (1983):378: "To admit that a trifunctional ideology could have preceded, or—worse yet—determined an articulation of society following the three functions would strike me as absurd."

58. While one cannot overlook the major role played by religious ideology and religious institutions in support of exploitative social orders, it is simplistic to explain this as the result of a cynical duplicity on the part of venal priests, as did Voltaire and his epigones in the history of western anticlericalism. While such a state of affairs may prevail in isolated individuals or epochs, much more important are the structural and systemic factors that control the sociopolitical stance and effects of religious institutions, professionals, and ideologies, quite apart from any individual volition. This is an extremely important and difficult issue. I have made some remarks on the topic in "Notes Toward a Theory of Religion and Revolution," in B. Lincoln, ed., *Religion, Rebellion, Revolution* (London: Macmillan, 1985), pp. 266–292, but much remains to be said.

59. See, e.g., *BG* 6.13, *Manu* 1.92, and Plato, *Rep* 442B.

60. Speaking of the cattle won through raids as wealth *and* food is accurate, cattle being the chief measure of wealth for the Proto-Indo-Europeans, but this formulation does not go far enough. Cattle were, in fact, the very means of production, converting raw materials (grass) into food (milk, cheese, butter, meat) and other usable items, including leather, tools (made from bones), fuel (from dung), disinfectants (from urine), etc. Moreover, cattle were also the

means of exchange for such culturally important transactions as bridewealth, wergeld, and the like. See *Priests, Warriors, and Cattle,* pp. 6–7, 174–175, and the literature cited therein.

61. See esp. *Rep* 431A–D and *Tim* 69D–70A; also *Rep* 415D, 441E–442B.

62. See esp. *Rep* 416A–417B. In Iran, it appears that warriors did actively contest priestly supremacy around the time when the *Gāthas* of Zarathuštra were composed. One of the signal accomplishments of Zarathuštra's career, as evidenced in the *Gāthas,* was the forging of a class alliance between priests and commoners in response to the warriors' threat. On this, see *Priests, Warriors, and Cattle,* pp. 140–162, and Kaj Barr, "Avestan *drǝgu-, driyu,*" in *Studia Orientalia Ioanni Pedersen* (Copenhagen: E. Munksgaard, 1943), pp. 21–40.

63. On myths describing and condemning specific "sins of the warrior" against the other classes and the social order in general, see Dumézil, *Mythe et epopée,* II, 17–132.

64. Greed was seen not only as characteristic of the lower class but as a subhuman, animal characteristic; the very word *greed* and its numerous cognates in various IE languages are derived from the onomatopoetic representation of the growling sounds of ravenous animals. See my "The Hellhound," *Journal of Indo-European Studies* 7 (1979):279–282.

65. An instructive example is found in Hdt 4.3–4, in which a rebellion of slaves against the upper-class Skythians is described. Unable to defeat these rebels without prohibitive losses, the Skyths hit upon the strategy of attacking them not with weapons but with whips, thereby refusing to treat them as equals even in mortal combat. The stratagem worked; seeing the whips, the slaves faltered, fled, and were reconquered. The Apologue of Menenius Agrippa, discussed in Chapter 3, provides another example in which ideological persuasion checks lower-class unrest when forcible coercion would be impossible.

66. The ambiguity of the protection is obvious: in part, the commoners exchanged material gifts for real protection against external enemies; in part, they paid extortion so that the warriors' violence would not be turned against them.

67. Trust in the king as the protector of peasants and humble people against the excesses of the upper classes persists for many millennia in European history. For its importance in recent centuries see E. J. Hobsbawn, *Primitive Rebels* (Manchester: Manchester University Press, 1959), pp. 118–121.

68. On this passage see Gregory Nagy, *The Best of the Achaeans* (Baltimore: Johns Hopkins University Press, 1979), p. 313.

69. To cite but a few further examples, the formal structures of poetic meter, kinship organization, urban planning, and coinage all seem to have been initially based on the logic of sacrificial dismemberment among many Indo-European peoples. On poetics see Jesper Svenbro, "La découpe du poème: Notes sur les origines sacrificielles de la poétique grecque," *Poétique* 58 (1984):215–232; and Sayers, "Fergus and the Cosmogonic Sword." On kinship see Sayers; on urban design, Jesper Svenbro, "A Megara Hyblaea:

Le corps géomètre," *Annales E.S.C.* 37 (Sept.–Dec. 1982):953–964; on coinage, Nicola Parise, "Sacrificio e misura del valore nella Grecia antica," *Studi Storici* 25 (1984):913–924.

70. I have treated the problem of the interrelation of cosmic and social concerns within systems of religious ideology in greater detail in "The Tyranny of Taxonomies," *Occasional Papers of the University of Minnesota Center for Humanistic Studies*, no. 1 (Minneapolis, 1985).

71. Clifford Geertz, *The Interpretation of Cultures* (New York: Basic Books, 1973), p. 131.

Primary Sources

Adaigh Con Rói. Rudolf Thurneysen, ed., "Die Sage von CuRoi," *Zeitschrift für celtische Philologie* 9 (1913):189–234.

Aitareya Brāhmaṇa. Martin Haug, ed. and trans., *The Aitareya Brāhmaṇam of the Rigveda,* rpt. ed. Delhi: Bharatiya Publishing House, 1976.

Aitareya Upaniṣad. See Upaniṣads.

Alvíssmál. See *Poetic Edda.*

Anaxagoras. See: Presocratic Fragments.

Atharva Veda Sanhita, ed. R. Roth and W. D. Whitney, 3rd printing. Bonn: Ferd. Dümmler, 1966.

Avesta, ed. Karl Friedrich Geldner. Stuttgart: W. Kohlhammer, 1896.

Ayādgar i Jāmaspīg. Guiseppe Messina, ed., *Libro Apocalittico Persiano Ayātkar i Žāmaspīk.* Rome: Pontificio Istituto Biblico, 1939.

Book of Leinster, ed. R. I. Best, Osborn Bergin, and M. A. O'Brien. Dublin: Dublin Institute for Advanced Studies, 1954–1956.

Boroma. Whitley Stokes, ed. and trans., "The Boroma," *Revue Celtique* 13 (1892):32–124.

Bṛhadāranyaka Upaniṣad. See Upaniṣads.

Caesar, *De Bello Gallico.* H. J. Edwards, ed. and trans., *The Gallic War.* Cambridge; Mass.: Harvard University Press, 1963.

Cath Maige Turedh. Whitley Stokes, ed. and trans., "The Second Battle of Moytura, "*Revue Celtique* 12 (1891):52–130, 306–308.

Code of Emsig. Wilhelm Heusler, ed., *Altfriesisches Lesebuch.* Heidelberg: Carl Winter, 1903.

Coir Anman. Whitley Stokes, ed., *Irische Texte.* Leipzig: S. Hirzel, 1891.

"Contra Vermes." Felix Genzmer, "Germanische Zaubersprüche," *Germanisch-Romanische Monatschrift* 32 (1950):21–35.

Cicero, Scholium to *Pro Plancio.* Paul Hildebrandt, ed., *Scholia in Ciceronis Orationes Bobiensia.* Leipzig: B. G. Teubner, 1907.

Curtius Rufus. John C. Rolfe, ed. and trans. *Quintus Curtius Rufus.* Cambridge: Harvard University Press, 1946.

Dēnkart, A Pahlavi Text; ed. M. J. Dresden. Wiesbaden: Otto Harrassowitz, 1966.

Dialogue of Solomon and Saturn; ed. M. Kemble. London: Aelfric Society, 1848.

Dialogue of the Three Saints. Vatroslav Jagič, ed., "Slavische Beiträge zu den biblischen Apocryphen. I. Die altkirchenslavischen Texte des Adambuches," *Denkschrift der kaiserlichen Akademie der Wissenschaften* (Vienna) *Philosophisch-Historische Classe* 24 (1893):60.

Dindsenchas. Whitley Stokes, ed. and trans., "The Prose Tales in the Rennes Dindsenchas." *Revue Celtique* 15 (1894):272–336, 418–484; 16 (1895):31–83, 135–167, 269–312.

Diodoros Sikelos. C. H. Oldfather, ed. and trans., *Diodorus of Sicily.* London: William Heinemann, 1933–1967.

Dionysius of Halicarnassus. Earnest Cary, ed. and trans., *The Roman Antiquities of Dionysius of Halicarnassus.* Cambridge; Mass.: Harvard University Press, 1937–1950.

Donne, John. *Devotions upon Emergent Occasions;* ed. Anthony Raspa. Montreal: McGill University Press, 1975.

Empedokles. See Presocratic Fragments.

Euripides, *Suppliants.* A. S. Way, ed. and trans., *Euripides III.* Cambridge, Mass.: Harvard University Press, 1979.

Gāthās. S. Insler, ed. and trans., *The Gāthas of Zarathustra.* Leiden: E. J. Brill, 1975.

Gellius. John C. Rolfe, ed. and trans., *The Attic Nights of Aulus Gellius.* Cambridge; Mass.: Harvard University Press, 1968–78.

Greater Bundahišn. Ervad Tahmuras Dinshaj Anklesalia, ed., *The Bundahišn, Being a Facsimile of the TD Manuscript No. 2.* Bombay: British India Press, 1908.

Grímnísmal. See *Poetic Edda.*

Gylfaginning. See Snorri Sturlason.

Herodotos, ed. and trans. A. D. Godley. Cambridge, Mass.: Harvard University Press, 1975.

Hippocrates, ed. and trans. W. H. S. Jones. London: William Heinemann, 1931. See also *Peri Hebdomadōn.*

Homer, *The Iliad,* ed. and trans. A. T. Murray. Cambridge, Mass.: Harvard University Press, 1967–1971.

Laws of Manu. See *Manāva Dharmaśāstra.*

Lebor Gabála Érenn: The Book of the Taking of Ireland, ed. and trans. R. A. Stewart Macalister. Dublin: Irish Texts Society, 1938–1956.

Livy. Robert Maxwell Ogilvie, ed., *Titi Livi, Ab Urbe Condita I, Libri 1–5.* Oxford: Clarendon Press, 1974.

Lucan, *Pharsalia.* W. E. Heitland, ed., *M. Annaei Lucani, Pharsalia.* London: George Bell, 1887.

Lucretius, *De Rerum Natura,* ed. and trans. W. and I. D. Rouse. London: William Heinemann, 1924.

Manāva Dharmaśāstra. August Loisleur, ed., *Les Lois de Manou.* Paris: Levrault, 1830.

Mēnōg i Xrad. Frederic Charles Andreas, ed., *The Book of the Mainyo-i-Khard.* Kiel: Lipsius & Tischler, 1882.

Merseburg Charm. Felix Genzmer, "Germanische Zaubersprüche," *Germanisch-Romanische Monatschrift* 32 (1950):21–35.

Moses Xorenaci. P. E. le Vaillant de Florival, *Moise de Khoréne, Histoire d'Arménie.* Venice: Saint Lazare, 1841.

Ovid, *Metamorphoses,* ed. and trans. Frank Justus Miller. London: William Heinemann, 1929.

Pahlavi Rivāyat Accompanying the Dādistān ī Dīnīk, ed. E. B. N. Dhabhar. Bombay: Pahlavi Text Series, 1913.

Peri Hebdomadōn. W. H. Roscher, ed., *Die hippokratische Schrift von der Siebenzahl in ihrer viefachen Uberlieferung.* Paderborn: Ferdinand Schöningh, 1913.

Pindar. C. M. Bowra, ed., *Pindari Carmina.* Oxford: Clarendon Press, 1947.

Plato. J. Barnet, ed., *Platonis Opera.* Oxford: Oxford University Press, 1901.

Pliny, *Natural History,* ed. and trans. H. Rackham. Cambridge, Mass.: Harvard University Press, 1938–1963.

Plutarch, *Life of Romulus.* Bernadotte Perrin, ed. and trans., *Plutarch's Lives* I. New York: Macmillan, 1914.

"Poem on the Dove King" (*Stič o golubinoj knig*"). Stanislas Schayer, "A Note on the Old Russian Variant of the Puruṣasūkta," *Archiv Orientalni* 7 (1935):319–323.

Poetic Edda. Gustav Neckel, ed., *Edda: Die Lieder des Codex Regius,* 4th ed., rev. Hans Kuhn. Heidelberg: Carl Winter, 1962.

Pomponius Mela. Gunnar Ranstrand, ed., *Pomponii Melae, De Chorographia Libri Tres.* Göteborg: University of Göteborg, 1971.

Presocratic Fragments. Hermann Diels, *Die Fragmente der Vorsokratiker,* 5th ed., ed. Walther Kranz. Berlin: Weidmann, 1934.

Raleigh, Sir Walter, *The History of the World,* ed. C. A. Patrides. London: Macmillan, 1971.

Rennes Dindsenchas. See *Dindsenchas.*

Ṛg Veda. Theodor Aufrecht, ed., *Die Hymnen des Rigveda.* Bern: Adolph Marcus, 1877.

Rituale Ecclesiae Dunelmensis: The Durham Collector. ed. A. H. Thompson and U. Lindelöf. London: Andrews & Co., 1927.

Śānkhāyana Gṛhya Sūtra. Hermann Oldenberg, ed., "Das Çānkhayanagṛihyam," *Indische Studien* 15 (1878):1–166.

Śatapatha Brāhmaṇa. Albrecht Weber, ed., *The Çatapatha-Brāhmaṇa.* Varanasi: Chaukhambā Saṃskṛta Sīrīja Auphisa, 1964.

Šāyast Ne Šāyast, ed. and trans. Jehangir C. Tavadia. Hamburg: Friedrichson, de Gruyter, 1930.

Second Enoch. André Vaillant, ed. and trans., *Le livre des secrets d'Hénoch.* Paris: Institut d'études slaves, 1952.

Senchus Mór. The Ancient Laws of Ireland: Senchus Mór. (n.e.) Dublin: Alexander Thom, 1865.

Simon Grunau's Preussische Chronik, ed. M. Perlbach. Leipzig: Duncker & Humbolt, 1875.

Skaldskaparmál. See *Snorri Sturlason.*

Škend Gumānīg Wizār. Jean Pierre de Menasce, ed. and trans., *Škand-Gumānīk Vičār; La solution décisive des doutes.* Fribourg: Librairie de l'Université, 1945.

Slovo O P"lku Igorevě. Tatjana Ciževska, *Glossary of the Igor' Tale.* The Hague: Mouton, 1966.

Snorri Sturlason, Edda. 2nd ed. Anne Holtsmark and Jon Helgason. Copenhagen: Muuksgard, 1976.

Strabo. Horace Leonard Jones, ed. and trans., *The Geography of Strabo.* London: William Heinemann, 1923.

Tacitus, *Germania.* Rudolf Much, ed.; rev. H. Jankuhn. *Die Germania des Tacitus.* Heidelberg: Carl Winter, 1967.

Táin Bó Cúailnge from the Book of Leinster; ed. and trans. Cecile O'Rahilly. Dublin: Dublin Institute for Advanced Studies, 1967.

Táin Bó Cúailnge (From the *Lebor na Huidre*). R. I. Best and Osborn Bergin, eds., *Lebor na Huidre: Book of the Dun Cow.* Dublin: Royal Irish Academy, 1929.

Táin Bó Cúailnge (From the *Yellow Book of Lecan*). Cecile O'Rahilly, ed. and trans., *Táin Bó Cúailnge: Recension I.* Dublin: Dublin Institute for Advanced Studies, 1967.

Upaniṣads. S. Radhakrishnan, ed. and trans., *The Principal Upaniṣads.* Rpt. of 1953 ed. London: George Allen & Unwin, 1978.

Vergil, *The Aeneid,* ed. J. W. Mackaid. Oxford: Clarendon Press, 1930.

Vīdēvdāt. See *Avesta.*

Vǫluspá. See *Poetic Edda.*

Yasna. See *Avesta; Gāthās.*

Yašt. See *Avesta.*

Zad Spram. Behramgore Anklesaria, ed. and trans., *Vichitakiha-i Zatsparam.* Bombay: Trustees of the Parsi Punchayet Funds, 1964.

Selected Bibliography

Reference Works

Boyce, Mary. *A History of Zoroastrianism,* vols. 1–2. Leiden: E. J. Brill, 1978–1982.

Buck, Carl Darling. *A Dictionary of Select Synonyms in the Principal Indo-European Languages.* Chicago: University of Chicago Press, 1949.

Chantraine, Pierre. *Dictionnaire étymologique de la langue grec.* Paris: Editions Klincksieck, 1968–1977.

Ernout, A., and A. Meillet. *Dictionnaire étymologique de la langue latine.* Paris: C. Klincksieck, 1951.

Feist, Sigmund. *Etymologisches Wörterbuch des gotischen Spraches.* Leiden: E. J. Brill, 1939.

Frisk, Hjalmar. *Griechisches etymologisches Wörterbuch.* Heidelberg: Carl Winter, 1973.

Gonda, Jan. *Die Religionen Indiens,* vol. 1. Stuttgart: W. Kohlhammer, 1960.

Guthrie, W. K. C. *History of Greek Philosophy.* Cambridge: Cambridge University Press, 1981.

Hoffman-Krayer, E., and H. Bächtold-Stäubli. *Handwörterbuch des deutschen Aberglaubens.* Berlin: Walter de Gruyter, 1930–1931.

Liddell, Henry George, and Robert Scott. *A Greek-English Lexicon.* Oxford: Clarendon Press, 1968.

Marstrander, Carl, general ed. *Dictionary of the Irish Language.* Dublin: Royal Irish Academy, 1913–1966.

Mayrhofer, Manfred. *Kurzgefasstes etymologisches Wörterbuch des Altindischen.* Heidelberg: Carl Winter, 1956–1976.

Pokorny, Julius. *Indogermanisches etymologisches Wörterbuch.* Bern: Francke Verlag, 1959.

Schrader, Otto, and Alfons Nehring. *Reallexikon der indogermanischen Altertumskunde.* Strassburg: Walter de Gruyter, 1917–1929.

Ström, Åke V. *Germanische und baltische Religion*. Stuttgart: W. Kohlhammer, 1975.

Vasmer, Max. *Russisches etymologisches Wörterbuch*. Heidelberg: Carl Winter, 1953–1958.

Vendryes, Joseph. *Lexique étymologique de l'irlandais ancien*. Dublin: Dublin Institute for Advanced Studies, 1959–1978.

Vries, Jan de. *Altgermanische Religionsgeschichte*. Berlin: Walter de Gruyter, 1957.

———. *Altnordisches etymologisches Wörterbuch*. Leiden: E. J. Brill, 1961.

Walde, Alois, and Julius Hofmann. *Lateinisches etymologisches Wörterbuch*, 4th ed. Heidelberg: Carl Winter, 1972.

Widengren, Geo. *Die Religionen Irans*. Stuttgart: W. Kohlhammer, 1965.

Books and Articles

Bader, Françoise. "Autour de Polyphème le Cyclope: diathèse et vision." *Die Sprache* 30 (1984): 109–137.

Bailey, H. W. *Zoroastrian Problems in the Ninth-Century Texts*. Oxford: Clarendon Press, 1971.

Barkan, Leonard. *Nature's Work of Art: The Human Body as Image of the World*. New Haven: Yale University Press, 1975.

Barr, Kaj. "Avestan drəgu-, driγu-." In *Studia Orientalia Ioanni Pedersen*, pp. 21–40. Copenhagen: E. Munksgaard, 1943.

Bauschatz, Paul. *The Well and the Tree: World and Time in Early Germanic Culture*. Amherst: University of Massachusetts Press, 1982.

Benveniste, Emile. "Les classes sociales dans la tradition avestique." *Journal asiatique* 221 (1932): 117–134.

———. "Traditions indo-iraniennes sur les classes sociales." *Journal asiatique* 230 (1938): 529–549.

———. "La doctrine médicale des indo-européens." *Revue de l'histoire des religions* 130 (1945): 5–12.

———. *Le vocabulaire des institutions indo-européennes*. Paris: Editions de Minuit, 1969.

Biardeau, Madeleine, and Charles Malamoud. *Le sacrifice dans l'Inde ancienne*. Paris: Presses universitaires de France, 1976.

Börtzler, Franz. "Ymir: Ein Beiträg zu den eddischen Weltschöpfungsvorstellungen." *Archiv für Religionswissenschaft* 33 (1936): 230–245.

Bonfante, G. "Microcosmo e macrocosmo nel mito indoeuropeo." *Die Sprache* 5 (1959): 1–8.

Brandenstein, Wilhelm. "Die Abstammungssagen der Skythen." *Wiener Zeitschrift für die Kunde des Morgenlandes* 52 (1953–1955): 183–211.

Briquel, Dominique. "Tarente, Locres, les Scythes, Théra, Rome. Précédents antiques au thème de l'amant de Lady Chatterly?" *Mélanges d'archéologie et d'histoire de l'école française de Rome* 86 (1974): 673–705.

———. "Mahābhārata, crépuscule des dieux, et mythe de Prométhée." *Revue de l'histoire des religions* 193 (1978): 165–185.

Burkert, Walter. "Caesar and Romulus-Quirinus." *Historia* 11 (1962): 356–376.

———. *Homo Necans: Interpretationen altgriechischer Opferriten und Mythen.* Berlin: Walter de Gruyter, 1972.

Campanile, Enrico. *Ricerche di cultura poetica indoeuropea.* Pisa: Giardini, 1977.

Chadwick, Nora K. *The Druids.* Cardiff: University of Wales Press, 1966.

Christensen, Arthur. *Le premier homme et le premier roi dans l'histoire légendaire des Iraniens.* Uppsala: Archives d'études orientales, 1918–1934.

Crevatin, Franco. *Ricerche sull' antichità indoeuropea.* Trieste: Edizioni LINT, 1979.

Dalton, G. F. "The Ritual Killing of the Irish Kings." *Folklore* 81 (1970): 1–22.

Daraki, M. "Aspects du sacrifice dionysiaque." *Revue de l'histoire des religions* 197 (1980): 131–157.

Darmesteter, James. *Ormazd et Ahriman.* Paris: F. Vieweg, 1877.

Detienne, Marcel. *Dionysos Slain.* Baltimore: Johns Hopkins University Press, 1979.

Detienne, Marcel, and Jean-Pierre Vernant, eds. *La cuisine du sacrifice en pays grec.* Paris: Gallimard, 1979.

Dieterle, Richard. "The Hidden Warrior: The Social Code of the Vǫlundarkviða." Manuscript.

Drobin, Ulf. "Indogermanische Religion und Kultur? Eine Analyse des Begriffes Indogermanisch." *Temenos* 16 (1980): 26–38.

Dubuisson, Daniel. "The Apologues of Saint Columba and Solon, or the 'Third Function' Denigrated." *Journal of Indo-European Studies* 6 (1978): 231–242.

———. "L'équipement de l'inauguration royale dans l'Inde védique et en Irlande." *Revue de l'histoire des religions* 193 (1978): 153–164.

———. "Le roi indo-européen et la synthèse des trois fonctions." *Annales: Economies, Sociétés, Civilisations* 33 (1978): 21–34.

———. "Structure sociale et structure idéologique: l'apport de Georges Dumézil." In J. Bonnet, ed., *Georges Dumézil*, pp. 147–158. Paris: Centre Georges Pompidou, 1981.

Duchesne-Guillemin, Jacques. "Persische Weisheit in griechischem Gewande?" *Harvard Theological Review* 49 (1956): 115–122.

Dumézil, Georges. "La préhistoire indo-iranien des castes." *Journal asiatique* 216 (1930): 109–130.

———. *Jupiter Mars Quirinus*, vols. 1–4. Paris: Gallimard, 1941–1948.

———. *L'idéologie tripartie des indo-européens.* Brussels: Latomus, 1958.

———. "Métiers et classes fonctionnelles chez divers peuples indo-européens." *Annales: Economies, Sociétés, Civilisations* 13 (1958): 716–724.

———. "Le Rex et les Flamines Maiores." In *La Regalità Sacra*, pp. 407–417. Leiden: E. J. Brill, 1959.

———. *Les dieux des Germains.* Paris: Presses universitaires de France, 1959.

———. "La société scythique avait-elle des classes fonctionelles?" *Indo-Iranian Journal* 5 (1962): 187–202.

———. *Mythe et epopée.* Paris: Gallimard, 1968–1973.

Dumont, Louis. *Homo Hierarchicus: The Caste System and Its Implications.* Chicago: University of Chicago Press, 1970.

Durand, Jean-Louis. "Le rituel du meurtre du boeuf laboureur et les mythes du premier sacrifice animal en Attique." In B. Gentili and G. Paioni, eds., *Il Mito greco,* pp. 121–134. Rome: Ateneo & Bizzarri, 1973.

Ebenbauer, Alfred. "Ursprungsglaube, Herrschergott und Menschenopfer: Beobachtungen zum Semnonenkult (Germania c. 39)." In M. Mayrhofer et al., eds., *Antiquitates Indogermanicae: Gedenkschrift für Hermann Güntert,* pp. 233–249. Innsbruck: Innsbrucker Beiträge zur Sprachwissenschaft, 1974.

Ebermann, Oskar. "Blut- und Wundsegen." *Palaestra* 24 (1903): 1–25.

Eis, Gerhard. *Altdeutsche Zaubersprüche.* Berlin: Walter de Gruyter, 1964.

Eliade, Mircea. *The Myth of the Eternal Return.* Princeton: Princeton University Press, 1954.

———. *Zalmoxis: The Vanishing God.* Chicago: University of Chicago Press, 1972.

———. "Druids, Astronomers, and Headhunters." In G. Piccaluga, ed., *Perennitas: Studi in Onore di Angelo Brelich,* pp. 173–183. Rome: Ateneo, 1980.

Evans, J. M. "Microcosmic Adam." *Medium Aevum* 35 (1966): 38–42.

Filliozat, Jean. *La doctrine classique de la médecine indienne.* Paris: Imprimerie nationale, 1949.

Förster, Max. "Adams Erschaffung und Namengebung." *Archiv für Religionswissenschaft* 11 (1908): 447–529.

Frenkian, Aram. "Puruṣa—Gayōmard—Anthropos." *Revue des études indoeuropéennes* 3 (1943): 118–131.

Genzmer, Felix. "Ein germanisches Gedicht aus der Hallstattzeit." *Germanischromanische Monatsschrift* 24 (1936): 14–21.

Götze, Albrecht. "Persische Weisheit in griechischem Gewände." *Zeitschrift für Indologie und Iranistik* 2 (1923): 60–98, 167–177.

Gordon, R. L., ed. *Myth, Religion and Society.* Cambridge: Cambridge University Press, 1981.

Grottanelli, Cristiano. "Cosmogonia e sacrificio, I e II." *Studi Storico-Religiosi* 4 (1980): 207–235; 5 (1981): 173–196.

———. "Temi Duméziliani fuori dal mondo indoeuropeo." *Opus* 2 (1983): 365–389.

Grottanelli, C., N. Parise, and P.-G. Solinas, eds. "Sacrificio, organizzazione del cosmo, dinamica sociale." *Studi Storici* 25 (1984): 829–956.

Güntert, Hermann. *Der arische Weltkönig und Heiland.* Halle: Max Niemeyer, 1923.

Guthrie, W. K. C. *In the Beginning: Some Greek Views on the Origins of Life and the Early State of Man.* London: Methuen, 1957.

Hamel, A. G. van. "The Game of the Gods." *Arkiv for Nordisk Filologi* 50 (1934): 218–242.

Hammerich, L. L. "Horrenda Primordia: Zur 'Germania' c. 39." *Germanischromanische Monatsschrift* 33 (1952): 228–233.

Hauck, Karl. "Carmina Antiqua." *Zeitschrift für bayerische Landesgeschichte* 27 (1964): 1–33.

Henry, Victor. *La magie dans l'Inde ancienne.* Paris: E. Leroux, 1904.

Hinnells, John. "Aspects of the Mithraic Bull-Slaying." In J. Hinnells, ed., *Mithraic Studies*, pp. 290–312. Manchester: University of Manchester Press, 1975.

Hoang-sy-Quy, Hoang-son. "Le mythe indien de l'homme cosmique dans son contexte culturel et dans son évolution." *Revue de l'histoire des religions* 175 (1969): 133–154.

Hoffmann, Karl. "Gayōmart und Martāṇḍa." *Münchener Studien zur Sprachwissenschaft* 11 (1957): 85–103.

Jensen, Alfred. *Die getötete Gottheit.* Stuttgart: Syndikat Verlag, 1968.

Kirste, Johann. "Indogermanische Gebräuche beim Haarschneiden." In *Analecta Graeciensia: Festschrift zum 42 Versammlung deutscher Philologen und Schulmänner in Wien*, pp. 53–59. Graz: Styria, 1893.

Ködderitzsch, Rolf. "Der zweite Merseburger Zauberspruch und seine Parallelen." *Zeitschrift für celtische Philologie* 33 (1974): 45–57.

Koppers, Wilhelm. "Pferdeopfer und Pferdekult der Indogermanen." *Wiener Beiträge zur Kulturgeschichte und Linguistik* 4 (1936): 279–411.

Kristensen, Anne K. G. *Tacitus germanische Gesellschaft.* Copenhagen: E. Munksgaard, 1983.

Kucharski, Paul. "Anaxagore et les idées biologiques de son siècle." *Revue philosophique* 154 (1964): 143–159.

Kuhn, Adalbert. "Indische und germanische Segensspruch." *Zeitschrift für vergleichende Sprachforschung* 13 (1864): 49–74, 113–156.

Lévi, Sylvain. *La doctrine du sacrifice dans les Brahmanas.* Paris: Ernest Leroux, 1898.

Lincoln, Bruce. *Priests, Warriors, and Cattle: A Study in the Ecology of Religions.* Berkeley: University of California Press, 1981.

———. "Die politische Gehalt des Mythos." In Hans-Peter Duerr, ed., *Alcheringa, oder die beginnende Zeit*, pp. 9–25. Frankfurt: Qumran Verlag, 1983.

———. "The Tyranny of Taxonomy." *Occasional Papers of the University of Minnesota Center for Humanistic Studies* 1 (1985).

———. "Ancora il mondo alla rovescia: Aspetti dell' inversione simbolica." *Annali della Facoltà di Lettere e Filosofia, Università di Siena* 6 (1985).

———. "Notes toward a Theory of Religion and Revolution." In B. Lincoln, ed., *Religion, Rebellion, Revolution*, pp. 266–292. London: Macmillan, 1985.

———. "Mito, Storia, Sentimento, e Società: Osservazioni preliminari su un grande tema." *Thélema* (Cagliari), forthcoming.

Lindow, John. *Comitatus, Individual, and Honor.* Berkeley: University of California Press, 1976.

Lommel, Herman. "Mithra und das Stieropfer." *Paideuma* 3 (1949): 207–219.

———. "König Soma." *Numen* 2 (1955): 196–205.

Macdonald, A. W. "A propos de Prajāpati." *Journal asiatique* 240 (1953): 323–328.

Mahler, Elsa. *Die Russische Totenklage.* Leipzig: Otto Harrassowitz, 1935.

Martin, John Stanley. *Ragnarok: An Investigation into Old Norse Concepts of the Fate of the Gods.* Assen: van Gorcum, 1972.

Mayrhofer-Passler, E. "Haustieropfer bei dem Indoiraniern und den anderen indo-germanischen Volkern." *Archiv Orientalni* 21 (1953): 82–205.

Molé, Marijan. *Culte, mythe, et cosmologie dans l'Iran ancien.* Paris: Presses universitaires de France, 1963.

Müller, Carl Werner. *Gleiches zu Gleichen: Ein Prinzip frühgriechischen Denkens.* Wiesbaden: Otto Harrassowitz, 1965.

Nagy, Gregory. *The Best of the Achaeans.* Baltimore: Johns Hopkins University Press, 1979.

———. "Patroklos, Concepts of Afterlife, and the Indic Triple Fire."*Arethusa* 13 (1980): 161–195.

O'Brien, D. *Empedocles' Cosmic Cycle.* Cambridge: Cambridge University Press, 1969.

O'Brien, Steven. "Indo-European Eschatology: A Model." *Journal of Indo-European Studies* 4 (1976): 295–320.

Olerud, Anders. *L'idée de macrocosmos et de microcosmos dans le Timée de Platon.* Uppsala: Almquist and Wiksells, 1951.

Parise, Nicola. "Sacrificio e misura del valore nella Grecia antica." *Studi Storici* 25 (1984): 913–924.

Polomé, Edgar. "Vedic Speculations on the Ultimate." In E. Polomé, ed., *Man and the Ultimate,* pp. 39–52. Austin: American Oriental Society, 1980.

———. "The Background of Germanic Cosmogonic Myths." In B. Brogyanyi, ed., *Klingenheben Festschrift.* Amsterdam: Benjamins, forthcoming.

Puhvel, Jaan. "Mythological Reflections of Indo-European Medicine." In G. Cardona et al., eds., *Indo-European and Indo-Europeans,* pp. 369–382. Philadelphia: University of Pennsylvania Press, 1970.

———. "Remus et Frater." *History of Religions* 15 (1975): 146–157.

Quellet, Henri. "L'apologue de Menenius Agrippa, la doctrine des souffles vitaux (Skr. *prāṇa*) et les origines du stoïcisme." *Travaux neuchâtelois de linguistique* 3 (1982): 59–167.

Ramat, Paolo. "Linguistic Typology and Reconstruction." *Journal of Indo-European Studies* 4 (1976): 189–206.

Ramnoux, Clémence. "La mort sacrificielle du roi." *Ogam* 6 (1954): 209–218.

Reitzenstein, Richard, and H. H. Schaeder. *Studien zum antiken Synkretismus aus Iran und Griechenland.* Leipzig: B. G. Teubner, 1926.

Rönnow, Kasten. "Zur Erklärung des Pravargya, des Agnicayana und der Sautramaṇī." *Le monde oriental* 23 (1929): 113–173.

———. "Zagreus och Dionysos." *Religion och Bibel* 2 (1943): 14–48.

Roth, Rudolf von. "Die Sage von Dschemschid." *Zeitschrift der deutschen morgenlandischen Gesellschaft* 4 (1850): 427–433.

———. *Der Mythus von den fünf Menschengeschlechtern bei Hesiod.* Tübingen: L. T. Fues, 1860.

Rudhardt, Jean. "Les mythes grecs relatifs à l'instauration du sacrifice: les rôles corrélatifs de Prométhée et de son fils Deucalion." *Museum Helveticum* 27 (1970): 1–15.

Sayers, William. "Fergus and the Cosmogonic Sword." *History of Religions* 25 (1985): 30–56.

Scheid, John. "La spartizione a Roma." *Studi Storici* 25 (1984): 945–956.

Schlerath, Bernfried. "Zu den Merseburger Zaubersprüchen." In R. Schmitt, ed., *Indogermanische Dichtersprache*, pp. 325–333. Darmstadt: Wissenschaftliche Buchgesellschaft, 1968.

———. "Ist ein Raum/Zeit Modell für eine rekonstruierte Sprache möglich?" *Zeitschrift für vergleichende Sprachforschung* 95 (1981): 175–202.

Schmitt, Rüdiger. *Dichtung und Dichtersprache in indogermanischer Zeit*. Wiesbaden: Otto Harrassowitz, 1967.

Schröder, Franz Rolf. "Germanische Schöpfungsmythen: Eine vergleichende religionsgeschichtliche Studie." *Germanisch-romanische Monatsschrift* 19 (1931): 1–26, 81–99.

Sergent, Bernard. "Les trois fonctions des indo-européens dans la Grèce ancienne: bilan critique." *Annales: Economies, Sociétés, Civilisations* 34 (1979): 1155–1186.

———. "L'utilisation de la trifonctionalité d'origine indo-européenne chez les auteurs grecs classiques." *Arethusa* 13 (1980): 233–278.

———. "Penser—et mal penser—les indo-européens." *Annales: Economies, Sociétés, Civilisations* 37 (1982): 669–681.

Smith, Brian. "The Domestication of the Vedic Sacrifice." Ph.D. Dissertation, University of Chicago, 1984.

Solinas, Pier Giorgio. "Caccia, spartizione, società." *Studi Storici* 25 (1984): 897–912.

Solmsen, Friedrich. "Tissues and the Soul: Philosophical Contributions to Physiology." *Philosophical Review* 59 (1950): 436–441.

Ström, Åke V. "Indogermanisches in der Völuspa." *Numen* 14 (1967): 167–208.

Svenbro, Jesper. "A Megara Hyblaea: Le corps géometrique." *Annales: Economies, Sociétés, Civilisations* 37 (1982): 953–964.

———. "La découpe du poème: notes sur les origines sacrificielles de la poétique grecque." *Poétique* 58 (1984): 215–232.

Tierney, J. J. "The Celtic Ethnography of Posidonius." *Proceedings of the Royal Irish Academy* 60, sec. C, no. 5 (1960): 189–275.

Tristram, H. L. C. "Der 'homo octipartitus' in der irischen und altenglischen Literatur." *Zeitschrift für celtische Philologie* 34 (1975): 119–153.

Vernant, Jean-Pierre. *Mythe et pensée chez les grecs*, vol. I. Paris: Maspero, 1974.

Vidal-Naquet, Pierre. "Le mythe platonicien du *Politique*." In J. Kristeva et al., eds., *Langue, discours, société: pour Emile Benveniste*, pp. 374–390. Paris: Editions du Seuil, 1975.

Wackernagel, Wilhelm. "Die Anthropogonie der Germanen." *Zeitschrift für deutsches Altertum* 6 (1848): 15–20.

Wayman, Alex. "The Body as a Microcosm in India, Greek Cosmology, and Sixteenth-Century Europe." *History of Religions* 22 (1982): 172–190.

Widengren, Geo. "Microcosmos—Macrocosmos." *Archivio di Filosofia* (1980): 297–312.

Wikander, Stig. "Germanische und indo-iranische Eschatologie." *Kairos* 2 (1960): 83–88.

Wright, M. R. *Empedocles: The Extant Fragments*. New Haven: Yale University Press, 1981.

Zuntz, Günther. *Persephone: Three Essays on Religion and Thought in Magna Graecia*. Oxford: Clarendon Press, 1971.

Index of Words

Note: The alphabetical order of modern English has been followed in all cases.

Index of Texts Cited

Index of Subjects

Adam: christianized first-man figure in anthropogonic accounts, 4, 12–16, 20, 26, 84, 178n27; in sociogonic and regiogonic myths, 4–5, 145, 224n18, 225n31, 228n56

Agamemnon, 168; tripartite body of, 228n52

Aging: as process of erosion, 99, 119; reversed in Age of Kronos, 135

Agni, *see* Fire

Agnicayana (Vedic sacrifice), 60–61, 193n63

Agriculture: and rebirth, symbolism of, 120–121; charged to commoner class, 142, 144, 148, 152, 158, 224n17

Ahriman, 66, 81, 115; as serpent, 213n45; assaults against cosmos, 66, 81, 181n51

Ahuna Vairya prayer, 91, 92, 207n21

Ahura Mazda, *see* Ohrmazd

Air: homologized to breath or soul, 28, 39, 84; in Empedoklean system, 35, 39, 53

Aither: homologized to soul, 39; receives souls at death, 120

Akhilles, 168

Alba Longa, 43, 44

Alban Mount, 43, 44, 185nn14,15

Alloforms, 5–9, 16–25, 141–143; consubstantiality of, 5; defined, 5; graphic representation of, 21–25, 113–114, 143, 153–154; homologize body and cosmos, 1–40; in analysis of food, 66–75; in analysis of society, 141–171; summarized, 16–20, 141–142; use in healing, 106–117; variation and innovation in, 8–9. *See also* Homologies

Anaxagoras, 76–78, 80, 96, 136–137, 203nn39,42; on death and rebirth, 136–137; theory of nutrition, 76–78

Anaximander, 35

Ancestors, eponymous, 47, 48, 146, 157–158, 227n42

Animals: death of, 125; relation to food and plants, 65, 71–72; wild and domestic, 200n23. *See also* Carnivores; Cattle; Goats; Horse; Serpents; Vermin; Worms

Anthropogony, 4–5, 10–16, 59, 84–86, 107–110, 120, 139–140; Armenian, 178n30; Celtic, 13–14, 84–85; cosmogony reversed in, 20, 26, 31–35, 40, 59, 78–81, 85–86, 138–140; death, resurrection, and, 127–130, 132–138, 138–140; Germanic, 13–14, 178n27, 188n29; Greek, 132–134, 221n47; healing and, 107–110, 117; in cures for baldness, 93, 97; Indic, 31–35, 78–81; nutritional process as continuation of, 84–86; ongoing nature of, 14, 84–86, 134; Roman, 132–134; Rumanian, 15–16; sacrifice and, 59–61, 78–81, 85–86, 138–140; Slavic, 4–5, 7, 11–13, 15. *See also* Body; Cosmogony; Microcosm

Anthropophagy, 185n12

Grass, 11, 16–17, 87, 196n3; contrasted to edible plants, 87; disposal of hair in connection with, 88–93; homologized to hair, 11, 13, 16–17, 31

"Great Man" (in Pravargya sacrifice), 61, 193n63

Greece (in mythic geography), 223n15

Greed, 152–153, 168–169, 224n64; animal nature of, 229n64; commoner and, 142, 152–153, 163, 166; kings and, 163, 168–169; results from excess stone in body, 14. See also Appetite; Generosity

Greek materials: anthropogonic, 132–134, 221n47; cosmogonic, 35–37; cosmologic, 27–30; eschatologic, 132–135; healing, 100–102, 105–106; on death and resurrection, 120, 132–138; on the nutritional process, 76–78; on the treatment of hair, 95–97; regarding social institutions and formations, 151–156; regiogonic, 156; sacrifices, 51–53, 199n18; sociogonic, 153–156, 225n30

Greetings, formalized, 100

Growth, bodily, 17, 77, 88, 119

Gruel: as primal food, 202n3

Hair, 16–17, 30, 39, 87–98; as bodily extremity, 112, 213n43; disposal of, as cosmogonic process, 88–93; homologized to plants, 1, 9, 10, 11–12, 13–14, 16–17, 26, 31, 32–34, 39, 87–98, 128, 206n18; ladanum and, 95–97; relation to flesh, 88; to nails, 92, 206n18; to nerves, 11. See also Baldness; Plants

Hands: as bodily extremity, 111, 112; homologized to ridges of cosmic mountain, 10; to warriors, 146; primordial bull created from, 176n11

Haošyaŋha Paraδata (Iranian king), 157

Hardness: of bodily parts, classification by, 112; of character, 14

Head, 5, 19, 141, 154; as bodily extremity, 112; as sacrificial portion, 50; commands rest of body, 154; homologized to dawn, 56; to heaven, 1, 3, 5, 7, 19, 26, 175n11; to mountaintop, 10; to political sovereigns, 145, 154, 161, 224n18; to priestly class, 141, 144, 146, 162, 163, 222n2, 226n33; and

powers of intellect and speech, 141; represented by pot in Pravargya sacrifice, 61; smallest, most perfect organ, 154. See also Brain; Heaven; Mouth; Skull

Healers, 99–100, 140

Healing, 99–118, 138–139; alloforms manipulated in, 108–109, 117–118; anthropogony, cosmogony, and, 107–108, 110, 117, 138–139; Celtic, 105, 107–108; dismemberment and, 107–108; Germanic, 102–103, 106, 109–110; herbs used in, 66, 101, 104, 106–108, 211n31; Hippokratic, 100–102, 105–106; Indic, 104, 106–107, 108, 110–111, 212n40; injuries to limbs, 102–110; infestations, 110–112; Iranian, 101, 108, 115–117, 208n7, 212n40; nutrition and, 99, 108; restores wholeness, 100, 117–118; Slavic, 104, 111–112, 210n15; specialists in, 99–100; systems of, related to social classes, 100–102; works on microcosm and macrocosm, 115, 117. See also Body; Charms; Herbs; Hippokratic medicine

Hearing, 34–35; and alloforms ears/cardinal directions, 32, 34–35; and alloforms flesh/earth, 12

Heart, 13–14, 32, 141–142; and warriors' courage, 141–142; as seat of thought or emotions, 32, 182n54; homologized to moon, 32; to wind, 13–14; relation to breath, 14

Heat, bodily, 28, 30–31, 80, 81–82, 122, 142; homologized to celestial spheres, 29; to fire, 84; to sun, 30–31; warrior class and, 142, 222n3

Heaven, 5, 7, 9–10, 19, 27, 55, 124; as vault and shell, 5, 10, 19; homologized to back of sacrificial animal, 56, 192n50; to head, skull, or brain, 1, 5, 7, 19, 26–27, 176n11; to skin, 9–10, 19, 26, 28–30, subcategorization of, 26–27. See also Atmosphere; Head; Sky; Sun

"Heaven and Earth," 109

Herbs, healing, 66, 87, 101, 104, 106–108, 197n9, 211n31; mode of healing appropriate to commoner class, 101; origin of, 66, 107n108